THE
SACRED WELL
MURDERS

By
Susan Rowland

CHIRON PUBLICATIONS • ASHEVILLE, NORTH CAROLINA

www.ChironPublications.com

Interior and cover design by Danijela Mijailovic
Cover photo by Richard Peterson at shutterstock.com
Printed primarily in the United States of America.

ISBN 978-1-68503-005-6 paperback
ISBN 978-1-68503-006-3 hardcover
ISBN 978-1-68503-007-0 electronic
ISBN 978-1-68503-008-7 limited edition paperback

Library of Congress Cataloging-in-Publication Data Pending

ACKNOWLEDGEMENTS
AND APOLOGIES TO CELTS

The Sacred Well Murders is a work of fiction. The notorious Reborn Celts who cause so much trouble are entirely my invention. No modern Celts would ever re-enact what is generally considered to be Roman propaganda: that the Celts practiced human sacrifice as a regular part of their religion. Similarly, while divinities and figures such as Manannan Mac Lir are to be found in historical writings, the intoxicating drug, Danu's Root, is entirely the product of my fevered imagination.

As well as Celtic gods and their reverence for the sacred in water sources, the details of Celtic London and its historic wells are as accurate as I could make them. Celtic offerings are frequently recovered from the Thames and its tributary rivers. While 'Walbrook,' a name for a policeman in the story, is an actual London river, the Eponia is made up.

This is not a story criticizing the ancient Celts nor those inspired by them today. Rather the novel explores the dangers of psychic possession. It looks at people traumatized by war or family breakdown in the context of acute anxieties about the climate emergency. *The Sacred Well Murders* argues that there is a psychic and social dimension of ecological crisis hitherto neglected by the powers that be.

Just as Mary Wandwalker discovers that she cannot address her splintering world alone, so too this work owes more to others than can possibly be expressed here. My kind colleagues and students at Pacifica Graduate Institute, have been inspirational over years of teaching and exploring the interplay of nature and human nature. My family, and friends have been essential in their kindness, patience, and good humor.

Leslie Gardner, fantastic agent, and even better friend got me started writing novels and is in no way to blame for the results. Gay Kinsman and Meredith Taylor offered invaluable late critiques and the artist, Kathryn Le Grice has been a splendid supporter and volunteer editor.

My husband, Joel Weishaus, is almost as good an editor as he is a poet and arts-based researcher.

Finally, this story pays tribute to my friend of over forty years, the wonderful writer, Wendy Pank (1961-2021).

The Sacred Well Murders began as an act of Jungian arts-based research into how personal trauma might invite psychic possession and culminate in domestic terrorism. I did not foresee, but welcomed the presence of, a character *after* she had been murdered, and one arising from prehistory. Moreover, when I finished a draft in December 2020, I did not expect it to be so pertinent to events in the American Capitol on the 6th of January 2021.

Above all, I was determined that the novel not to be about me. And yet, writing it became an excavation of my childhood immersion in the wet woods of Surrey, England. It seems that I am a Celt, after all; not in exile in California but one whose triple goddess of crone, matron and maiden, lives in my three detectives, Mary Wandwalker, Caroline Jones, and Anna Vronsky. May she bless my words.

Susan Rowland, September 2021, Ojai, California.

CONTENTS

PROLOGUE

Faced with bloodstains, the old woman had a daring idea. It involved that nosy parker, Mary Wandwalker, and her dubious detective agency: deep. . .depth something. Janet clicked her tongue, so pretentious the agency's name. Nevertheless, with Wandwalker on board, Janet could persuade her fellow witches that the girl performing forbidden rites had to go.

Blood desecrating the ancient well was bad. Even worse, the drops had been fingered into symbols. Under the midnight moon, the old woman smelled rust and candle wax. A conjuring charm, decided Janet, gritting her teeth. The air trembled. Such practices possessed power, even for a witch as experienced as she. Deep inside herself lived creatures she did not want to see again.

Pulling on the white roots of her red hair, Janet cursed. Turning away from the well, she caught the hiss of wings. Owls hooted from the trees, a welcome comfort. Foolish to be unnerved by silly girls acting out. Yet, who knew what swam in from the dark when disturbed adolescents summoned gods?

The full moon flooded the garden of the Holywell Retreat Center. Working outside tonight was unnerving for Janet because she was spooked by the moon. Long ago, her brother nearly drowned following the bright orb into their family's pond on the farm. He was long cold in the earth, and Janet was now an old, old woman. Yet, the leaves must be harvested when they were at their most potent. Janet was the Center's chief grower, after all.

She'd almost finished gathering the herbs when she'd spotted trouble at the old well.

Janet bit her lips. Keep calm and think this through, she told herself. Known for therapeutic rehab, Holywell no longer guarded a fearful secret. Today anyone could know its history of medicinal magic. First the Church and then the Law forbad witchcraft. For centuries, Holywell ostensibly housed religious women dedicated to prayer and homemade remedies for the ailing poor.

Many decades ago, the Holywell women decided to re-frame their mission. Formally training as therapists meant they could enter the National Health Service. Going mainstream offered income without taking money from patients. They could focus upon those most in need. The only snag was, they were required to give up using their magic on patients. Today, women like Janet practiced the craft only for each other. Holywell provided regular psychotherapy for vulnerable women whom they sheltered in body and soul.

Janet rejoiced in Holywell's deep roots in the earth and the goddess of nature.

"Magic brews itself in the gardens," she would say. "Spells, as well as labor, built the medieval house; we see them carved in the rafters of the barns."

Just one person resisted Janet's enthusiasm: Mary Wandwalker. Janet remembered.

"Nonsense. Dangerous nonsense," Mary had muttered. In another kitchen chair her friend Caroline sat with shining eyes on Janet.

"It would be dangerous," retorted Janet, "if we let the gels get involved. They know before they get here: spells are for resident witches who can distinguish between the light and the dark. Any gel who thinks otherwise has to go." Janet glared at Mary, who sipped her tea and sighed at Caroline before guiding her to the car.

Janet scowled at Mary's firm stride, a neat figure in a plum vintage suit and grey bob. Something made her keep watching as the car swung round to the track that led from Holywell. Yes, that was it, that defiance, even in Mary's driving. Janet resolved to remember a spirit so unlike her own and so. . .managing.

Tonight, it was stubborn Mary who came to mind when Janet found occult symbols on the well stones. Holywell is the *holy well,* said Janet to herself. Any spell by a fool is dangerous, let alone one written in blood. This. . .this *thing,* cannot continue.

She snorted into the dark. Janet's big idea was to use outsider, Mary Wandwalker, to remove the violator.

"Wandwalker is bloody minded enough," Janet muttered. Ha, bloody minded – that's good, she thought. I suppose I must take another look to be sure.

She edged up to well just as the moon sprang from a cloud. Streaming light froze Janet. Drying pools of blood had eyes that flickered.

"Trouble, trouble. . .trouble," Janet said aloud. She wouldn't sleep until this was sorted. That could not happen before daybreak.

Back inside, Janet paced the remaining night hours. Some mornings deer swam through the misty fields surrounding the Retreat Center. Janet envied their elegant gait on model-thin legs. No deer today though. They would have smelled the offering and shied away.

With a scrape and a click, Janet unfastened the back door and straightened her elderly spine. Plunging into the dawn she approached the well for a third time. It was no dream. The spell on the stones was wet with dew; too red. Janet's stomach revolted.

No good, Janet concluded. I'll call Wandwalker. How would she, a skeptic, talk about sacred wells? Janet reflected that the woman was twenty years her junior, formidable in her way. Yet she's so ignorant, blessedly ignorant, of the gods. Yes, she could hear Wandwalker on holy wells, speaking like a guidebook:

Finds from Holywell's actual well include votive offerings of great antiquity. Veneration of the spring goes back to the ancient Celts, whose practices are

3

so little known. This rural well has a twin at the University. Visit that historic well on open days at Exmoor College, between High Street and Blackwell's Art Bookshop.

Too right, Mary Wandwalker. The sour taste in Janet's mouth gave way to a wicked grin. The Mary in her head was the very Mary she wanted. Go on Wandwalker, she plotted, tell us about the Oxford well at Exmoor College. You don't know it yet, but that's where you are going to take my girl. You'll keep her long enough to drain away the dark, thought Janet.

Relief washed away Janet's tension until it pooled beneath her feet. She relaxed her eyes to gaze beyond the mossy walls to the Oxfordshire hills that hid the city. Her plan unfolded of its own accord, like red paint flowering in water.

Wandwalker, you are marvelously unsentimental and insensitive, Janet mused. Bull headed, too fond of being in charge. . .exactly who I need. Moreover, you owe Holywell a favor for our treatment of Caroline Jones, your friend and fellow sleuth. I'm going to use your thick skin and unbelief. Janet put her tongue between her teeth. Her first move would be to remember the details of Wandwalker's new case. Caroline had spilled all on the phone.

"Hardly detecting. Mary is chaperoning a young American at one of those Oxford Summer Schools. You know, the one on ancient Celts at Exmoor College. Anna and I are going to check out one of the teachers—someone Mary knows has doubts about him. Nothing to it, really," said Caroline. "Of course. . ."

"Of course?"

"The new teacher is easy on the eye. Anna spent ages tracking him online."

"Ah," Janet said.

Caroline would not say more about Anna, her young lover. That woman was a hard nut in Janet's opinion; impossible to crack and famously taciturn.

Never mind, the three detectives were perfect for Janet's purpose. She would insist that the Holywell culprit stay with Wandwalker in the city for six whole weeks. In theory the girl would be taking the Summer School. In practice, she would be swamped by dry scholarship, quenching her desire for magic. Studying will turn her away from silly spells, Janet thought. And the beauty of the plan is that the girl is crazy to go. What is the course this year? Ah, 'Sacred Waters of the Celts: Wells, Rivers and the Great God Thames.' The girl had even printed out a list of classes: 'Celtic Gods and their Sacrifices,' 'Why the Celts Matter to the Climate Emergency,' 'The Sacred in the Land,' and 'Initiation and Rebirth: The Celtic Way.'

With no spare cash or transport, no Holywell girl could attend the Summer School alone. Janet was delighted to find another way. Thank the goddess, Wandwalker, Jones, and Vronsky are signed up. The gel can make herself useful, and in return, they'll take care of her.

Janet almost laughed, so great was her relief. Mary Wandwalker would organize and protect. Caroline had picked up some Hollywell healing skills. As for Anna. . .Janet's nose formed a drop of cold water. She is wild. She bore scars. No one had ever dared suggest therapy to her.

I'll never say it, Janet admitted. But I do admire Mary Wandwalker for becoming Anna's legal guardian. Wandwalker has contacts in high places. Janet shivered. High places meant London, where Janet herself had barely survived on the streets.

For the umpteenth time she repeated her talisman, said whenever her demons stirred: I'll never spend a night away from Holywell. It is my home, and I will keep it safe.

Janet took a deep breath and allowed her body to soak up the garden, its medicinal herbs, and ancient trees. I won't permit blood spells here. Let the girl take her monsters to Oxford. Maybe she'll pal up with that rich American.

Janet snorted with gallows humor and stumped off to pluck weeds. Those hardy beggars were trying to grab the precious drops of water she'd kept for the kitchen vegetables. Three hours

5

later she stood up and rubbed her stiff back. Kicking her hoe and trowel together, she marched to the main house. Breakfast was a leisurely affair, despite compulsory attendance for the young women in rehab.

"Coffee and cigarettes are not breakfast!" insisted Cherry the cook.

By a combination of intimidation and chores, Cherry got the girls to choose from a menu of porridge, or eggs and toast, or cereal and beans plus vegan sausages. Janet entered the kitchen through a gust of steam heavy with frying, ketchup, and tea. Twelve young female heads turned in her direction. A few had the instinct to duck away from the old witch's expression.

"Right, you gals," said Janet. "Listen to me. I've come from the old well. Enough is enough. I've a plan to end this dangerous nonsense."

What was that echo? Oh, 'dangerous nonsense' is what Wandwalker called Holywell. That woman has a lot to learn. Janet felt better. She scanned the sleepy expressions.

A choking erupted from the left corner of the table. Janet showed her teeth. "Time to get real, Sarah. No more human sacrifices, *got it?*"

CHAPTER 1
MARY WANDWALKER
IS DISTRACTED

Practical and determined Mary Wandwalker had no time for magic. None of that nonsense for her, thank you very much. Yet, her attitude to Holywell was more complex than she would own up to. For, as well as indulging depressed Caroline in her visits, if pushed, Mary Wandwalker would admit to a grudging respect.

I'm not saying this to Caroline and Anna, she thought. But I do see that despite the goddess gibberish, Holywell therapists work hard. They take in very vulnerable girls who need all the attention they can get. Trying to relieve psychological pain, they don't give up, I like that.

For this reason, Mary agreed that Janet's 'gel,' Sarah, could join the Depth Enquiry Agency, at least for the Exmoor Summer School. Janet had asked at the right moment, just as classes were about to begin. Indeed, the Celtic Summer School was doing pre-sessions for those unable to commit to the whole six weeks.

Mary settled that Sarah would arrive the night before classes officially started. Fortunately, Mary's rich American employer, Mr. North, had rented a big Victorian house in north Oxford for his daughter and her companion. Mary brushed aside Caroline's worries about the two young women.

"You agonize too much," Mary said. Never mind that Sarah is from the underworld of trafficking and Rhiannon from the starry skies of privilege. Don't fuss, Caroline, she was thinking. "They're about the same age. They'll make friends."

Mary failed to notice the shaking head, or she might have recalled Caroline's greater perceptiveness about relationships.

In truth, Mary was distracted by an unexpected summoning to London. Weeks ago, Mary Wandwalker's ex-boss, Mr. Jeffreys, learned of the chaperone position from a mutual acquaintance. He seized the opportunity of recruiting Mary's detective agency to snoop on a new teacher and those he represented, The Reborn Celts. Suspicious, Mr. Jeffreys wanted to know more about how the group operated outside the classrooms of Oxford.

Yes, that will be fine, a busy Mary had thought. She'd agreed to the added task because it was so straightforward. Since I've got to go to classes with the American girl, Caroline and Anna will come to keep watch. The fee from Mr. Jeffreys is most welcome, as well. With relief about extra money and confident of her management, Mary Wandwalker was taken aback by Mr. Jeffreys' later phone message. In a radical change of tone, he demanded a meeting.

"I insist you come to London so we can talk in person," he'd growled into her voicemail. "We'll meet outside the National Theatre. This mission is far riskier than I suspected. It's imperative that I see you."

Refusing to give details was typical of him, fumed Mary. She was determined to give him a piece of her mind. A few choice phrases accompanied the buttoning of her best lavender jacket, brushing her hair with unusual vigor, and applying her brightest lipstick (a subtle pink touched with gold). After all, he'd got used to her stubbornness when she'd worked under his supervision at the National Archives.

Arriving early within a stone's throw of the river Thames, she spotted the large Black man sitting outside the cafe. The sun burnished a steel table the size of a warrior's shield. After stilted pleasantries, and the purchase of a rather good cappuccino, nothing could stop her. She cleared her throat. Mr. Jeffreys must understand that he was merely the client and no longer her boss. Those days were far behind.

CHAPTER 2
MISS WANDWALKER IS WARNED

"I resent your phone message, Mr. Jeffreys. Too imperious by half. This meeting is a waste of my valuable time." Imperious, that was one of the words she'd tried out.

He looked closely at her. After a moment, his face relaxed with amusement. He is so *provoking*, Mary fumed. She continued.

"Our arrangement is simple. The Celtic Summer School is about to begin, and we've agreed to keep watch on Joe Griffith of the Reborn Celts, the teacher you mentioned. As we speak, Caroline is joining Anna at the pre-class workshop. Therefore," she leaned forward, grey eyes stormy, "why is it so essential to talk in person today? And why here of all places?" She jutted her chin and waited.

Mr. Jeffreys sighed. He smoothed the sleeve of his custom-made, silver-grey suit, giving his skin a bronze sheen.

"There's danger," he said. "More than I realized. I want your advice."

If Mary Wandwalker was shocked by his directness, she did not show it. Rather, she folded her arms. Sitting outside the National Theatre's brutal edifice, Mary faced Waterloo Bridge. If she craned her neck, she could glimpse the river Thames at low tide. Mr. Jeffreys had insisted on this very spot. If it had been his office near St Paul's, he would have brought out his single malt Scotch and ordered the Ethiopian coffee she liked. She waited until he continued.

"As I said in my message," he began again, "I want to upgrade your mission. Before, it was intelligence gathering about the Reborn Celts. You are on the spot as chaperone, or whatever, for that American girl." He pursed his lips. "Now, despite your lack of experience, I'm asking you to do more. It involves getting close to some disturbing personalities."

He stared at Mary in a way that made her grip the side of her chair. For the moment, she was lost for words.

"You will have noticed," Jeffreys said heavily, "that the brochure for the Summer School offers something extra. Higher membership of the Reborn Celts is possible through participation via three rites called initiation, immersion, and uprising. Sounds like a good challenge for you three extraordinary women. I want you to enroll." He glared at Mary. "The three of you will enroll in the optional initiations, even though I suspect all three involve illegality and physical peril."

Mary blinked. Usually, she relished his irony. Usually Mr. Jeffreys, Director of the National Archives, collecting material on groups of national significance, did not ask so much of her Depth Enquiry Agency. She waited for him to continue.

"You see, Miss Wandwalker, the Reborn Celts are more of a threat than we thought. The Oxford Summer School is just the beginning," Jeffreys went on. "If the hints on social media and the dark sites are anything to go by, they're planning acts of violence."

"The Reborn Celts? The Summer School in Oxford?" Mary dropped her coffee spoon. She really could not believe what she was hearing. Even this early the South Bank was busy with tourists. Mary had to speak loudly. "You can't be right about them. How can a group of antiquarian enthusiasts be a problem? They're *historians*."

She could feel the heat wetting her neck. London never used to bake in June.

"Are you too hot?" said Mr. Jeffreys, himself radiating comfort. "We can go inside if you like. I wanted you to experience. . .well, perhaps we could call it 'the scene of the crime.'

He stood up. "There is a breeze by the river. Come on. If we walk, there is less chance of being overheard. I want to show you something."

Mary opened her mouth to swallow the second half of her coffee. She glared at Jeffreys. If only that fee of his was not so tempting.

"I'll buy you another one," he said, nodding at her cup with bonhomie that he knew would infuriate her further. She stood up with perfect dignity and strolled ahead of him across the road, first dodging whizzing bicycles doing the Thames cycle route. She and Jeffreys arrived at the glittering river, swollen by the tide to hug Waterloo Bridge to their left. Mary stared at the moving water. Her body quivered with new awareness of her companion's serious expression.

"Miss Wandwalker, I am going to show you part of a report that reached my desk yesterday. He handed Mary a sheet of paper. It's white dazzled with black lozenges in the brilliant sunshine. She held it on the stone balustrade while she got out her glasses.

Ah, the black shapes were redacted material. Fortunately, one paragraph had been spared.

> Joseph Griffiths should be placed on the watchlist for two reasons: his psychiatric condition and his association with the group calling themselves 'The Reborn Celts.' Although set up for educational purposes, (principally the annual Summer School at Exmoor College), web surveillance suggests that group may be fronting a racist cell with terrorist ambitions. Suspects include all three members of the Morrigan family. Cross reference with Albert Edward Morrigan, deceased, who founded the 'Reborn Celts' as a dubious merging of history teaching and occult practices. I strongly urge my superiors to find funding to...

The rest of the sentence was redacted.

"Ah, that funding must be to pay extra fees to us, The Depth Enquiry Agency?" said Mary with a wry twist of her lips. Mr. Jeffreys narrowed his eyes at the government offices directly opposite them on the north bank of the Thames.

"Nice try. Funding to get in the professionals. Refused of course," he said, taking back the paper and returning it inside his jacket. "Instead, I've raided the budget for. . .well, never you mind, to find your fee, Miss Wandwalker. Of course, if you do find evidence of something serious. . ."

"Hazardous," broke in Mary.

"Then you will withdraw at once. I have no illusions about the competence of your so-called Agency."

"Depth Enquiry," said Mary, very stiff. "We go deeper than the police have time for. That is what it says on our website." She saw her companion's lips move and thought she heard him say 'amateurs' before he thought better of it. He turned to face Mary and leaned on the stone parapet. She remained straight backed.

"Let's talk about what this means for the Celtic Summer School. Take a hard look at the Morrigan family who are behind all this. Classes go back to that Celtic scholar, old Albert Edward Morrigan, mentioned in the report. Not only did he start the Summer School at Exmoor, but he also founded the Reborn Celts as more than scholars. Then, of course, he jumped off Waterloo Bridge, right here."

Jeffreys pointed at the bridge while not taking his eyes off Mary. As if he produced it by magic, thought Mary. She took a moment to make the connection.

"Waterloo Bridge. He jumped here?"

Mr. Jeffreys watched as Mary dropped her gaze to the river then up to scan the lean structure spanning the Thames like a greyhound. Steel railings above the parapet gleamed. Below, the river coiled like a huge boa constrictor. Mary glimpsed the heads of pedestrians.

She would not let Mr. Jeffreys have it easy.

"Scene of the crime, you said. What crime?" she hissed. "Don't tell me suicide is still a crime. How ridiculous is that? I don't understand why you couldn't just tell me scary stories in your office. Just what is so bad about the Reborn Celts that you are suspecting them of, of. . .violent stuff? It is a Summer School that teaches about pre-Roman Britain, not some terrorist training camp."

"You hate my office," said Mr. Jeffreys, deliberately ignoring her concerns. "The last time you were there. . ."

He was going *there*, was he? "You fired me. And replaced me with a computer. Very well, I see what you mean. Now. . ." she drew herself up like the lady her manner insisted upon, "why do you want to frighten me about a sensational suicide and a bunch of crazy Celts?"

In the old days, Mary Wandwalker would never have pressed her boss so far. While confident he relished verbal sparring, she drew on her reserve as well as her intelligence. This morning she was faced with circumstances far from her forty years as an archivist. Her response had an edge.

Mr. Jeffreys understood. He offered Miss Wandwalker his arm and walked her back to the National Theatre Expresso Bar. Fortunately, this time there was an isolated table where the droning of London traffic was sufficient to screen their conversation. After a second rejuvenating cappuccino, Mary no longer wanted to snipe at her ex-employer. He noticed.

"Are you ready to hear about some crazy Celts?"

He downed his hot coffee, wiped his mouth with his perfect handkerchief, and smiled at the trim woman with thunder in her eyes.

"I am not trying to frighten you, Miss Wandwalker. Merely to put you on your guard. Cast your mind back to the very public death of the Albert Edward Morrigan, Professor of Celtic Studies at Oxford's Exmoor College. His suicide on Waterloo Bridge provoked outrage that became overtly racist."

He put up a hand to forestall her reaction. "Perhaps you don't remember how Morrigan's death stirred up social media?"

"You're wasting time," said Mary. She rattled her cup so it could be heard over the background city noise. "We. . . that is, the Depth Enquiry Agency, don't do politics, as you well know." A bead of sweat was pooling at the base of her throat.

Mr. Jeffreys raised his voice as a trio of buses crossed Waterloo Bridge. "What I'm talking about is how Morrigan's death affected his family, now leaders of the Reborn Celts. His act of self-violence seems to have inspired them to, shall we say, redirect their destructive impulses. To be blunt, Miss Wandwalker, I fear they have taken up murder."

Mary gulped. He had her attention.

He sighed. "My colleagues in Whitehall dismissed this particular headache. That report I showed you is filed under 'paranoid.' I don't happen to agree with their risk assessment."

Before continuing, Mr. Jeffreys shot her a measuring glance. "If there's one thing worse than a group bent on violence, it is one driven by misguided beliefs that their gods demand it. And, if there's one thing worse than terrorist Celts, it's terrorist Celts with money." He sighed. Mary could see him decide to divulge something sensitive. She waited.

"It was in the press and on TV that Albert Edward Morrigan found a Celtic neck-ring, called it the Sacred Well Torc. Said he got it digging at Exmoor. When he refused to hand it over to the British Museum, there was an almighty row. Eventually, he said he lost it. No one believed that." Mr. Jeffreys banged the table. "Lost a gold offering to the Celts' water gods? I don't think so." He frowned at Mary.

"Now we're finding the torc on racist websites linked to calls for blood sacrifice."

Jeffreys paused to gauge her reaction. Or, to ascertain how close he was to his prey, as Mary would remark later to Caroline and Anna.

Mr. Jeffreys was a shrewd judge of character. "Come on Mary, get a grip! If that gold torc is genuine, it's priceless. You know that authorities here and in the US are not doing enough to track white supremacists. Just think what such people could unleash with money from genuine gold artefacts."

Jeffreys' voice became harsher. Mary noticed new lines around his jaw. He had strong feelings about racism, even though he never mentioned it in connection to himself. Mary knew because of how she and Jeffreys had first met. Over forty years ago, young Jeffreys had been assaulted while he and Mary were students at the same Oxford college.

In the dead of night, she'd been wrenched awake by the roars of the Rugby Club on a drunken spree. When the shrieks and shattering glass added taunts and the crunch of punches, she'd crept down the staircase to peek into the quad. Before running off, the bullies dumped their target into the central fountain. Mary never forgot the sight. Pulling himself up, young Jeffreys' dark skin gleamed in the lamplight. She could hardly *not* recognize the first black British student at St Julian's College. She herself was an impoverished orphan with a Grammar School education.

Young Mary Wandwalker ventured towards the bleeding victim. Using the hem of her dressing gown, Mary helped wipe the blood streaming from his nose. That night they exchanged no words on the matter, nor any since. Yet neither forgot the incident. Later, when unwed and pregnant Mary was desperate for a job, Mr. Jeffreys used his Civil Service connections to get her work in the Archive. The rest was water under the bridge and forty years of Mary's skillful dedication.

"White supremacists, you said." She was attending now. "Is the Archive gathering *that* kind of material?"

Mr. Jeffreys sighed. "You know, we collect everything that might assist the protection of the nation. Some. . .unfortunate topics have become more relevant. While MI5 watches the known terrorists, some of us. . ." He coughed. "Some of us are concerned that new groups may be tapping into the corrosive effect of the Climate Emergency. Miss Wandwalker, the point I'm making is that the Reborn Celts are just getting started. They are not the usual killers who keep it all in the family."

15

Mary opened her mouth and Jeffreys was quick to anticipate. "So why you, why your Depth Enquiry Agency?"

That's his shark expression, Mary thought. Now for the fatal bite. I wish we didn't need his fee. Mr. Jeffreys read her too well.

"Elementary, my dear Miss Wandwalker. Your respectability is impeccable. No one could suspect you of snooping at the Exmoor College Summer School. Pay extra attention to Joe Griffith. He will be grooming students to take part in acts of. . .well, unspecified violence," he ended lamely.

"That is the problem. We do not know what they are planning." He drummed his long fingers on the table. Mary nodded, which set Jeffreys on again.

"Make sure you are selected for the three rites I mentioned earlier: initiation, immersion, and uprising. Go along with the nonsense, then slip away when it gets. . .sticky. When you think about it, it's an easy assignment."

Had Mary any coffee left she would have choked on the word "easy" coming from Mr. Jeffreys.

"Yes, I get it," she said, refusing to rise. Jeffreys thought he could get information on the cheap, since an unlicensed DEA could not charge the rates of trained operatives.

Surely, Jeffreys was making too much of a personal tragedy, plus wasn't this just a bunch of students with too much time on their hands? Wasn't the suicide an old man's plea for attention? And he'd got it alright by ending his life in the famous river that bisected London. She turned a searching gaze to the large man in front of her.

"About these so-called racist Celts? Do you have actual evidence? Dead professor sets up a group to promote ancient history. *He* may have been crazy, yelling into the night before drowning. I'm not sure the Celts were even white. Not all of them, anyway."

"Probably not, agreed Jeffreys. "The history is complicated. Celtic artefacts have been dug up all over the Mediterranean. The problem is not what the Celts *were*, which is a mystery since they left no writing, but rather what they can become *today*. Don't you recall another Morrigan? A scientist—she must be in her forties now—goes by the name of Simmy."

Mary did indeed remember a taut woman with cropped hair.

"Simmy Morrigan? Good God, Jeffreys, I have not thought of her for ten years!" Mary was shocked by the reference to a woman whose defection had been, well, annoying. "She used the Archive for a few months," Mary said. "Researching England's lost rivers, London in particular."

Mary did not add that she and Simmy had twice shared a bottle of wine when Simmy stayed late.

"After a while she just. . .disappeared," Mary said. "Months later, I heard she'd gone on an expedition to the Antarctic, looking at glaciers, something like that. I never knew she was related to the old coot who jumped off the bridge. . .this bridge." Mary looked more curiously at Waterloo Bridge. A golden rippling reached the bridge itself. The river was rising, the tide coming in.

Jeffreys followed her gaze. "If you stood up now, you'd see water trickling from a big sewer pipe on the north bank. That's one of Simmy's "lost rivers," the Eponia. Broken axes, brooches minus pins, even little figurines have been washed into the Thames right there. It, too, was sacred in pre-Roman Celtic London."

"Eponia. . .," said Mary. Conversations with Simmy were drifting back. "Yes, that was the lost river Simmy could not find, apart from its outflow into the Thames. We located a few references to the Eponia in early medieval texts, nothing more. I remember Simmy getting fed up with the Archive and stomping out."

Mr. Jeffreys had more. "Your Simmy is Sulis Iseult Morrigan, younger child of Albert Edward."

"So that's why she said she hated her name, insisted on Simmy."

"Which as you now know stands for Sulis, for a Celtic goddess, Iseult from a story of tragic love and the Morrigan surname: S.I.M. Mr. Jeffreys smiled. Mary did not.

Back when you knew her, Simmy disowned her father's obsession with the Celts. She became a climate scientist, specializing in freshwater. Recently, she's had a complete change of heart. Today she's an enthusiastic Reborn Celt, along with her almost grown son, Colin; adopted I believe. You'll meet her at the Exmoor."

"How could Simmy change like that? I don't see. . ."

Mr. Jeffreys' patience was wearing thin.

"On the Reborn Celts website, Dr. Simmy Morrigan says that facing the Climate Emergency means rediscovering the Celt within. They revered water. All wild land belonged to their gods, or so this group insists. Water sources were divine because they were passages into what they called the Otherworld. Simmy says that reviving the Celtic religion is a matter of life or death."

"We have friends at Holywell who see the earth as sacred," Mary said, frowning. "With no hint of terrorism," she added.

Mr. Jeffreys was aware of the DEA's connection with the Holywell.

"The Reborn Celts are quite another matter than your therapist-witches," he said, his tone sharp. "This group barely conceals their rhetoric of shedding blood. We must know if their talk of violence is more than just talk. You know how such language converts casual racism into real attacks. To be specific, Miss Wandwalker, I find them too fond of alluding to the Celts' supposed belief that revival of spirit means human sacrifice."

"Ah," said Mary Wandwalker. "*Supposed* belief?"

"Roman propaganda insisted the Celts killed as part of their religion. These days, scholars disagree. Unfortunately, the Celts did have a fascination for severed heads. It can be misconstrued."

"Indeed," muttered Mary.

Jeffreys continued, "My sources. . ."

Mary pounced, "What sources?"

Mr. Jeffreys smiled the huge smile of one closing a trap. Here we go, Mary thought.

"My best source is your California friend Dr. Jez Wiseman. I know you kept in touch after that case last year. He has history with the man you will be watching, Joe Griffith. They served together in Afghanistan."

Mary shook her head. "No, you can't mean the same man. Dr. Wiseman's coming over with some US veterans for extra rehab. He said he was thrilled he could visit his best 'buddy' at the Summer School."

"The very same Joe Griffith," said a somber Jeffreys. "The story goes that after pulling out of treatment for Post-Traumatic Stress Disorder, Griffith discovered the crutch of racism and god, or rather, gods in the ancient Celts. These days he is studying for a PhD with Albert Edward's son, Barin. Morrigan's children are letting Griffith be the public face of the Reborn Celts. After all, he has the scars that suggest Celtic warrior."

Mr. Jeffreys fixed his stare on Mary's strained expression. He's really worried, she thought.

"Let me repeat, Miss Wandwalker: the Morrigans and Griffith are behind the so-called triple rite taking place this month. Initiation happens at the Exmoor sacred well in a few days. Immersion will be at some lake cut from the Thames near Reading. Then the whole shebang decamps to London— we've no idea where— for the uprising at the summer solstice. I don't like it, and I want you and your team to be my eyes and ears."

"Alright," said Mary slowly. "Untreated PTSD, mysterious water rites. I can see how it could get out of hand. Dangerous, I agree. Especially with Joe Griffith, a trained killer, and a lost lump of gold."

"Ring," said Mr. Jeffreys. "Ring, or a torc of gold. More precisely, a man's neck ring, illegally exported for a small fortune. The Sacred Well Torc is thought to have gone to the States. Best guess is that it was snapped up by your billionaire employer. Yes, Mary, I'm referring to the father of the girl you are to chaperone. The whole family is crazy for their Celtic heritage. You've not yet had the pleasure of the little princess?"

Mary groaned and clapped a hand to her forehead. "I don't need to meet her. Spoiled in a way only the uber rich can do. Bloody Rhiannon," she said.

CHAPTER 3
RHIANNON NORTH ARRIVES
IN OXFORD

The suitcases arrived first. All seven of them, in dark blue leather, monogrammed RN. The unsmiling limo driver denied all knowledge of Miss Rhiannon North's plans for the rest of the day.

"Dropped her at Exmoor College like she insisted," he mumbled and disappeared.

"She was supposed to come straight here," fumed Mary.

"Behaving like royalty," said Caroline, amused.

Mary was glad to see Caroline's mood improving. After she'd returned from London, Caroline was too stressed to listen to Mr. Jeffreys' warnings. Mary had assigned Anna the task of getting to know Joe Griffith, which Caroline felt her lover was taking too literally.

"Positively flirting with him over lunch, she was. I couldn't bear it, so I left. Let's go to Exmoor together, Mary, and drag her away with us. She'll listen to you. I'm getting a bad feeling about exposing Anna to the Reborn Celts. You and I can do the Summer School."

Mary dismissed Caroline's fears. She kept to herself the conviction that Anna did not listen to either of them. Anyway, she was too wrapped up in Mr. Jeffreys' warnings. Sparring with him on the banks of the Thames left her drained. Nevertheless, she would accompany Caroline to Exmoor for the final session of the pre-summer school events: dinner and a special lecture by Joe Griffith.

21

Then the text came.

At Exmoor with hot Prof. Meet me 6p.m.

It was signed, R.

"What?" said Mary, showing her phone to Caroline. "What is she thinking?"

"Ah," said Caroline. "Must be Miss RN. Sensible to have her luggage delivered.

"Is she summoning me? Me! How old is this girl?" Mary wanted to stamp her foot. Too juvenile. After all, she prided herself on tolerating the younger generation. Yet Rhiannon had irked her twice, and they hadn't even met.

"She's eighteen," said Caroline, comfortably. "Come on Mary. She and Anna need us at Exmoor College."

To Exmoor they went with modest hopes. These would be dashed as events began to spiral out of control. Caroline learned, to her horror, that Anna had disappeared with Joe Griffith. As for Rhiannon, the first meeting with her chaperone was not a success. Rhiannon, too, was in love with the man who represented all things Celtic.

Trouble began soon after Mary Wandwalker and Caroline Jones stumbled, hot and breathless, into Exmoor. The porter, sweating into his red beard, insisted that Mary sign into the Celtic Studies Summer School, even for tonight's lecture. Reluctantly, she put on the inevitable plastic badge. She hated feeling like a tourist at her own university.

In her anxiety about Anna, Caroline refused to wait with Mary. Watching the slightly overweight woman in her forties stamp around the quad, Mary experienced a ripple of unease. Caroline was walking as if heading to a trial for her life. Clinical depression: it was sucking her down into the mud of her own nature. Chronic, they said. Learn to manage it, they said.

By contrast, Anna behaved like a wounded animal of an alien species. She was ungovernable, yet not always unpersuadable.

She was the last person Mary thought suitable for Caroline. Yet the relationship worked, usually.

Ah, well, Rhiannon first, she said to herself as Caroline disappeared. No, no, she decided. That infuriating child can wait. I want to examine the so-called sacred well.

For the first time Mary thought seriously about Janet's story of occult symbols daubed in blood. All nonsense, of course, decided Mary. Yet, there was a piece of what Mr. Jeffreys also feared. If a trafficked girl is drawn to ideas about human sacrifice, then. . .Mary was suddenly uneasy, as if sensing water below ground. They say that the Holywell and Exmoor wells both go back to a Celtic shrine. Time to check this one out, thought Mary.

So still was the college in the sinking sun that her footsteps on the worn flagstones echoed off the stone walls. She passed through three succeeding squares, or quads, each with bottle-green grass and central fountains. Dreadful waste of water, Mary noted automatically. Chapel Quad, Hall Quad. . .and the other one, she mused.

After seeing a printed sign for the Summer School, she peered at the discreet plaque that simply said: Well Garden: No Entry. It directed her to a rounded arch, unlike the Gothic style of the surrounding buildings. Could it really be Norman? The medieval well enfolded the past with its Roman masonry and Celtic artefacts in the depths.

She surveyed the empty quad and then darted through the old arch and into the forbidden garden, feeling absurdly young. There was the well in the far corner, cleaned, restored and, Mary guessed, operational. No weird symbols, thank goodness. Small in comparison to the grand quads, the garden was a simple space. Her eyes were drawn to rose bushes in full red bloom. They lined the stone wall that was surely also medieval. Then Mary noticed the girl in the well's shadow.

In coordinated blue skirt and jacket, her long blond hair had a tint that reminded Mary of a yellow moon. At least it distracted from the discontented expression. Throwing her thick tresses back over her shoulders, the girl knelt over a wooden bucket of water. Over the surface the sulky well maiden dangled a circle of gold.

Mary Wandwalker opened her mouth to speak. No sound emerged. Instead, she heard a loud and annoyed male voice from behind her.

"Girl, what the hell you doing here? This garden is forbidden."

Mary jumped and turned. Delight softened her features. She knew this man in a wheelchair. She had been expecting him, though not so soon.

"Dr. Wiseman. I didn't hear you. I am so glad you managed to get to the Summer School."

After what Mr. Jeffreys had told her, she was relieved to see him. Six months ago, they had met at his graduate college in California, where Mary had chased a client. She impressed the President, Jez Wiseman, enough for him to recommend her services to his wealthy donor, Frederic North.

"Miss Wandwalker, always a delight." Pain wracked his body, for Wiseman was relegated to a wheelchair by a roadside bomb in Afghanistan. Mary stared at him thoughtfully. Looking older than his thirty years, this man of Native American descent had served with the dangerous Joe Griffith and called him 'my best buddy.'

It was an opportunity. The unknown girl could wait. She turned to indicate the way out of the Well Garden. Wiseman, watching her, shook his head. "First, I want a word with Miss North, here," he said quietly.

"She's Rhiannon North?" Mary peered with new interest at the young woman. She raised her head to scowl back before returning to dangling the golden hoop in the water. Mary stepped aside to allow Wiseman to wheel ahead. It gave her time to ponder. Mary knew that she lacked Caroline's natural sympathy with strange creatures like this rich American.

"Harrumph," she said.

Sweating with effort over the grass, Wiseman waved away Mary's attempt at assistance; she was surprised by his grumpy mood. Instead of the laidback humor he'd demonstrated in California, the man was upset. He beckoned Mary closer so he could whisper into her ear.

"Let me talk to Rhiannon first. I know her father. Then, I'll tell you what's really at stake in your mission for Jeffreys. You see, for me, it's personal."

Mary nodded in reply.

"Miss North," Wiseman said, loud enough to echo off the well.

Rhiannon took no notice. Her ignoring of Wiseman and Mary became outright rudeness. The teenager stared soulfully at her reflection. She wants her own well, Mary realized. She wants all this to be about her. Part of Mary wanted to laugh. Yet even with her ignorance of teenagers, she judged it not a good idea. She followed Wiseman's lead and watched.

After about a minute, the girl shrugged.

"I know who you are, Dr. Wiseman," she muttered. She ran her hand through the artificial waves of her hair. "You're that man my father is funding. He's Frederic North, you know, CEO of Mer-Corp."

Wiseman was in no mood to chat.

"Ms. North. Take that precious torc out of the water. If it is what I think it is, it's no toy."

The girl pouted as if she'd had a lot of practice. Mary thought for a moment she might even stick out her tongue.

Wiseman cleared his throat. "Your father's people messaged me about your arrival. I've also seen photos of the famous Sacred Well Torc." He turned to Mary. "See that? It's the one that Professor Morrigan found right here at Exmoor. Mr. North warned me that his daughter might bring the torc with her. He's not happy."

Ah, no export license, thought Mary. Mr. Jeffreys was right. An illegal sale with money going to the Reborn Celts. No doubt Mr. North's one of those billionaires who thinks money buys everything. He must be worried lest the torc be seized. Rhiannon is careless, not to mention rude.

A flush began to compete with the girl's cosmetics. Mary realized that the perfect complexion owed everything to makeup. Was that the remains of acne beneath? Even she could tell that Rhiannon's simple outfit with matching shoes cost thousands of dollars. She was indeed from another world.

Rhiannon lifted the torc, shook off droplets of water, and placed it around her neck. Wiseman wasn't giving up.

"Ms. North, let me put the torc somewhere safe before I phone your father."

Mary raised her eyebrows. Wiseman stopped to choose his words with care.

"Mr. North would never let you wave it around where anyone could see it. You could be putting yourself in danger."

Rhiannon saw that she would have to talk to the wheelchair guy with the ancient woman in a wrinkled suit. (The house rented by Mr. North had no iron. Mary was planning to speak to 'his people' about it.)

The girl sniffed. "My name's Rhiannon, after a Celtic Goddess. I've come to meet my Summer School tutor," She simpered. "The hot professor, Joseph Griffiths. He's going to love this torc."

"Griffith," corrected Wiseman. He was cold. "His name's Joe Griffith."

"Whatever." She stretched out her long limbs. "You see, I'm finding where I belong: my roots." She giggled to show that she did not care about boring old people.

A little forced, thought Mary, while Wiseman remained concentrated on the torc. Rhiannon wore it like a child dressing up. Then, Mary thought: she's trying to grasp something bigger than she is.

Time to intervene, Mary decided.

"We've not met officially, Rhiannon. I'm Mary Wandwalker," she said, trying for a pleasant tone. "You sent me a text.

I'll be your chaperone throughout the Celtic Summer School. You do understand what that means?"

The girl looked stunned. My age, or my manner? wondered Mary. "Yes, your father signed the contract. Dr. Wiseman kindly recommended me. I see you are wondering about my name." Mary knew she wasn't. "Wandwalker is a corruption of Anglo-Saxon: Wind Talker. They were old women who talked to the gods."

Not registering Mary's history lesson, Rhiannon appeared horrified at this old woman speaking to her like that. She returned to her reflection in the water. Perhaps if she ignored her, the crone with the funny accent would go away.

Meanwhile, Wiseman had made up his mind.

"Rhiannon, Ms. North, enough now. Give me the torc. Your father and I need to discuss its future. It's extremely valuable."

"It doesn't even belong. . ." Mary broke in, then thought better of it. "I've seen such torcs in the British Museum. Plus, I've um. . ." Belatedly she caught Wiseman's eye and coughed. "That is, Rhiannon, hand it over so I can have a closer look."

Rhiannon was disconcerted. A slight breeze was cooling the moisture on the would-be goddess's naked arms. Mary's body language was immutable. She stuck out her hand for the torc. Without thinking, Rhiannon passed it over, her pout becoming a sulk.

The almost-circle of twisted gold strands was damp from the well or from Rhiannon's sweaty neck. Mary rested the torc on her lap while she reached for her glasses. Individual strands of gold had been braided together, then pressed into serpent-like markings. As Mary turned the torc in her hands, its tiny facets caught the remaining sunlight. Each end of the torc was fashioned into an open mouth. Mary touched its tiny teeth and tongues.

"Sharp teeth. Are they lions?" Wiseman asked. He seemed mesmerized by the torc, calmer now that it was out of Rhiannon's hands. He must be nervous about Mr. North's money, thought Mary.

"Dragons," said Mary, remembering details from Mr. Jeffreys' emailed file. She spoke low to Wiseman: "It must have been a secret sale; black market." She raised her voice to the petulant princess. "I can see why the torc is said to be priceless. The workmanship is astonishing. So, Rhiannon, how did your family acquire such an historic treasure?"

Mary's mischievous question was rewarded by a screwed-up mouth. Rhiannon pawed the ground with one expensive shoe.

"My father," she muttered. "Can I go now?"

"Yes, of course," said Mary without thinking. She turned to Wiseman in apology. He nodded.

With a whirl of blue and shoes tapping on stones, Rhiannon was gone. Mary's eyes were drawn to the well itself. It was too old, with those two thousand years of stone. And it was too new, with that restored top and winch. The stripped wood was as naked as a man about to dive in.

As the sun dipped below stone spires, a set of small dark wings flitted from a tree in the adjacent quad: a blackbird. Landing on the rim of the bucket, the bird cocked its inky eye at the intruders in his garden. He dipped a golden beak, then head, into the water. Darting back to the old wall, its wings gave off a minute spray that became a million sparks. Mary held her breath.

"Back home it would be a hummingbird," said Wiseman. "Every morning I hope to catch sight of one during my exercises." He cleared his throat. "I arrived late yesterday so this morning I tried my crutches before people were about."

Keeping her eyes on the bird hopping along the wall, Mary said: "Are you trying to get out of the wheelchair?"

There was a pause; the blackbird vanished. No, it had darted up to that big oak tree. She swallowed, wishing that Caroline had not rushed off after Anna. She knew how to talk about painful stuff.

"Don't know," came the answer at last. "Probably not." Before Mary could apologize, he went on. "You see, my doctors in LA want to give me artificial legs. New research means they can do a digital fitting. Here comes the cyborg Wiseman, the whole nine yards."

His tone raw, Mary looked at the torc in her lap. The spoiled child must assume she could collect it any time.

"Miss Wandwalker, I don't want to give up my legs," Wiseman continued. "Even if they are useless. Even though therapies found no life in them, I'm asking for another six months. But I gotta say, it doesn't look good." He paused. "Not enough blood. They feel like the legs of a dead man."

Mary gripped the torc in both hands, as if she could will it to heal Wiseman's legs. Then she passed it to him without looking up. He held it up to his eyes.

"What a miracle. So beautiful, and so old. Good as new after being lost in the earth, or was it water down that well?" Wiseman was deep inside his suffering. His mouth twisted as he continued to address the torc. "Won't cure this cripple, but I can see why it's driving my buddy Joe crazy.

He handed back the artefact. Mary saw that he wouldn't be able to carry it and maneuver his wheelchair at the same time. Before she could ask him about Joe Griffith, Wiseman began talking again.

"Joe Griffith is, or rather was, my best buddy. That's why I'm here, and it is why I need your help, Miss Wandwalker. In fact, I need more than an Enquiry Agent. You have to understand about Joe and me."

Mary waited.

"This story is… well the simple truth, is he saved my life."

Mary sat very still, hardly breathing. A crow made a hoarse cry overhead. Wiseman directed every word onto the trembling skin of water in the bucket. It reflected his large boots, combat fatigues, and the face of the haggard man who kept an army buzz cut.

"In Afghanistan, Joe and his squaddies, as you Brits say, were blended with my platoon. I was getting over the weird accent when our truck detonated a bomb hidden in the road. Joe

pulled me from the explosion. I'd be dead if it weren't for him."
He paused. "You know, sometimes I wish I had died that day."

He had shocked Mary. He tried again.

"Three of us were driving through the desert when it
happened. Joe was thrown clear. Our driver was killed instantly.
I found myself under the SUV, or rather my legs were. Joe
dragged me out as the whole thing blew up. Last thing I recall
is fire spouting from pools of oil on the track. The sky rained
flames, they said."

He glanced at Mary. "By then I was out of it. You see, Joe
wasn't. He stayed conscious and that's a big problem."

Wiseman shifted uncomfortably in the chair. Mary guessed
he had chronic pain from the top of his non-working legs. In
the tension the background of birdsong was a heartbeat. This is
where Caroline would touch his arm, she thought. She put out a
hand and touched him with the tips of her fingers. It seemed to
work because he went on.

"One of the Medevac guys came to see me in hospital.
'Man, that Griffith,' he said. 'Drenched in your blood', he says.
'The bits not red 'n wet burned to black, skin hanging off like
a ripped shirt. The docs in the chopper couldn't believe he was
still alive. He was yelling that he was just fine. Crazy adrenalin
over-reaction, the docs said.'"

Another pause. "No one is fine," said Wiseman. "Not after
seeing body parts, bits of your buddies lying about on the road
while you live."

Wiseman stared into the tree where the blackbird had fled.

"It ain't natural," he said. "Soon, Joe had a terrible
breakdown. Of course, he got an Honorable Discharge. Then.
. ." Wiseman banged a fist. Mary winced. "Then comes the
real PTSD, 'episodes of psychosis,' say the shrinks. He started
refusing treatment. I got him to come over. Saw how bad it was,
then took him to a veteran's healing program run by one of the
New Mexico tribes. I got the contacts because my grandparents
were born on the Reservation."

Wiseman checked his watch and became brisk.

"Back in hospital, someone passed him a book by Albert Edward Morrigan. I don't know when he got. . .well, obsessed. Online he learned about the Reborn Celts. Since he had a degree in engineering, he could enroll straight into the Oxford Ph.D. program. That's when we lost touch.

A few weeks ago, he called to say his doctorate is practically done and to rave about teaching at the summer school. Would I come and see for myself because it would be perfect for classes at our school in California?

He knew I'd be interested because we're about to launch an Indigenous Studies degree. Many Americans reckon on Celtic ancestry. With Albert Edward dead, Joe's been studying with the son, Barin, another Oxford tight ass. Sorry Mary."

He faced her.

"I told him I'd come and check it out for my graduate college. Then I started doing more digging about this group, the Reborn Celts. Trouble is, I have a bad feeling about the Morrigans. Joe wasn't straight with me. He still won't talk, not really. He just smiles, pats my shoulder, and says wait. 'The power of the gods will come upon you,' or some such nonsense. Something's not right."

Wiseman looked hopefully at Mary. She knew that he and Mr. Jeffreys had talked.

"Like I promised, we'll investigate," she said. "I've not met Professor Barinthus, Joe's supervisor. Although I was once acquainted with his sister, Simmy." She paused. "Dr. Wiseman, you know that Mr. Jeffreys wants my Depth Enquiry Agency at the summer school to report back on the Reborn Celts."

"All three of you?" said Wiseman, a smile playing on his lips. The smile died. It was unlike him.

"What are you really worried about?" said Mary, as her intuition clicked in. "What are you *not* telling me?" Clients must be straight with us, she thought.

Haunted eyes locked on Mary.

"I got a call," Wiseman whispered. "About what really went down with Joe in New Mexico. It was real bad, Miss Wandwalker."

He pursed his lips. "They were in a sweat lodge. The others were doing just fine, when Joe started screaming. They had to sedate him to stop him hurting anyone." Wiseman shut his eyes. "Holy Mother, he was yelling that the gods need more blood, more sacrifices. He lashed out at anyone he could reach. Four of them it took to hold him down."

There was more, Mary could tell.

"He shouted that white people had to be warriors, had to fight for their survival."

Mary could see how much saying this cost Wiseman.

"Joe was the man who saved my ass, and I'm not white! Just look at me! I'm Native American by blood, even though not by upbringing, to my sorrow. Joe…he was never a racist before… before those damn fuckin' Celts."

Wiseman stopped. Anguish strained his entire upper body as he reached for his chair's wheels.

Mary helped him by pushing from behind. When they were back under the stone arch, Wiseman took Mary's hand.

"You'll stay for the lecture tonight, won't you? I reckon it will be Joe's big speech— getting everyone fired up."

He gripped her hand.

"Take care of him for me, Miss Wandwalker, please. Joe is in big trouble. And the worst thing is, he doesn't know it."

CHAPTER 4
JOE GRIFFITH IS INSPIRED

Arriving early for the lecture, Mary Wandwalker gripped her knees and scrutinized the hall. It was an old-fashioned setup, rows of wooden chairs on a polished floor. The modest numbers attending the Celtic Summer School did not rate Oxford's new facilities.

While middle aged people rattled cups and saucers in their excitement, Mary Wandwalker stared at each newcomer. A cold hand gripped her stomach at the impossible decision ahead. If Caroline was right about Anna and Joe Griffith, then the case was already out of control. What to do next?

Mary could feel the rising tension. These people were breathless for Joe Griffith, war-hero, and front man for a new religion. The cold in Mary dripped ice water as she forced herself to think rapidly. Of all the Reborn Celts, Griffith was the most dangerous. With Caroline consumed with worry about Anna, and Anna involved with Griffith, only Mary remained. Suppose Anna had told Griffith about the investigation? In the next few minutes Mary would find out if she had been betrayed.

Drip, drip went the cold inside her. She glanced at the exit, where a young man with white-blond hair was fastening the door. I'll leave, she thought in some desperation. I'll drop the case rather than continue it alone. She remained frozen, gazing at the door. Either course risked her fragile "family," Caroline and Anna.

Should she make a getaway and abandon Anna and Caroline to the entanglement with Griffith? Or should she stay and carry on alone? If Anna was having an affair with Griffith, then continuing with the case put all three of them at risk. Mary groaned in silence. Valued all her life for her rationality, reason suggested telling Mr. Jeffreys to find other, more sophisticated, spies. And desert Anna and Caroline? came an inner voice. Mary was shocked to find reason accompanied by a desire to hurt others.

Suddenly half the lights in the hall snapped off. The lecture must be about to begin. Mary patted her suit pockets in vain for a handkerchief.

She might let loose a tear, were it not for the fact that she never cried. Remember Mary, she told herself. You knew the vulnerabilities of Caroline and Anna when you proposed the Depth Enquiry Agency. It was a wholesale reinvention of our lives. Too bad we might drown in this case. I'm used to loneliness, she thought. I am not, however— she drew her trim figure tall in her seat— I am not in the habit of deserting those I am responsible for. In her years as an archivist, she always knew what to do. Now, after a few months as an Enquiry agent, she was baffled by the wild minds of her companions. Mary Wandwalker relished irony. Tonight, it had a bitter taste.

A murmur rippled from the door and, yes, it was him, the bronzed and scarred Joe Griffith. Mary's hands clenched as Joe locked his arms around Anna. The gesture proclaimed it was a done deal, a relationship consummated.

Heads automatically took in the couple. Someone hissed. Could that be Rhiannon? Mary could not see past a tall man and a woman with even taller hair. Turning to the entwined body that was Joe and Anna, Mary could at last see the man who attracted so much desire and danger.

Joe's scars were part of his magnetism. The rim of his sunburned face had a silvery pattern of burns like a river delta. With brown curls tipped with grey, his brilliant blue eyes swept the room like a cool breeze. Women sighed; men noticed. A thickset man, his tight denim pants advertised muscular thighs and buttocks; the sexual invitation overdone, in Mary's opinion.

Joe was a toucher, Mary recalled Caroline saying. Laying hands on male arms, he moved closer to women until they allowed him to flick a lock of hair in tender affirmation. It wasn't straightforward flirting, although women could and did see it as such. No, for Joe Griffith every sinew in his honed body, every wrinkle of skin, every scar, all steamed conviction. All was for the cause of the Reborn Celts. Once he achieved intimacy, he would whisper about old gods and their ecstasies.

Tonight, Anna and Joe radiated sexual satisfaction. Joe grinned in acknowledgement of the naked envy of the couple. He bent his curly head to kiss Anna on the lips before sauntering into position near a lectern. Anna shut her eyes and cupped a breast as if still feeling Joe's hand. Her blue silk shift trembled as she took a seat next to the one reserved for him.

Mary was furious with Anna. This was her interpretation of "getting to know" Joe? Becoming his lover without consulting her? No wonder she's broken off all contact. Now to all appearances Anna is one of *them*. Mary gulped.

Her eye was caught by a movement near the door. It was Caroline beckoning. "Later" mouthed Mary. "Let me hear this." Caroline banged the door on her way out.

Caroline was off to the shared house to meet Janet's protégé, the wayward Sarah. Mary groaned inwardly. What with the Celtic princess a few rows in front and a dabbler in blood magic back at the house, this was getting to be too much.

Damn you Mr. Jeffreys, why us? She could answer her own question. Because no one would suspect this dysfunctional trio of spying. He knew the Depth Enquiry Agency was less a business and more Mary's last-ditch attempt at making a family. Yet in this, only their second case, she was already out of her depth.

Mary leaned forward to take a tissue from a box left on a seat and then wiped her forehead. She would stay to hear Griffith make his recruiting pitch. After all, there was Jez Wiseman in the front row, demonstrably unhappy. And Mr. Jeffreys suspected Joe was planning a murder.

To be fair, rational Mary argued, he's done nothing criminal so far. He's making us wait. It's working. Her bones ached. She had had enough of being played like an instrument, when the man in question raised his voice.

"All that matters is that we live in Celtic times," he said, teasing. "You wait and see. On the summer solstice the waters will rise, but only if we make the right sacrifices."

There he goes, thought Mary. The esoteric hints Caroline told me about. His Celts are the answer to everyone's anxieties, including the climate crisis. I don't believe it. Do people listen because he is so attractive? Or is he so seductive because he offers everything, while spelling out nothing? Ah, that's it, she decided: Joe's peddling the ultimate drug: divine, inexhaustible meaning.

Comforted by her skepticism, Mary stared at Joe. Are you as dangerous as you appear to be? Can you destroy more than the three of us? The next few minutes would tell.

Joe Griffith stood still at last. The audience stopped shuffling. Joe raised his arms. His shirt sleeves fell revealing more burn scars. The silence was total.

"The earth has spoken. This planet wants its gods back."

His voice boomed a powerful wave. Mary sat up.

He threw his arms wide as if summoning a flood. The audience leaned forward. Without warning, the small screen behind him broke into a blue sky with swan white clouds. With a dizzying swing, the camera rose like a skylark to reveal a great river with many tributaries and no signs of human habitation. There was something familiar about the serpentine channel.

"London," announced Griffith. "London at the time of the Celts, before the great river was polluted, desecrated, and emasculated. Before its satellite rivers were forced underground. Before the river was left to gulp for breath in sacred wells. In those untamed days the river we call the Thames was holy." He paused, measuring the audience's attention.

"No!" he shouted to the roof. "The great Thames was a god!"

The audience gasped.

"We are going to get our divine rivers back." Joe lowered his voice to a musical intensity. "The Climate Emergency is howling through us. That is why here at Exmoor in Oxford, and soon at a new graduate college in California, we will bring back the Celtic gods. Together we will re-sanctify the Earth!"

That was Jez Wiseman's college, he was talking about. Mary half stood to catch his horrified expression. Joe noticed as well. He gave a placating wave to his old buddy.

"Well actually, folks," he said with a self-deprecating laugh. "We're offering you classes in Celtic Studies." There was a ripple of nervous laughter.

That was not what Joe wanted.

He looked up to the skylight for his invocation. When it came there was a general intake of breath.

"It is time for the Celts to be reborn in water and in blood."

Dammit, he's good, thought Mary. He's good because he believes in what's he's saying, said a voice inside her.

Joe paused, dipped three fingers in his water glass and sprinkled drops onto his forehead: a baptism. Sacred water. The audience sighed in unison. Joe was their hero guide, their psychopomp to the otherworld. Appreciative muttering broke out. One or two people stood up and began clapping. Oh no, that's Rhiannon, thought Mary. Her heart sank as she saw Anna rise. Now everyone was getting up. The applause grew wild. Joe Griffith was getting a standing ovation. And he'd hardly begun.

Mary Wandwalker prided herself on being able to make up her mind. Joe Griffith was destroying the Depth Enquiry Agency, her family. The words in her head would not stop. If I continue this case, I push away Anna and Caroline, perhaps forever. If I drop the case, I'm abandoning Anna to danger and Caroline to despair. Mary swallowed at the thought of Caroline's chronic depression. Despair could be dangerous too. Her decision was no decision because there was no choice.

Even without hope of saving the DEA, she would go on. Damn Mr. Jeffreys for being right. The Reborn Celts are big trouble. They must be stopped.

CHAPTER 5
FEARFUL AND ANGRY

The passionate speech over, Joe stepped aside glistening and supercharged. He shook his head like a dog emerging from a pond, and sprayed drops of sweat around him. Some landed on the quiet man in the wheelchair. Joe dropped on one knee for a word with Dr. Wiseman.

I guess we count Jez Wiseman as a client too, thought Mary, given his fears for Joe. She watched as after a brief exchange and a pat on the back, Joe bounded over to a group of older fans. Sadder after the exchange, Wiseman slowly wheeled toward the back of the hall and to Mary.

"I didn't mention earlier about Joe's plans for me," he said in a taut voice. "The field trip he's got organized in a couple of weeks— calls it 'the immersion rite'— he's got my veterans involved. It is supposed to be a tryout for my college. Tomorrow, I'm off to the clinic." He smiled sadly. "More consultations about my legs. I'll be away for a couple of weeks and then join you with the vets. We're gathering by the river Thames near a town called Reading, Joe said."

"Reading's halfway from Oxford to London," said Mary, absently. "Are you really going to let Joe teach at your college in California?"

"We want Celtic Studies to be part of our new Indigenous degree," said Wiseman, not looking at her.

"Would this have anything to do with your rich donor, Rhiannon's father? The Celt enthusiast."

"He's not alone. Many Americans have Celt ancestors, or think they do. It's better to study heritage than to fantasize about it."

His tone was sharp, Mary was reproved. Yet she knew there was more to it. Wiseman suddenly looked older.

"Try to understand, Mary. It's Joe. It's like he's part of me," said Wiseman. "I'm scared for him. No, it's much worse. I thought he was my buddy forever. Now, I'm starting to be afraid *of* Joe."

Mary shut her eyes briefly and thought of Caroline and Anna. It was up to her alone, she reflected. Nowhere online or off do the Reborn Celts spell out the exact nature of their secret rituals. Was the emphasis on blood a metaphor? Or could it indicate something far more deadly?

Wiseman was getting ready to leave.

"Let your Mr. Jeffreys know what I've said about Joe," he said. Mary could see how torn he was. Fortunately, he and Mr. Jeffreys had already communicated over the Reborn Celts. Mary recalled Mr. Jeffreys parting words. "Old gods are all very well. But not when they demand ritual murder."

"I'm so grateful you are on the case, Miss Wandwalker," said Wiseman, putting his papers in the side pouch of his chair. "Please keep in touch."

"Absolutely," muttered Mary. She nodded slowly at his worried expression. As Wiseman wheeled away, he called over his shoulder, "And good luck with the girl."

The girl? Mary had momentarily forgotten the girl. He meant Rhiannon. If it were not for the state of the DEA's finances, Mary would have nothing to do with "the girl." So where was she? As if Mary didn't know.

Despite the emptying auditorium, Joe was visible behind a clutch of excited women. Warily Mary made her way to within earshot. Joe's arm was around Anna. The blonde teenager was pushing others aside to get to the spot directly facing him. Rhiannon had haunted him all day. Such was the buzz around Joe that only Anna noticed.

"Can I touch them?" Mary heard her ask. Her manicured hand hovered over the warm hollow of his neck where his shirt was open. She was referring to the animal heads on his copper torc peeking from under his collar. They had pointed teeth, Mary noticed. His reply was muffled. Anna pulled Joe towards the door. The group dispersed, apart from the Rhiannon who was staring after Joe. Something in her scowl was desolate. Oh no, thought Mary. I've seen that look on Caroline's face.

Rhiannon caught sight of Mary. She stuck her chin up.

"The limo guy will be at the gate. He'll take me to the house my father rented." With her nose in the air, she slammed the door behind her.

"Thank you for offering me a ride, Rhiannon." thought Mary.

Back at the house, the domestic drama of getting two young women settled took longer than Mary could have believed possible. It was very late before she could sit down with Caroline.

"I'm going away," Caroline said as soon Mary joined her. "I won't go back to our home in Surrey because it is full of *her.* I'm going to stay with Janet at Holywell."

Sick at the thought of Caroline leaving, Mary could not leave it there. One person could keep Caroline at the Summer School, and it wasn't Mary.

"Anna needs you. She may not know it right now, but. . ."

Caroline grabbed Mary's arm to make her stop.

"OK, not Anna. What about Sarah? She's only just arrived; it's you she is clinging to. Janet refuses to take her back, you know. I called earlier with the news from Mr. Jeffreys. The Summer School isn't the desiccated scholarship she thought. It could be dangerous: out of the frying pan and into the fire for her dabbler in blood magic."

Caroline had an answer ready.

"Didn't she say that fires are necessary to defeat some frying pans? At any rate, she texted me that Sarah should be with us; Janet feels in her waters. No idea why, given what you've done, Mary."

Caroline's white face glittered. Mary flushed. She homed in on the practical.

"You have to stay. Even one teenager's too much for me. Be here to support Sarah, or Rhiannon will eat her."

Caroline was in too dark a place for Mary's humor.

"It's really important," Mary continued. "You see, Rhiannon's not just the daughter of the CEO of Mer-Corp. . ."

"You don't need to spell out what I can see with my own eyes. She thinks she's in love with Joe. Poor child."

Caroline swallowed. She was coming to a decision.

"Alright, I'll stay in Oxford to support Sarah. But don't think that I'm going to the Summer School classes with *her*."

Mary was shocked at how bleak she felt, how alone.

"Caroline, I don't think I can do it without you. There's Rhiannon to keep an eye on as well as Joe and the other Reborn Celts."

"No, no, *no*! I'm not going near Exmoor College. You don't know what you're asking of me." Caroline's faded copper curls shook.

Mary was at a loss. She'd been so confident that her cogent arguments would sway Caroline. Sometimes Mary resented the way that the DEA finances were left for her to sort out. To her dismay Caroline had more to say.

"You have not been listening." She fixed Mary with haunted green eyes. "This thing with Anna and Joe. It is your doing."

"Dear Caroline," began Mary. She was awkward—not a people person. "You mustn't be too upset about Anna and Joe Griffith. They are just. . .what do the young people call it? 'Hooking-up.'"

Caroline stared at her. Enormous stones were dragging her underwater. "Caroline?" Mary held out a tissue. Caroline took it. With slow strokes she scrubbed her face. In her forties, she never wore make up. "Caroline, talk to me. You don't think. . ."

The words would not come, not to Caroline, who understood far more than she could bear.

Mary tried to explain. Suddenly the waters between them were treacherous.

"I didn't ask her to. . .you know. I wouldn't. That's. . .that's not what we do."

Caroline's reply bit deep.

"No, you didn't ask her. Not in *words*. But this is Anna we're talking about. *Anna*! You didn't think about how she was trafficked as a child, educated to use sex as a weapon. Did you? She doesn't have boundaries. Of course, she fell too far into whatever Joe is offering."

Mary blanched. Caroline was right. Mary had not thought about what asking Anna to befriend Joe would mean to someone with Anna's past.

"I. . .I. . ." Mary searched for justification but found none. "I had hoped. . ."

"Hoped!" Caroline was too drained to be properly angry. "For all her life Anna had to use sex to get what her captors wanted. She was passed from gang to gang until she learned to— well, manipulate them. Janet says that if you've once been in the underworld. . .you know, it's always there, waiting to drag you back down."

Mary was stung. "I'm not Anna's boss, nor yours," she snapped. "We're *partners*. Very well, Caroline. Maybe I regret asking Anna to get close to Joe Griffith. But do you really think I forced her into this. . .this affair? Do you really believe I'd do that to you?"

Caroline sniffed. She might have said that it didn't matter what Mary thought she was doing, that there were many types of coercion. However, she didn't say these things. Even so, Mary could see her thinking them.

The depressed woman took out a bottle of pills from her battered handbag and swallowed two with a swig from a bottle of water. She and Mary were alone in the shabby living room. Upstairs, two teenagers slept at opposite ends of the house. It gave Mary a headache, thinking of the morning. At last Caroline sighed.

"You'll find a way, Mary. You always do. You'll get the case back on track."

"I don't know how!" said Mary, trying to quash her panic. What she wanted to say was her greatest fear: If Anna and Joe were in love, it was a dark thing because the wounded warrior and the trafficked woman connected through mutual pain.

Wrapped in an oversize pink dressing gown that did nothing for her figure, Caroline created her own dignity as she departed for the stairs and bed. Mary watched her go. Her throat was constricted with a feeling she hardly recognized. Not guilt, surely?

She recalled Rhiannon standing by the podium, staring at Joe. That girl is going to be trouble, thought Mary. Rhiannon's obsession with Joe began with a fascination for all things Celtic. Eighteen years ago, Frederic North had named his only child after a Celtic shapeshifter. Something of those fluid passions must have been passed to Rhiannon, Mary mused. It had been a very long day. Almost too tired to brush her teeth, Mary Wandwalker crawled into bed. I refuse to anticipate what will happen tomorrow at the summer school, she thought falling down a deep tunnel of sleep.

CHAPTER 6
SKIRMISHES WITH RHIANNON

The next morning Mary realized that tussles with Rhiannon had only just begun. An hour after the time specified in Mary's written instructions, the young woman flounced down to breakfast, unrepentant. After attempting small talk, which Rhiannon ignored, Mary captured the girl's attention with a shocking remark. She announced to the group that they would be walking to Exmoor College.

"Walk! You mean actually *walk*? What about the limousine?" Rhiannon's incredulity made Caroline hide her smile. Sitting next to Caroline was Sarah, a nervous African woman of around twenty. Covering needle-damaged arms in a green t-shirt, her eyes grew huge as Rhiannon shook her dazzling locks in the morning sun. On the opposite side of the kitchen table, Mary had spent a restless night with Caroline's reproaches streaming through her dreams. She was not amused by the Celtic princess.

"No limousine. Oxford is choked with traffic as it is. Everyone walks if they can."

"I don't. I never walk. I *can't* walk."

"Why not? Is something wrong with your legs?"

Even Mary could see that this was a bad start. Caroline got up to clatter dishes in the sink. Sarah leaned over to finger up the last crumbs on her plate.

"The décor is so last century," Rhiannon had dismissed.

Mary shot a rueful grin of recognition at the battered brown Formica cabinets, orange floral tiles, and white electric stove; this student kitchen was familiar from her 1970's shared house.

Only the large scrubbed wooden table had any 21st century kudos. Sarah stole glances at Rhiannon, who could touch up her makeup, scroll her phone, and argue all at the same time.

"Walking's so. . .so *demeaning!*" Rhiannon pronounced the word as a triumph. Mary was impressed by her vocabulary. Her expensive education counted for something after all.

"Try to like Rhiannon," Caroline had whispered that morning. Mary had been shocked to realize that Caroline was right. She *didn't* like Rhiannon, the spoiled, overdressed offspring of Mer-Corp's ultra-rich CEO. Nevertheless, in Mary's book, liking did not require giving in to someone's whims. The girl had to understand who was in charge.

"Walking's not demeaning," she said, determined to be firm. "It's good exercise and makes sense in this city. You're not in Los Angeles now. On foot it's twenty minutes to the College."

Rhiannon stared in outrage.

"Remember, too, Rhiannon, that the Summer School is about the Climate Emergency. Walking is in your future."

The Celtic princess made a rude noise. She pushed her propped up mirror away until it banged against the half empty plate of sugar cookies she had brought down. Naturally the breakfast offerings set out by Caroline were unacceptable. Now Caroline intervened.

"Walking to class is what Joe Griffith wants. I'll come with you, see you to the class," Caroline offered Rhiannon a subdued smile. Only Mary knew what it cost. The girl sniffed.

Moving as slowly as she dared, Rhiannon began to pack up her extraordinary array of cosmetics in tiny glass bottles. Upstairs Rhiannon's suitcases had shrunk her large bedroom to the size of the one Mary occupied.

Mary tapped her foot. Caroline looked with meaning in her direction, then thoughtfully at the Celtic princess. Sarah, who'd been ready to go for an hour, made use of the delay by putting the washed dishes back in the cupboard.

Mary had wondered at Sarah's offering to do chores when she arrived. Caroline explained that Sarah found housework reassuring. It gave her a way of feeling safe around people. Sarah wanted tasks even without the deal with Holywell. With the DEA paying Sarah's fee for the Summer School (Mr. North had included a generous amount for 'incidentals and entertainment'), Janet had instructed Sarah to pay back by helping in the house.

Mary caught Sarah's relaxed expression as she turned from putting away the washing up. I see what Caroline means by the work helping Sarah, she thought. Without it she'd be like a frightened horse. What a contrast to Rhiannon.

"What's bothering you, Rhiannon? Still jetlagged?" said Caroline. She was trying to melt the girl's resentment. Rhiannon sniffed again. Nevertheless, her aggressive energy was visibly draining.

"I feel worse than on our vacation in Japan," she admitted. "Suppose I get a migraine from the sunshine. It's so bright out there."

Was that an eruption of spots in those tiny bumps under all that foundation?

"Walking is good for migraines."

Yet Mary was beginning to feel brutal. Caroline was right. That was more than petulance in the girl's taut features. Could she be afraid? And if so, was it the Celtic Summer School, or Joe Griffith? Could she be afraid of Oxford? There must be some European cities that her exclusive rearing had overlooked.

Alright Caroline, Mary thought. You are trying to tell me something with that look. With a jolt, Mary realized that, yes, Rhiannon could be afraid. . .of her. She cleared her throat.

"Migraines? I see. Alright, Rhiannon, jet lag can be. . .uncomfortable. Um. . .I'll call a taxi. If you really don't feel well, that is. Just for today."

Mary wanted to be unambiguous about who was in charge. She had never lived with a teenager. Rhiannon resembles those dopey graduates at the Archive, she mused. Washed in on a tide of educational privilege, they were all confidence and no experience. Such recruits had been brought up sharp by Miss Wandwalker.

47

They called me the Princess of Darkness, or POD, thought Mary with grim appreciation. Their joke was that I never left the vaults. My work was formidable. I was no princess educated to spend Daddy's money. Mary sniffed. Gotta get real, as Anna might say. The Princess of Darkness is no more, and investigator Wandwalker requires more lubricating tactics. Rhiannon's hanging her head. Caroline is cross enough about Anna. Even Sarah seems to be waiting for something other than commands.

Mary put her handbag down on the kitchen table.

"Let's not get this Summer School off to a bad start, Rhiannon," she said. "I'll get the taxi while Caroline makes you a flask of my special coffee to take. If you really want to go today, that is."

"Of *course,* I'm going," said Rhiannon, then winced. Her headache was real. "Joe expects it. He needs me; he said so. When we met at the online interview, he said he was so looking forward to seeing me in Oxford."

She stood up and shook down a long frock in shades of pink that made her skin glow. Her pout suggested she was ready to combat any dispute of her importance.

I guess I can feel sorry for her, Mary thought. The unfortunate girl is going to hate seeing Anna with Joe as much as Caroline does.

"Of course, Rhiannon" she said. "It goes without saying that you're needed. After all, we have all signed up for the three rites. We cannot do them without the first few classes. The Reborn Celts are relying on us, I mean you." There was a tiny pause. "Taxi in nine minutes. Pack up what you are taking. We'll meet you outside."

CHAPTER 7
FIRST RITE: INITIATION PART ONE

For the next two weeks of classes, Mary pondered the enigma of the Reborn Celts. Anna only appeared when Joe Griffith was doing the teaching. A special chair at the front was reserved for her. All Anna's ties to the DEA had melted like late frost in the sun.

Caroline bore the regime of the Summer School with determination. She told Mary that she'd decided to go for Anna's sake. There would come a time when her lover would call for help. Mary tried to look as if she agreed. It did not work. Caroline and Mary barely spoke.

In each class, the climate emergency was implied as the product of a world that had lost its sacred ties to nature. So far, the year had set a British record for heat and drought. Now in scorching June, Celt enthusiasts and bored retirees were ready for the Reborn Celts to re-shape their world. The summer school taught that water sources were divine to the ancient Celts.

That much Mary could accept. However, she was highly suspicious of what the Reborn Celts' next step would be; for Joe was fond of repeating that when such a worldview was desecrated, blood sacrifices are necessary to restore the balance of life.

"What kind of blood sacrifices?" asked Mary with all the innocence of her sixty odd years. Anna narrowed her eyes, Rhiannon scowled at her for interrupting Joe.

"All in good time, Miss er. . .Walker," said Joe, beaming. He never lost his divine conviction, Mary noted.

The days rolled on; Exmoor College became hotter and heavier. Despite the fans, older attendees dozed during lectures. There was no air conditioning anywhere, to Rhiannon's disgust. Mary longed to put her head down on her arms in the drowsy afternoons. No wonder the regular Oxford term ended when it did. With the teaching term over, exams done, champagne parties thrown, and undergraduates all tidied away, the city had shifted into slower, heavier waters.

Each day Mary and her household passed tourists trailing from college to college. Some were herded like livestock, some roamed in ones and twos bearing massive backpacks. They paddled around the city with little disturbance to its essential rhythms.

Mary knew that almost all the tutors or dons had migrated to country homes. One exception to the summer travels was Professor Barinthus Morrigan, known as Barin, son of the late Albert Edward. Appointed as a Junior Research Fellow to teach his eccentric father's classes, he had assumed the professorship after the dramatic suicide.

Being that it was Oxford, there were raised eyebrows. Colleagues muttered about the large donation to Exmoor College in Albert Edward's will, whose executor was Barinthus. For the last two years Barin had expanded the famous (some said infamous) Celtic Studies Summer School. Rumors of wild rites in the old professor's time gave way to the son's obsession with secrecy. This year, much of the teaching was in the scarred hands of his most talked-about research student, Joe Griffith.

Although the Summer School admitted recruiting for the secret activities of the Reborn Celts, they divided the regular classes from the three rites that would mark entry to the inner circle. Not just anyone would be invited by unnamed 'elders, or druids.' Mary, together with Rhiannon, Caroline, and Sarah, ticked the box to be considered for membership. Mary pursed her lips at the list of rites: 'Initiation at the Sacred Well,' 'Immersion in the Sacred Water,' and the final, 'Solstice Uprising.' Her eye caught Rhiannon's. No way was she going to allow the young woman into these occult rituals. She sighed at the battles to come.

While pouring over the first day's paperwork, Mary caught the curious glance of Simmy Morrigan, who gave her a slight nod. Before Mary could claim prior acquaintance, Simmy stuffed her notes on lost English rivers into a cheap briefcase and vanished. OK, so *not* friends then, thought Mary.

Two weeks in, a bland email confirmed that all four of them were invited to the next stage, Initiation, and would then be considered for the two final rites. Rhiannon danced around the kitchen blowing kisses to an imaginary Joe. The next day was a holiday for the regular students, so it was to an eerily quiet college that the four arrived at the appointed time in the Hall Quad of Exmoor. Next to Joe, Anna stood in the shade, her body language an extension of his. Mary dared not look at Caroline.

It was the first time they'd come close enough to speak to Anna since that first evening. The young woman had dark half-moons under her eyes. Even her scarlet sundress was dusty. Most unlike her, thought Mary. She could see that Caroline was surprised and worried.

Joe Griffith, on the other hand, was more relaxed than ever. He grinned at the women in the rising heat. Clad in beige, the shirt opened at the neck to display curly chest hairs growing on a sunburn. Mary could see Rhiannon quivering. The girl almost sniffed him as she dodged around for a place as close to Joe as Anna would tolerate. Joe took no notice. He had bigger fish to land this morning.

"Welcome, future members of the sacred circle of the Reborn Celts. You've been chosen from this year's Summer School. By blood and by water, today begins your spiritual awakening."

He threw his arms wide to embrace them all. Mary coughed. "Dr. Griffith," she began.

"Not quite 'Doctor.' Joe will do fine, Mary," he said.

Mary noted his condescending tone. "Joe, then," she said, starting again, with feigned diffidence. "Your website does not say much about. . .what the Reborn Celts actually *do*. I read that it takes courage, imagination, and the ability to keep. . . 'blood-born' secrets?"

Mary played down her everyday steely look. She would be a lost older woman looking for directions instead. She *wanted* to march Joe Griffith into the nearest office and fire hard words at him until he released the intoxicated Anna and shifted the Reborn Celts away from talk of blood. Mary had not needed Dr. Wiseman's revelation to distrust Joe Griffith. She was all naive admiration on the outside; inside, she was seething.

"The initiation will come at the right time, Miss. . .er Walker," Joe explained. "It's a matter of finding your sacred springs first. Which gods speak through you. The third and final rite happens at the Blood Rising on the summer solstice, a ceremony of tremendous sacrifice and renewal." He paused for breath.

"We rise in the holiest of Celtic shrines, in London. The sacred river will wake." Joe's voice increased in volume until "London." He noticed puzzlement on a couple of faces and calmed. "Today is fourteen days from the solstice. Time to get you started so that you may be ready for something very ancient and. . ." he paused for effect, "very new."

The younger recruits shuffled in excitement.

"Yes, this solstice will be special. Something never tried before, even by the Reborn Celts," he beamed.

Mary's jaw dropped; she was not acting. Catching Rhiannon's enraptured expression, Joe was back to business. "So today we're getting you started at our sacred well. Follow me."

He strode across the green lawn and ducked through the arch that led to the oldest part of the college. For a second, he turned back. Framed by the stones like a hero from the distant past, he called to his warriors. "This way. Simmy and Dr. Barinthus are waiting at the well."

Doesn't Simmy have a Ph.D. too? thought Mary, bringing up the rear. He hasn't answered any of my questions. Not properly, at least. Simmy's session on Celts and lost rivers had been the only class to stir any enthusiasm in Mary. With Caroline grieving and Rhiannon bathed in lust, it was Sarah who was most fascinated by stories of nature gods.

Trafficked from her village in the Congo, Mary remembered that Sarah had been caught at Holywell trying moon rituals with her own menstrual blood. Out of the frying pan, thought Mary. I do hope Caroline is keeping Janet updated. I must make time to call her.

It was Caroline who visited the witches at Holywell with some regularity and enthused about their eco-therapeutic magic. She tried to find the same energy when Simmy spoke about the Celts treating springs and rivers as sacred doors to the Otherworld. To the Celts, Simmy said, a river was a vein of blood in the land's divine body. Yet now Caroline was drooping, a sign of returning depression. Mary had to speak to her.

She tried to catch Caroline as they were passing through the cool interior of the arch. Mary now knew more about this college, an upstart from 1609. The Exmoor website cited the fortunate purchase of much older ruins of a monastic hospital. Exmoor's builders reused the ancient stones and kept the old well in service.

Like other colleges, it was named for its founders, here the Earls of Exe. A family with the traitorous taint of the "old religion," meaning Catholicism, they'd decided to quash suspicions once and for all by setting up an Oxford College to train priests for the Anglican Church. However, they refused to pay for a new well, whether for secret religious reasons or parsimony went unrecorded.

The others were chatting at the well when Mary pulled Caroline aside. She waved to Joe to signal that this would not take long.

"Caroline, please try to get through this morning. You've been doing so well." Mary wanted to say, 'for Anna,' but those words could not be spoken. She noticed Rhiannon staring at her and mouthed, 'Coming.'

Caroline looked drowned; her face was puffy. She's put on weight, realized Mary.

"I'm trying to help. Seeing Anna is. . .hard. Even though I'm here to look after Sarah."

Mary was considering her response when Caroline pulled her shoulders back. "OK, Mary, OK, I'll do my best. I can't promise."

Mary forced a smile. "Onward then."

A silence greeted them when they rejoined the group. Forlorn Caroline moved further from Anna. Joe's raw fingers reached for Anna's hand. Mary registered the erotic tension between them. Rhiannon scowled at the oblivious couple. Mary could also see Simmy, a lanky boy, and a hairy man, who must be Barinthus, standing near her. Barin is supposed to be in charge, yet he's leaving most of the teaching to Joe and Simmy. I wonder what that's about, thought Mary.

They were looking at Mary expectantly. Sarah moved so that she could see the well in one corner of the lawn. Mary decided to keep quiet about her earlier visit and flashed a glance at Rhiannon. The young woman gave Mary a defiant sniff and turned away.

"Restored with funds from Professor Albert Edward's will," said Barinthus.

The well reminded Mary of pictures in storybooks with its wooden winch and little tiled roof.

"Come forward Mrs. Jones and er. . .Miss Walker. You two must greet our sacred well," said Joe.

Mary nodded to Simmy and the boy who'd already been introduced in class as Simmy's son, Colin. Barinthus looked a lot older than the photo on his website where his age was given as 48. His long hair covered everything, including his shoulders, in aluminum-colored strands.

Mary felt mischievous. Perhaps they'll reveal more if I drop a stone in the water.

"Oh, is this the well where Professor Morrigan found that gold torc? The one that mysteriously vanished?" she said.

The Morrigan siblings tensed. Rhiannon scowled, and Colin shifted from foot to foot at the mention of Albert Edward. Simmy shot out a restraining arm. Colin shook it off, moving to be close to Joe. Barinthus started to flicker pale eyelashes at Mary. She was reminded of a shark with a cultured cough. She wanted to laugh.

"You are correct," came Barinthus's precise tones. "My father directed a limited excavation. He found the torc; a priceless artefact that should have been. . .I digress. It was in the bottom of the shaft, where the spring enters. Celts, as you know, made offerings to their waters. Springs, rivers, and lakes joined this world and the Otherworld."

Peering at Barin, Mary was shocked to see Simmy's features in a male face. Barinthus Morrigan was Simmy's brother, except for too much hair and about fifty extra pounds. Simmy favored a cut Mary's father had called "a short back and sides," dyed blonde. As Barinthus studied each initiate, Mary caught a glint behind strands of beard. He was wearing a torc. Copper, like that one I saw on Joe, thought Mary.

"Reborn Celts call me Barin," he announced to no one in particular.

Mary pretended to be impressed. She'd learned to handle academics back in her days at the Archive.

"Let the initiates come one at a time." Joe Griffith was the sentinel at the well shaft. Last to peer down, Mary almost jumped at the old woman looking back at her. Oh, I'm forgetting.

"You're noticing the water, despite the drought. We're not sure where it's coming from, although a connection to the river is a possibility," said Simmy. The five students exhibited polite interest.

"Exmoor Well," Joe spoke in reverent tones. "Our sacred well is the only one of Celtic origin in Oxford." He moistened his lips. "It's coming alive. The water proves. . ."

Barinthus clasped his student's forearm. "Now then Joe. . ."

Simmy jumped in. "Hang on, Joe. I'm just getting to the Waking of the Waters," she said. Soothing his bubbling emotions, judged Mary. Are they afraid of him? Her mind went back to Jez Wiseman's warnings about Joe. She shivered in the heat.

With her sleek hair and crisp white shirt, Simmy adopted a lecturer's stance: hands on hips and a professional smile. Mary detected a current of anxiety about Colin, who was ignoring her. He's a boy, thought Mary. Could be about Rhiannon's age. He's imitating Joe's physical intensity. Pink skull peeked through Colin's moon-white spiked hair. It had the effect of rays shooting up above cobalt blue eyes. Mary caught Sarah's look of surprise.

"Contact lenses," she mouthed.

When Simmy had introduced him to the class as "my son, Colin," the boy had muttered, "Adopted. But I'm a real Morrigan," and slipped back into his seat. Mary noted he watched the other participants, and never took notes.

Mary remembered something else Mr. Jeffreys had mentioned. Around the time of Albert Edward's suicide, Simmy's lover deserted her, taking their child. Her ex vanished abroad with her baby. Since Simmy and she had not married, and the adoption process not even started, there was nothing Simmy could do.

"That was when Dr. Sulis Morrigan joined the Reborn Celts," Mr. Jeffreys added.

"Oh," said Mary. The loss of Mary's own baby, given up at birth, was something she never spoke about. Mr. Jeffreys knew that.

"What about that boy on the website? The one standing next to Simmy."

"Foster son," confirmed Jeffreys. "Perhaps adopted by now. Yes, she took on a troubled teenager. Both parents died of overdoses when he was fourteen. They were also members of the Reborn Celts."

"Oh," said Mary again. "Oh, do you think…?"

"Drugs in their rituals? Very likely. There are hints on social media that their secret events are secret— and ecstatic— for more than one reason. Be very careful, Miss Wandwalker."

Back at the sacred well, Simmy recounted tales of the riotous medieval rite of Well Waking. Mary kept part of her attention glued to Rhiannon's increasing excitement. According to Simmy, wild parties in late Spring would release healing powers in the water.

"A proven survival of Celtic worship," she concluded. "Now my brother will invite you to our own rite of awakening."

"Becoming a Reborn Celt means initiation by well, by river, and by blood," intoned Barin. Mary tried to look foolish while her insides quivered. Joe's eyes were too bright, and his face too flushed as he listened intently to Barin's words.

"We begin by the Waking of the Well." The five initiates tensed as Barin's tones got louder. Colin's unnatural eyes lit up, and for the first time he glanced at Rhiannon.

"Water calls to water." That was Caroline. She was not among those staring wide-eyed at Barin; rather she peered down mossy shaft of the well.

"Precisely," Barin said.

An unexpected voice bubbled into the brew. Sarah steeped closer to Caroline.

"Does it matter that I am not white?"

Sarah's accent was as English and as cultured as Mary's, whom in fact she was imitating. Mary held her breath. She had not expected Sarah to speak at all. In fact, she was not sure that she had *ever* heard her speak at Exmoor.

Then Mary remembered something she had not thought about at the time. A middle-aged woman of Indian origin and a Chinese man had left the Summer School after the first week. Had they sensed an unwelcome atmosphere? Why hadn't Mary asked about them? Right now, Anna looked curious, and Colin glowered. Something swam behind Barin's eyes. He avoided looking at Joe.

"All blood is the same color." Joe's reply was almost inaudible. Colin stiffened. Simmy took her cue.

"Right then. Thank you, Barin. You see, you initiates will attend the Waking of the Well tomorrow night; the first of three rites. The second, immersion in the sacred river, will occur on the field trip, and the third, the Blood Rising, in London at the solstice itself. However, before we leave today, I want to show you another discovery by my father, Professor Morrigan. I mean father to myself and Barin, of course."

Her brother shot her an enigmatic glance that turned colder when his eyes rested on Colin. Simmy ploughed on. "This stone here," and she went to the part of the well closest to the Exmoor boundary wall. "Come on round to this stone. You see, it's reused from Roman times. We know because of the inscription. The Roman Britons were also Celts. The invaders adopted the Celtic gods and synthesized them with their own."

Caught behind Joe's broad shoulders, Mary could not see the letters. Whereas she *could* decipher Rhiannon's impatience.

"Awesome stone. . .but, but. . .hang on." Rhiannon was prancing, cheeks flushed in the heat.

"Yes, Miss North?"

Drat, Rhiannon's batting her eyes at Joe again, thought Mary. Simmy doesn't like Rhiannon. And is that resentment of Colin making Barin look like he's swallowed a frog?

"Um, Professor Griffith," Rhiannon lost no chance at drawing in Joe. "You said that the medieval people weren't Celts, were they? They were Christians. They did not worship the spring or the well."

Rhiannon waited to be praised. Instead, Joe gestured at Simmy. Anna couldn't help looking smug.

"The *Roman* inscription is Sulis, Great Goddess," said Simmy, an icy tone to her voice.

"My mother's name." It was the first time Colin had spoken. Simmy gave one of her rare smiles to her son.

"You see, Rhiannon," broke in Joe. "This Waking Ceremony, a sort of party for the Summer School, proves that there *is* a continuation of holding the well sacred. In medieval times. . .Oh, sorry, Simmy. I know you've published on this."

Simmy nodded. "Yes, you're right, Joe. Celtic rituals were kept by the Romans. *Sulis* is important because this inscription is only the second to be found in the whole of Roman Britain. The Romans considered Sulis to be their Minerva. By the time they abandoned England it was nominally Christian. Yet the new festivals continued religious reverence begun by the Celts. Officially, the country was Christian, but the Church could not stop all of the old ways."

That's the connection between the ancient Celts and the witches at Holywell, thought Mary. A sceptic when it came to magical 'hocus pocus,' she'd not considered how the witches saw themselves as part of a tradition thousands of years old.

Simmy instructed further. "We have Christmas grafted onto to winter solstice feasting, Easter at the spring equinox, etc. Waking the Well happened once a year, close to summer solstice. It was a gathering with food, wine, singing, music, celebration. . ."

"A party!" Rhiannon clapped. Her greedy expression was painful to Mary.

"Prayer, sacrifice, renewal," concluded Simmy, with a glare.

"And we're going to do all this?" asked Mary.

"Think of it as a ritual gathering in honor of the Reborn Celts," said Joe, easily. "Tomorrow night. Bring a bottle. Food will be provided by the Summer School. Old clothes please. Come around 9:00 p.m. The special rite begins at sunset."

"Medieval Well Waking would last all night until sunrise," explained Simmy. "Not this time. Most of us have an early train the next day for the field trip to the immersion. Your second rite," she added.

"Dreadful timing," agreed Joe, too cheerful. He could see what Mary was about to ask. "We have to do the Well Waking first, and that cannot happen until after two modules. The College is a bit sniffy about parties and insists we do it before the conference next week. Then we can't delay the immersion because you initiates will be joined by a group of veterans brought by my old buddy, Jez Wiseman. They are on a strict schedule for their therapy."

His eyes rested thoughtfully on Mary. He must have noticed Jez and I talking, she realized, returning the blandest of smiles. He turned away, as Anna pulled him in for a brief kiss.

"I could get us a limo," pouted Rhiannon.

"Certainly not," snapped Simmy. "We practice carbon reduction every day."

Rhiannon frowned. Mary was glad she was wise enough not to argue. On the email received that morning, the initiates should be on the 9:11a.m. train to London via Reading. From Reading station, a minibus would transport the group to a mysterious sounding 'lost moon of the Thames' for several days in nature. The highlight of the trip would be the immersion rite with Wiseman's veterans.

They would be American, Mary realized, coming over here to taste British post-combat-trauma therapy as part of joint research. Mary wondered how Wiseman got permission to replace regular treatment with Joe's untried rituals. Perhaps The Reborn Celts were not so wild after all? Contractions in her stomach suggested otherwise.

'Rhetoric of blood and soil,' had said Mr. Jeffreys. It's true, she thought. Anna is already drowned. Joe has severed half her vitality. I know the Reborn Celts pose some threat; it's getting ever closer. Looking at the faces circling the well, Mary smelled cold water from down below.

"Ha," Rhiannon interrupted Mary's fears. "My father's already arranged for a limo to be on call for me. We'll be able to take it to Oxford train station." She gave a skip, delighted to have trumped the alien notion of walking.

That's what you think, resolved Mary Wandwalker.

It was over. Barin dismissed the new recruits while Simmy added a reminder about getting the right train the morning after the Well Waking. Dutifully, Mary, Caroline, Sarah, and Rhiannon followed Joe with Anna hanging on his arm. They trooped through the quad where perfect window boxes bubbled with scarlet geraniums.

All at once the sensation of something slimy made Mary gag. She put her hand over her mouth. Her clothes reeked of the sodden vegetation clinging to the inner sides of the sacred well.

Behind the parade of Oxford clichés, the gurgle of punting, and memories of students spraying champagne on these same lawns, it was always there: that shaft into the dark. Smelling of mold, it was a gate to the underworld rather than some Celtic otherworld.

Mary shivered. Minus the undergraduates, Exmoor lost its patina of carefree youth. Young Sarah worried about race, Mary could see, while Anna was too quiet. An eerie silence accompanied Mary, Caroline, Sarah, and Rhiannon to the Porter's Lodge.

CHAPTER 8
PARTY GAMES

The quiet evaporated outside the college gate. First, Caroline, Sarah and Rhiannon clustered around Mary, waiting for direction. Mary paused a few meters from Exmoor to gather her intuitions about the Waking of the Well party. Specifically, when should she address the touchy subject of who was not going?

Caroline was wearied with other burdens. She set her back to the College interior where they had glimpsed Anna disappearing with Joe. Sarah gazed at Caroline with huge eyes, while Rhiannon, of course, was scrolling through her phone. Perhaps it was the noon heat, for street noises were mild, even for out of term. They could see a corner of the Covered Market where delivery lorries, laden with coffee, fruit or new baked bread, blocked the passage, adding to Oxford's chronic traffic jam.

"I've been Googling thrift stores in Oxford, but nothing's coming up," Rhiannon accused Mary.

"What's a thrift store?" said Mary, not really listening. The more she reviewed that morning's events, the more ominous they appeared. If the Reborn Celts were involved with drugs, then the so-called 'party' presented a big problem. She tried to squeeze out a plan. Hell, I'm supposed to be good at plans. Everyone is relying on me. Just look at them.

Mary sighed. If only the DEA would work as it used to, then she could get Anna to do her cybermagic and dissolve the thickest firewalls. In those secret online dungeons, someone knew what the initiates were being pulled into. By Caroline's pained looks she was thinking of Anna too. Yet Anna was submerged, out of reach.

Before Mary could articulate a plan for the Well Waking, Rhiannon broke in.

"A thrift store? You don't know *that*?" Her disbelief was positively comic. It even distracted Caroline. "Thrift stores are where poor people get their clothes, of course."

"Oh, you mean a *charity* shop," said Mary. "Well, Oxfam's just around the corner in the Broad. We can call in on the way back to the house. What do you want it for?"

"Well… for tomorrow night. You heard Joe… old clothes…"

A sixth sense kicked in. Rhiannon glanced at Mary, her paid 'chaperone,' as Mary insisted. Mary cleared her throat. Alright then, the tricky conversation would be now.

"No, Rhiannon, you're not going to the Waking of the Well. Absolutely not. Remember what we discussed with your father's secretary. No risky nights out, whatever the Summer School does."

Mary expected resistance. She was quite prepared to take Rhiannon on in a public street. In fact, she'd had quite enough of 'the little madam.'

Caroline coughed; Mary knew it was a reminder. The younger woman tried to tell Mary about Rhiannon's fragile self-esteem. She was tossed like a paper boat on the waves of mercurial Joe. Alternately flirtatious and dismissive, whatever he did, he stoked Rhiannon's adoration. Mary determined it would go no further. Rhiannon had other ideas.

"I *have* to go to the Waking of the Well. Joe needs me. You know he does."

She was daring Mary to contradict her. "Old people like you and Caroline don't understand. This initiation is *so* important. You'll see. Just give it a chance." Rhiannon's whole being flowed into her insistence.

Caroline blinked at being described as old and placed her hand on Sarah's arm. That young woman smiled back. Rhiannon always ignored Sarah, and it didn't seem to bother her.

The American girl soaked up all the energy. Mary would not give in.

"Rhiannon, you must not take everything at face value. The Reborn Celts are not telling us everything. They are dangerous, and so is the Well Waking. You will stay with me in the house. Caroline will take Sarah to the early part."

Rhiannon gaped. Mary thought fast.

"Listen to me, young lady. There will be no ritual messing about in the dark. I don't care what Joe said. It's not safe. As soon as Caroline and Sarah return, I'll investigate the. . .the ceremony."

Rhiannon stamped a foot. What was it to her that a man stood staring, momentarily forgetting his strawberries, warm juice staining the bottom of his paper sack?

"Weren't you listening. . .you old. . .old crone? Staying for the ritual is compulsory for the initiation. I *must* become a Reborn Celt. I *must*." Tears appeared on her makeup. "Daddy promised."

Her last word was drowned by a sputtering van edging out of the Covered Market. The man with the strawberry stains on his hands leapt into the passenger seat. The engine roared as the van shot past the women. As soon as the noise died away Mary made up her mind.

"Alright, we'll discuss this matter somewhere cool. We've all got class tomorrow before any party and reading to do this afternoon. Lunch will be at that pub you like, Rhiannon, the Tolkien one."

"The Eagle and Child," said Sarah, ready to move off.

"*Real* Oxford people call it the Bird and Baby," said Rhiannon, flouncing angrily. She sped along the pavement towards another chance to assert her overpowering love for Joe.

"There are many ways of being a child," said Mary Wandwalker, sadly. Her troop was forced to walk in single file down the Broad. They dodged several ambulatory tour groups and tight mouthed locals hauling groceries to the bus stops.

Midday had a blinding sky. Smog flavored sweat leaked into their mouths and dripped off chins. Mary was rueful as she wondered if Rhiannon had a point about an air-conditioned limo.

CHAPTER 9
MARY WANDWALKER'S
BIG MISTAKE

"Miss Wandwalker, wake up! It's late, very late. Wake up. Please."

Mary grunted and turned over. Undaunted, the young woman began to tap her exposed arm. Working in an Oxford College, she was used to rousing undergraduates who smelled far worse. When gentle pressure failed, she grasped Mary's arm and shook it.

"Miss Wandwalker!" she said. "MISS WANDWALKER! THERE'S A TAXI WAITING FOR YOU AT THE PORTER'S LODGE."

Mary sat up, instantly furious. She dared not open her eyes because pain was flooding her whole body, as if someone had thrown her down a well. Who put weights on her skull? No, *in* her head.

"Owwwwww," she croaked. "Aaaargh. My head. Wa. . . water. Too. Much. Light." Between her eyelashes she glimpsed a human figure. "Who are you?"

Wait, this was not her bedroom in the Norham Gardens house. Why was she still wearing last night's skirt and blouse? Before she could demand an explanation, her leather tongue dried. The awful person in her room leaned over and banged the wooden headboard three times.

No. . .Rubbing grit from her eyes, Mary peered into the strange room. Filling a glass from the tap was a girl with a scraped back ponytail. The creaking of pipes and water crashing into beaker deafened Mary. She heaved her eyelids up again. Something bothered her about the girl in the college servant uniform.

"Eugh. . .Olga? Olga from Holywell?" she whispered through dust. "Is that you? Wha…s going on?"

"Yes, Miss Wandwalker, it's me, Olga from Holywell. Drink this."

The girl put the glass in Mary's shaking hands and helped guide it past her dry lips. Mary downed the contents and held the glass out for more. Olga obeyed. Mary noticed her surroundings, the bare white wall with matching bed covers. There was an empty noticeboard with nothing but pin holes and a fire safety notice.

"College dorm?" she rasped in between gulps of the second glass.

Olga nodded. "Keep drinking, Miss Wandwalker. You'll feel better if you hydrate. That must have been some party. And you old people criticize *us* for going to clubs in Oxford."

Mary took the third helping of chalky water. Its surface wobbled. Her stomach sympathized.

"You got Leni's job?" she muttered, telling herself not to panic. There *would* be answers as to how she got here. Of last night, she had no clear memory, only dirty water swirling. Fragments floated across her mind: flotsam of words, masks, hideous laughter. Did she hear a distant flute? No, it was too dark with flaming torches, sour syrupy drinks, and then… nothing.

Mary put the glass down. She had to find the way back to *her* world. Right now, she was with Olga from Holywell. The girl had put on much needed weight. Her face no longer had the gaunt, secretive look Mary remembered.

"I'm at St Julian's," she said with relief. Her old College had given jobs to the recovering young women from Holywell.

"No, Miss Wandwalker. You're at Exmoor."

Mary paled.

"I transferred to this College. They offered higher wages."

Mary finished drinking. She looked for her clothes; no, she was wearing them. Not good.

"I suppose someone put me to bed after the Waking of the Well. How. . .embarrassing. I'm not sure. . ."

There was a crash of a heavy door followed by pounding on wooden stairs. Caroline fell into the room lugging a backpack. She was so out of breath that she must have been running across the quad.

"Mary, the taxi. You're going to miss the train. You need to meet up with Rhiannon at the station. She's already gone."

Caroline tugged open the curtains to dazzling sunshine. Mary groaned, throwing her arms across her burning eyes.

"You're not ready." said Caroline, shocked.

"Obviously."

"What happened?"

Mary subsided onto the pillow.

"I don't know. Go away. . .both of you," she said. She could hear Olga backing out of the room with her mops.

"No, *you're* going away," said Caroline with merciless volume. "Don't you remember? The field trip with Jez Wiseman's Veterans Retreat' starts tomorrow near Reading. You've got a train to catch this morning, so you don't miss the minibus."

Caroline indicated the backpack. "I packed this for you. Don't forget that I'm staying in Oxford to look after Sarah. Poor child, she's sick from what she ate last night. At least, we thought it was the food because I didn't have any. I tried waiting up for you but couldn't keep my eyes open. Why didn't you come home?"

Mary took her hands down from her eyes and scowled at Caroline. Sarah sick? The food? She was starting to get a bad feeling about last night. If only Caroline would go away. The words 'taxi' and 'train' were churning her stomach.

Caroline stood still, watching Mary.

"We slept like the dead. Sarah's suspicious. You know she has a history with drugs. It's a bit worrying because Rhiannon left without either of us seeing her. Once we found you, I booked a taxi from Exmoor to the station. Go now, and you can just make the train."

Mary's limbs hugged the bed. I feel tied up, she thought. I wish I was tied up.

Caroline stepped forward.

"Mary." She ripped the sheets from Mary's fingers. "Get up!"

Mary swallowed with difficulty. Nothing in her body felt right, from the throbbing headache to the sticky mouth, to her wobbly legs. Miss Wandwalker is not at home.

She shot a resentful glance at Caroline. Wait a minute. Hadn't Caroline mentioned Rhiannon? The girl had not been seen since last night. Rhiannon is missing. At once Mary's spine stiffened. Chaperone to the naughty American princess was her job, and she always did her job. The field trip was about to begin.

"God, the train."

Mary swung her feet to the floor. Next challenge, stand up, she told herself.

"Are you going to throw up?"

Caroline looked around for a bucket. Unfortunately, Olga had gone.

"No," said Mary Wandwalker, on her feet, just about. "No, I refuse to. Help me to the taxi. Something bad happened last night. Don't ask, I can't remember."

As Caroline helped her downstairs, Mary tried to find word for images drifting back.

"I heard a drum beat. After that came chanting, it went on for hours."

She stopped to rummage in her handbag. Caroline handed over aspirin. "Dancing, if you can call it that. They put on robes. I saw a torc like the sun around his neck. People wore masks, at least I hope they were masks. We drank bitter stuff from a horn. Weird smoke made us dizzy, herbs maybe. Like incense, it was sort of orange. Then I must have fallen asleep."

"Should you be going today?" Caroline was worried. She started wringing her hands. Mary knew that gesture. For Caroline anxiety could tip into depression-as-exhaustion.

"Yes, absolutely, I'm going," she said. "I have to find Rhiannon. The people who can answer our questions about last night are on Platform 3, waiting for fast train to Reading and London Paddington."

Twenty-two minutes later, Mary Wandwalker scooped her belongings out of the taxi and handed over a ten-pound note, waving away the change. Too much in the bright light, all those noisy coins. She strode, a little unsteadily, up the ramp of Oxford Station.

First, she dipped into Boots, the Chemist, for three bottles of water and more painkillers. Downing one bottle, she nipped through the ticket barrier, and looked for the coffee shop only to mutter curses at the queue. Turning on her heels, she walked as fast as her stomach would allow to Platform 3.

It was easy to spot the Reborn Celts with Joe's pumped-up magnetism. Even in a public place, he infected his people; they were a whirlpool around his hypnotic presence. Mary scanned for Anna. She almost missed her because her hair no longer shone like a waterfall at night. Rather it hung in clumps like seaweed. Close by huddled Simmy's boyish blonde haircut, Colin's white spikes, and Barin's metallic messiness. It was Joe who spotted Mary.

"Miss Wandwalker, you've found us. Over here." He waved with enthusiasm.

He's got my name right at last, thought Mary.

"Yes, I made it, er. . .Joe. Despite the traffic. I must have overslept. Caroline and Sarah are recovering from last night."

Joe beamed. Nothing dimmed his lust for life today. By contrast, Simmy offered a wan grimace before turning back to Colin. She pulled train tickets out of her trouser pocket and handed one to him. Barin ignored Mary. He had positioned himself furthest away from Colin and fussed with a panama hat that complimented his cream-colored suit. Colin was pretending insouciance while attuned to Joe. Mary registered all this in an instant. Her real attention was captured by Anna.

In addition to bad hair, Anna's summer frock was grubby. As Mary moved closer, she detached her arm from Joe. Anna's too pale, thought Mary, she's sick. *Joe has taken all her color; he's bubbling with it.*

Colin's watching him, she decided. Wants to do as he does, be the big Celt warrior. Mary became aware that Joe was chatting about the field trip. His skin was very pink, apart from the silver and maroon scars. Perhaps he thrives on little sleep, pondered Mary. She opened her second bottle of water.

"Ladies and Gentlemen. The train on Platform 3 in five minutes is the 9:11 for London Paddington, calling at Reading only."

The crowd rippled. Rucksacks were heaved onto backs, and bags on wheels were positioned where the train doors would gape open. The hungry mouths of the serpent, mused Mary. Then she gave a start: she'd forgotten the crucial question: "Where's Rhiannon?" she asked aloud. No doubt re-doing her makeup, Mary sighed.

The group around Joe Griffith stopped. Mary's skin prickled.

"With you, of course," said Simmy at last.

"No, she's not. I missed the limo at the house. Rhiannon should have arrived long ago."

"We haven't seen her."

"Not since last night. Ouch."

That was Colin. The adjacent group of backpackers was so solid that Mary could not see who kicked him. She stepped back from the platform edge to scrutinize all the Reborn Celts.

"You mean none of you have seen her here at the station? You're sure?"

They shook their heads. Even disinterested Barin gave a shrug.

Mary's weak stomach flooded with acid. The Celts exchanged blank glances, shuffled, and set their faces to the direction of the incoming train. Mary stamped her foot.

"She's not here? Why didn't you call me?"

This time Joe turned back. The others circled around him. Simmy continued to monitor the train snaking towards them. Colin, not Anna, hovered by Joe.

"Miss North is going to miss the train," said Joe, stating the obvious.

He looked at Mary hopefully. None of them seemed worried by Rhiannon's defection. Simmy tugged Colin back into the best place to dash for seats.

Time sped up for Mary. It wasn't just that she was being paid to watch Rhiannon. She had not missed Colin's admission that the girl had gone to Exmoor last night. Even though she'd promised not to go to the Waking of the Well, Rhiannon had been there. Today she was conspicuously absent. Why wasn't she waiting for the train to the second rite?

Last night, Mary had been certain the girl was asleep when she'd checked in on her. I even locked Rhiannon's bedroom door, she reflected indignantly. Then I was out doing my job by scouting the so-called initiation rite.

Mary shut her eyes. If only I could rewind to where I lost consciousness. Did not expect to wake in a strange bedroom after imbibing substances I can't identify. That's what teenagers do. Like Rhiannon, oh God.

Mary choked as more impressions surfaced. Images flowed of hairy men waving spears, misty hillsides, and a drumming that became rain, despite the heat and drought of June in Oxford. Yet on the hot and crowded platform there arose a memory of how Mary had left the Well Garden. So where was Rhiannon?

"The train arriving on Platform 3...."

Joe made a decisive turn. The Celts closed around him by the nearest door, already engorged with backpackers.

"Wait!" called Mary. "Joe, hang on a moment. She was there wasn't she? Rhiannon was at the Waking of the Well."

It was not a question. To Mary's surprise it was Anna who pulled Joe back to where Mary stood aside. Joe nodded.

"We need a plan," said Mary. "I'll go back for Rhiannon. We'll get another train later. I'll ring and you can send back the minibus to collect us both. Joe, listen to me." He blinked.

Mary felt rather than saw the passengers shrink to the Celts waiting for Joe and Anna. About to step aboard, Barin frowned at the mention of Mer-Corp. Mary addressed Joe's back in loud tones.

"I'll phone Dr. Wiseman. He's expecting to see me today, so tell him not to worry."

"No one is worrying, Miss Wandwalker," said Joe, sweetly.

"I'll come back with you, Mary," Anna announced. Mary was taken by surprise. Joe too.

"You can't, Anna. I need you on the field trip. I don't want to do it without you." He was confident of his influence.

Anna threw a tormented glance at Mary.

"Babe," said Joe. "Come on now. You know that Rhiannon's a spoiled child. Miss Walker will find her."

"*Wandwalker*," muttered Anna, not looking at him.

Yes, for a second, it was her Anna, the girl Mary knew, a glimmer in those black watchful eyes. For a few seconds Mary grinned at the woman she. . .well, sort of loved. Bugger you Celts, she thought in a moment of swagger, give back Anna. For Caroline's sake, if not for mine.

"The train on Platform 3 is about to depart. Stand clear of the closing doors."

"Come *on* Anna. I can't. . .You know I. . ."

He was hanging out of the door, stopping it from closing. A man with a flag and whistle glared at her from further down the platform. Joe pulled on Anna's hand. So far, she was letting him drag her on board.

Mary's phone pinged. She checked it, then back at Anna in amazement. As if it was a cue, Anna leapt into Joe's arms and the door swished shut. With a great shudder the serpent began to glide out of the station. Mary glued her eyes to Anna's moving lips. Unfortunately, she was addressing Joe.

At the last moment before she melted into a blur, she turned to Mary. *Message, see message,* Mary thought she heard in her ear. *I've seen it,* whispered Mary.

Her feet were stuck to the platform, as if it were mud by the Thames. I cannot believe it. Don't want to. Anna sent these words at 10p.m. last night. The ping just now was an extra notification because I'm always missing texts.

DANGER, STAY AWAY it said in capital letters, and nothing else.

Mary felt up to her armpits in liquid mud. She waded down the platform to the exit. Afterwards she could barely remember explaining to the ticket collector that she had changed her mind about taking a train. She had to swim against the incoming tide of people. Got to find another taxi because no time for anything else. Seeing the taxi rank ahead, made her push faster. Not even time to pause at the kiosk selling much-needed coffee.

CHAPTER 10
FIRST RITE: INITIATION PART TWO

Mary called Caroline after securing her taxi's seatbelt. She groaned when Caroline confirmed that Rhiannon was indeed missing. No grumpy teenager stumbled home this morning. Sarah had turned away the limo due to take Rhiannon to the train station to meet the other Reborn Celts. Of course, she and Caroline had checked that Rhiannon did not linger under the mound of discarded clothes, spilt makeup, and sour smelling dishes that once held ice cream.

Should they contact the police? Mary called the number of the Oxford Station, to be told that they couldn't do anything about Rhiannon's disappearance for 48 hours. She phoned Exmoor. No, they'd not found an American teenager taking an unplanned sleepover. Yes, they were sure. All the rooms had now been cleaned in preparation for the incoming conference.

And by the way, as a registered student at the Summer School, could Miss Wandwalker account for the terrible state of the Well Garden? Professor Morrigan? Why, he is gone to an important event near Reading, don't you know? The professor is far too distinguished to be bothered, was the unspoken undertone.

Mary ground her teeth. She ended the call. In minutes Mary banged on the front door of the rented house to find a white-faced Caroline behind it. Mary beckoned her into the car. They did not need any words. She directed the driver to chart a course for Exmoor in a voice that did not sound like her own.

"At once, please. A young girl we're looking for was last seen there."

Speeding like a powerboat, the taxi sailed through the usual congestion and drew up at the silent college. Exmoor in its scrubbed pre-conference incarnation displayed windows gleaming their multiple eyes. The stillness resembled a forest pool expecting decorous sprites.

Mary had a strange sensation that she ought not to breathe. Even the porter at the Lodge had disappeared. The green quad shimmered in the high sun. Mary and Caroline's footsteps echoed as they made their way to the scene of last night's party. At the Well Garden, they halted. It was worse than Mary had imagined.

The scouts, Olga included, must have refused to tackle the wreckage. Alongside empty bottles, broken glass, crushed beer cans, paper cups, and plates with half-eaten messes of pies and cakes, there were darker indications. Mary caught the whiff of vomit. Turning away she found herself treading on a couple of discarded syringes and items of underwear. Several used condoms were strewn together with knickers that could belong to either sex.

While Mary was staring, Caroline approached a pile of dirty laundry. She moved the top T-shirt with her foot. As it fell open, Caroline leapt back.

"Mary, over here," she hissed. "Come quick. That. . .stain. It's blood, isn't it?"

Mary found herself next to Caroline looking at a mangled yellow shirt with brownish red spattered all over it.

"Yes, that's blood," she said. Her voice was starting to shake. "A lo. . .lot of blood." Caroline lifted her head to the well. Unlike the rest of the garden, it was clean. She did not move.

Mary kept her eyes on the bloody cloth. "Shirt's too big for. . .you know, her," she said, hoping against hope. Seeing Caroline frozen like a dog on a hunt, she grasped her arm. Cold sweat soaked through her shirt.

"There's just one place left to look," Mary said.

Caroline nodded.

"Not you," sighed Mary. "I'll do it. Stay right here."

Caroline nodded again; a flush flooded her chalk white jaw. Scratching the waistband of her too tight jeans, she waited.

Alone amongst the wreckage, the sacred well had been scoured until its smooth stones glistened. Even the moss had been stripped. Someone used strong bleach, concluded Mary. Why? Must be getting rid of evidence. Yes, I see now I'm close enough to touch, a few brown threads in the mortar cracks. More blood.

She shut her eyes and told herself to shut out the noxious smells that hovered throughout the garden. Putting both hands on the top of the well to steady herself, the heat of the midday burned the back of her neck. There was sweat in her grey bob, and her hands were baking an unhealthy red. The stones absorbed heat like sponges. Trying not to breathe, Mary bent her head and forced open her eyes.

At first, she couldn't make it out, the thing in the water. Her eyes saw black from the sun's brightness. No, there it was floating, a nightmare. It couldn't be. Yet she'd been unconsciously expecting this, hadn't she?

Something deep in Mary peeled away and stood aside. It watched her senses piece together the long stain on the well shaft, the white wet skin, the flash of gold. Her mouth opened in a silent scream. Mary's chest convulsed. Blood does boil, came the thought. Then the smell. It reached up to her. She jerked up, gulping to wash out her lungs.

This is no good. She tipped back down to the poor thing that bobbed in the dark: a girl's severed head. Tendrils of blond hair floated like weeds, or a mermaid's hair. The water was dark, oily with slicks of red. *To see this is a sacrament.* No. No, *sacrilege,* she insisted to the voice inside her.

Drained of blood, flesh translucent, hair colorless, the head nevertheless gleamed with a golden torc worn as a crown. The Morrigan torc had come home to its very own sacred well. Crammed onto the delicate brow, snaky dragons' mouths bit through soft skin. Mary could not tear herself from the wide blue eyes that fixed her with a fierceness beyond all knowing.

Rhiannon had achieved her dearest wish. She had become a goddess.

Mary felt the touch of a sweaty hand on her shoulder. Someone groaned and shuddered: herself. Caroline hauled her up and took her into her arms.

CHAPTER 11
ONE OF LONDON'S LOST RIVERS

The next morning Mary and Caroline descended from the clouds into London and the bank of the Thames. The police wanted them to identify the torso of a young woman. For as the sun was rising over the glass towers of Canary Wharf, a Thames mudlark, licensed to glean treasure from the foreshores, made a gruesome discovery. She reported the headless corpse to the River Police.

Minutes later computers streamed the image onto police screens in Oxford, splashing cold evidence in the faces of tired officers. Fortunately, little time was lost in checking out the mudlark. A woman of eighty-five who walked ten miles each day along the river's beaches, she was well known to the river authorities. Wading in Thames mud for decades, she was famous for discovering Roman and Celtic offerings now in the British Museum and the Museum of London. Mary was in no mood to appreciate the irony.

An hour later, two expressionless and plain clothed policemen banged on the doors of the rented house. Mary and Caroline were fast asleep. Caroline was comatose due to doubling her medication on medical advice, Mary, because after hours of restless turning, she'd dozed off at 5:30 am. Both were drained from police interviews that had lasted into the night.

As well as biting questions from the police, Mary had to consider Rhiannon's living parent, Frederic North. This august personage declined to speak to the British police. However, his assistant did have a message for Mary Wandwalker. Between interviews, Mary checked her voice mail. A woman identifying herself as Mr. North's Senior Aide informed her that she and the Depth Enquiry Agency would be hearing from Mer-Corp's UK lawyers.

Mary was past caring. Every bone in her chest ached. Her prized cream-colored linen suit smelled of stewed tea. It meant she could not forget the indelible stains on the sleeves from spills. Her head throbbed from trying to comfort Caroline. Back in Norham Gardens, Miss Wandwalker threw her handbag on the sofa, staggered upstairs, and dove into bed. Even so, the day's bloody waters lapped at her door.

That night her bedroom was no place of safety from her demons. Instead, lying down summoned what pervaded the whole house, the sodden head with inhuman eyes. Rhiannon was pulling Mary down. Sleep was impossible. She'd seen those eyes looking up at her. Now they would not let her go.

Mary sat up in bed. The eyes from the well floated around the room. She switched on the lamp, and the eyes ducked into the shadows. Mary tried to face the young woman. *I let you down. I should have protected you, Rhiannon North, age 18 and a quarter*. The dead girl haunted Mary from outside her body and inside her mind. She buttoned up her nightgown and glared at the flowered wallpaper.

"I didn't like you, Rhiannon. I admit it," she said out loud. "But I was supposed to keep you safe and I didn't. . ."

Each word dropped like a stone into the bottomless well. Mary found it hard to breathe.

". . .I didn't try hard enough."

Mary closed her eyes and whispered: "I will find out. . .I will find out what happened to you, Rhiannon." Without thinking, she called out: "If it is the last thing I do, I will bring you home."

Home, why on earth had she said that? Where was home for that child?

Mary recalled her room in the house she shared with Caroline and Anna. Furnished to her personal taste with William Morris prints, it represented a statement to the world. "Fragile gallantry," Caroline had said. Mary sighed. A tiny rattle shook the wall behind the bed. That was Caroline snoring.

"Home," whispered Mary again to Rhiannon, to herself.

The eyes in the shadows abated some of their intensity.

Mary had another flash. A pair of dead eyes the exact color of her own, George's eyes, Caroline's murdered husband's eyes, the eyes of the son Mary had never known. My eyes, thought Mary, for you, Rhiannon, my eyes searching for your killer. Weren't you trying to find a place to belong?

At last, she fell into a troubled sleep until the police banged on the door. It was 7:00 am. The two young men had dodged charm school. *Miss Wandwalker and Mrs. Jones must come to Oxford Airfield, no time to waste. . .you are required in central London before the tide destroys a crime scene. . .it's a beach on the River Thames. . .yes, Miss Wandwalker, it is believed to concern the death of Rhiannon North. . .no, there's no time for coffee. We leave right now. . .the police chopper departs in twenty minutes for London City Airport.* Mary winced at the word for helicopter. Caroline stuffed extra pills in her handbag.

Later that morning the two wary women descended wooden steps slippery with weeds. Below, the Thames lapped hungrily at a narrow spit of sand. The tide was on the turn, or so their escort said. Mary saw a series of oily swirls with screaming gulls. As well as a yellow tent, tightly closed, persons in plastic coveralls searched the grey beach. They began to point and look at their watches.

Mary and Caroline held onto each other while putting on blue booties and gloves. Caroline shivered at the smell of tar, weeds, and ripening sewage. Facing the river, yet not seeing it, she held her summer coat, several sizes too large, tight across her chest.

They came for Mary first. A young woman on tiptoes like a ballet dancer escorted her to the tent. Mary stumbled over stones that had soaked in every tide since the Bronze Age. With them were half buried bricks and shards of glass mixed with sodden bits of splintered wood. She winced. The coffee on the ride had been sour and insufficient. At the tent's flap, a tired looking Asian woman in donned in white plastic poked her head out, nodded, and emerged.

"Have her taken to the morgue," she said back into the tent. "I've done all I can for now."

"Wait a minute, doctor!" called a young man from a group of figures on the foreshore with similar protective clothing. One detached himself and retreated after the doctor who was beginning to climb the stairs.

"Please come in, first Miss Wandwalker. Then we'll bring over Mrs. Jones."

The calm male voice came from inside the tent. Grotesque, thought Mary, involuntarily; a grotesque invitation she could not refuse. She could not get her mind to focus with these people concentrated on their mysteries. They had their rituals too, she noticed, trying to ignore the smells inside the tent. Feeling stubborn, she remained at the entrance.

"Why can't we see her at the morgue?"

"Protocol."

"What? I don't see why. . ."

"Miss Wandwalker, I've been hearing about you from my superiors. Just let us do our job."

Bound to have been Mr. Jeffreys, thought Mary.

"And for our job we need you to see her here," the voice continued. "In situ."

This had to be Inspector Walbrook; the name they'd heard as the helicopter descended. He'd ordered their transportation through the clouds. Walbrook of the Met commanded this crime scene.

Stooping into the tent, Mary peered to see the owner of the male voice. No way will I look down until I absolutely must, she thought. Intending to argue with Walbrook, she was stopped by the grey tinge of his ebony features.

He continued. "Your friend, or former boss, Mr. Jeffreys, said we could rely on your impeccable professionalism."

"Humph," grunted Mary, not taken in. Delay now over, she had to look at the thing at her feet. The blood stink mixed with the dank odor of the river. I hope it is the river that smells of rotting fish. I can do this, she said in silence. I made promises, I can steel myself. She felt the heat of liquid steel flowing up her backbone before she bent over. Open your eyes Mary, pin them if you must. Whatever you do, don't breathe. Several seconds passed until she ran from the tent, retching into the river.

Caroline made dogged progress towards Mary until she was intercepted. The constable whispered, "This way, Mrs. Jones. I'm afraid, we must."

Moments later, Caroline backed out from the tent tight mouthed. She headed for her handbag by the steps, where she fumbled with her emergency pills. The constable walked her up to a seat on a bench overlooking the swelling river. Mary saw her give Caroline a fresh bottle of water. Deciding that was a good idea, Mary started towards them, when she found herself being steered back to Walbrook. He had left the tent and was peeling off his overalls.

Mary faced a densely muscled man in his forties who wore his authority like a cloak, visible and elegant. Everyone on the beach was acutely aware of his presence, Mary noted. Dressed in black cords with water stains at the ankles, Walbrook radiated reassurance.

"Miss Wandwalker, I know you've had a shock, but what can you tell us?"

"Nothing. What do you want me to say?"

"Is this the body of Rhiannon North? Minus the head, of course."

His stark words took Mary back to bleak. She let her eyes slide over the tent. Such a tiny house for a corpse. Or maybe it was a shroud? Shroud: a comforting word for no comfort. About to insist she'd never seen Rhiannon naked; Mary did a double take. There was something strange between the tent and the river edge.

"Is that a stream? I thought it was too wet... Couldn't work out what..."

Walbrook nodded her to go on.

"There's water making a channel from the tent to the river. Inside it too. The body is being *washed.*"

Mary pointed to the flow. Approval softened Walbrook.

"Well done, Miss Wandwalker. You see, the body was placed on the bank of one river, *and in the bed of another*. Look at the brick wall behind the tent. Do you see that rusty pipe? It is very old. There is no map of where it goes because this is the Eponia, one of London's lost rivers. No one knows where it begins, just that it enters the Thames near Waterloo Bridge."

He was watching her minutely for her reactions. When he saw she was too wary to reveal much, he continued.

"You see, this isn't any old Thames killing. The body was placed so that water from the hidden river runs over, and beneath it. Doc says that's why there so little blood."

"Eponia, Eponia," muttered Mary. "I've heard that name."

For the first time since arriving, she looked up to take in the whole scene. Bleached stone mansions near the river were just catching the morning sun. Dominating everything was the bridge, huge and bluish in shadow, a running dog across the Thames. The bridge she remembered well.

"Waterloo Bridge," she said in wonder. "It looked familiar, but I was so dreading. . .I was here, right here, not long ago. I didn't notice. Too preoccupied with. . .what you found."

"Understandably," said Walbrook, scrutinizing Mary even more closely. She met his gaze and realized how controlled he was with his emotions. He was prepared to squeeze every drop of information from her. A possible ally? After all, he had mentioned Mr. Jeffreys to reassure her. She decided to tell it as she saw it.

"If this is Waterloo Bridge, and the. . .body was placed in the Eponia, then, yes, it could be Rhiannon North. The head... well you must know about it. The Celtic Summer School is where Rhiannon lost her head."

Oh no, she wasn't going to laugh, was she? Cackle like a witch? Mary swallowed hard. She spoke fast and with formality.

"Finding the body here suggests a Celtic connection. Eponia was sacred to the Celts. We know because of the finds, the offerings."

Mary tried to take short breaths while ignoring the smells. Oh Rhiannon, is that what your headless body is now? An offering? Mary's eyes met Walbrook's impassivity. He wanted more.

"She. . .with my colleagues and I, are. . .were taking the Celtic course in Oxford, at Exmoor College. Mr. Jeffreys, you mentioned him, well he asked us to. They talk about London's lost rivers there."

Inspector Walbrook nodded with deliberation. He'd guessed as much, Mary realized. Perhaps he's as formidable as I am, she said to herself.

"Odd though," she added.

His head snapped back: "Why's that?"

"So brazen. You can do DNA, confirm its Rhiannon. Its position makes the Celtic connection so obvious. How could they hope to get away with it? This isn't a usual murder."

"Not murder." Walbrook corrected himself. "I mean, your Mr. Jeffreys would call it terrorism. These kinds of killings are meant to be attributed; they are a message to the world. Does this group, the Reborn Celts have an agenda?"

Of course, he would know about the Reborn Celts by now, thought Mary. This is a test.

"An agenda, yes, we believe so. They say all will be revealed later this month at the summer solstice. We are trying to discover. . ."

"No, you are not," interrupted Walbrook. "This is a matter for the police. The police alone, Miss Wandwalker."

He is not taking me seriously as an investigator, Mary saw. Her hands curled into fists in her jacket pockets. Right, that's enough. I'm not saying any more. She stood up straight. No reason for the DEA to give up the case. We know from the Oxford Police that Mr. North's lawyers got the American Ambassador to quash publicity about his daughter's demise. We won't be overrun by the media. She felt her phone vibrating and recollected three unopened voice messages, all from Mr. Jeffreys. Later, she promised.

Walbrook looked thoughtful. Another officer, so fat he looked like a defunct moon wrapped in plastic, started speaking into his ear. A young woman with a Hindu mark on her forehead beckoned Mary to the wooden steps. Walbrook nodded his permission, and Mary ducked away, impatient to leave the deadly beach.

"Can you be sure it's Rhiannon North?" the woman asked.

"Of course not," retorted Mary. "I've been telling your inspector that the placing of the body makes it more likely than not. That's all that I can say for now. Mrs. Jones too, I expect."

"Yes, so she said. Mrs. Jones is quite distressed. My colleague has taken her for a cup of tea. We'll get your statements, then the 'copter will return you to Oxford."

Before getting into the police car, Mary looked back at the river, now steaming and sunlit. It's like a vast snake, she thought, thrusting its tongue into the sea. The sea roars back, twice a day. She was reminded of the golden dragons facing each other on the torc; the same torc that was placed on Rhiannon's sodden skull.

CHAPTER 12
A DELIVERY OF CAKES

The following day, after the horrors of the Thames by Waterloo Bridge, Caroline slept late. By afternoon Mary had to rouse her. Sarah was cooking a huge summer soup for dinner. After her offer to help with chores, in return for the DEA paying for the Summer School, she had taken on much of the cooking. Mary was grateful.

"Caroline, can you get up? Come downstairs with me. I'd like to talk to you before I go."

Caroline was groggy; she muttered and turned over. Mary knew those emergency tablets could induce drowsiness. She pulled away Caroline's sheet. After all, you did the same to me, she thought, sadly. Time to get the crew organized.

"No, no more sleep. We need to talk." She was loud. "Come on, Caroline, I need you. Frederic North's people have been in touch. They insist I go on the Exmoor field trip to look for Rhiannon's killer. Mr. North fears the Reborn Celts will use it as an excuse to escape."

The figure hiding under her pillow stopped moaning, "Go away." Even so she was beginning to listen.

"You know Anna is with them. It occurs to me that she. . ."

"Alright, alright, that's enough. I'm up," Caroline heaved herself up. Her suffering was palpable. Mary tried to look sympathetic when in fact she felt like getting into bed herself.

"Kettle's boiling!" yelled Sarah from downstairs. Mary opened her mouth, then closed it. Those waters again; it was getting dark. Mary wobbled. She would have fallen if someone had not pulled her onto the bed.

"*Oww*, my head." Caroline clutched her temples then put her hands down as she saw Mary sway. Mary blinked as her vision returned.

Caroline took in what Mary had just told her. She did not like it.

"You look terrible, Mary. You almost fainted. Did you say something about going to find the Celts in a field? You can't go today. It'll kill you. . .like my head is killing me." She stopped. "So sorry, Mary, I keep saying 'head.'"

"Forget it," muttered Mary, getting to her feet. "Come downstairs. You heard Sarah. She's making tea for both of us. We've something to show you. But when I heard her voice. . ."

"Whose voice?" Sarah was at the door, trying to smile. Her jeans and pink T-shirt set off the watery sunshine through the curtains. "Did you tell her, Miss Wandwalker? Tell her what was in all those boxes we found on the doorstep?"

"Caroline should see for herself," said Mary, collecting her travel handbag from the floor. I refuse to be ill, she told herself. And I refuse to let Mr. North down again.

Mary waved Sarah aside to signal that they would continue over tea downstairs.

"I've got fifty minutes before the limo arrives. Come down and I'll update you, Caroline. Don't worry about me. Mer-Corp sent a First-Class ticket. They don't know our trains."

"Ludicrous," said Caroline, throwing on a baggy dress over her nightgown.

The smell engulphed the three women as soon as they reached the ground floor. Waves of sugar with overtones of butter and chocolate shocked their palates. Even so, nothing could have prepared Caroline for the kitchen table piled high with cakes.

A few glistened with cellophane, some flaunted pastel colors made of icing. There were loaves sticky with brown ooze and others with chocolate buttercream starting to melt. Spots, one had spots, worried Caroline. She could have laughed. It was a cherry cake, perfectly baked, unlike her own when the cherries formed a pool of red at the bottom of golden dough.

Mary and Sarah exchanged a glance. They could see that Caroline felt lighter. That smell: it was the scent of her childhood, Caroline explained. She was back in her mother's kitchen on baking days. Entranced, she circumambulated the loaded table, keen to soak in the gifts from another world.

"We've counted them," said Mary, watching Caroline sniff the fruit cake.

Caroline's stomach gurgled as she marveled at the exquisite professionalism of the frosting: Christmas scenes with Santa, a nativity cake, one for Easter with miniature eggs, another with sculpted roses, one with silver bells and 'Wedding' in blue icing, and a matching cake that said 'Christening.' At last Caroline let the sugar palace of memories dissolve. Comprehension flooded in.

"Of course, Rhiannon. . ."

"Yes, she ordered the cakes," said Mary. She sounded at a loss. "Sarah found a receipt for over four hundred pounds. But, *why?*"

"Four hundred is a lot, isn't it?" asked Sarah.

"That's right. I remember now that she asked for a batch of Celtic cakes to be delivered," said Caroline, sitting on a wooden chair and making it creak. "For all the traditional festivals. At first the bakery had no idea what she was talking about. We went to the shop at her insistence." She turned to Mary.

"It was while you were off registering us for the Summer School. Rhiannon asked for, well, she demanded, Celtic brownies she could bring to class. All they had was a batch of éclairs about to be frozen, and a couple of left-over scones. We'd saved that last éclair for you, remember? So, later, she phoned. They must have persuaded her to put in a massive order."

"Celtic cakes," mused Sarah. She put a fingertip to the rock-hard whirlpool of a red rose.

"Not Celtic, most of them," said Mary. She put on her severe look. "I should have a word with that bakery, taking advantage of an American teenager."

"Or we could just eat them," said Caroline. She smiled her sad smile at Mary. The older woman struggled to understand how an eating disorder was part of her depression.

"I've laid tea in the front room," said Sarah, keeping her tone bright. "Real china cups 'n all. I cut the ginger cake. Since Miss Wandwalker's going to be travelling, I was thinking of her stomach. Janet makes us ginger tea when we're off our food."

Ten minutes later the three had steaming cups and fragrant slices. None felt able to pretend normality. While sipping her tea, Mary began to wonder about Sarah. The young woman was skilled at concealing her reactions. No doubt it was a legacy of her trafficking. Rhiannon took up so much psychic space. Even so, I should have thought of Sarah before this. What can she be making of a head in a well and the body by a river in London?

Before Mary could think of an acceptable way to interrogate Sarah, Caroline choked over her cake and needed her back slapping. Gulping down her tea, Caroline took another slice, determined not to be beaten. Taking big bite speckled with crystalized ginger, she recalled a ritual origin that post-dated the Celts. Or did it?

"Ginger parkin," she said through crumbs, swallowing with care. "Really good, sticky with syrup. Just how my mother made it for bonfire night, November the 5th."

Sarah frowned.

"You've not experienced Bonfire Night?" queried Caroline.

"Well, I *was* at Holywell last November," began Sarah. "The witches said their fire festival was Celtic. Sam something, they called it. But there was nothing about. . .you know."

"Samhain," said Caroline, halfway through her slice. "Fire streaming into the night for renewal against the dark. It's been assimilated to. . .well. . ." Caroline stopped and frowned at Mary.

"Burning the effigy of Guy Fawkes, the parliamentary terrorist," she said, tart.

"Catholic resister, not the most guilty, likely to have been framed," returned Caroline, pouring more tea. "Although as well as Celtic Samhain, it can stretch to Hindu festivals of light about that time."

Of course, Caroline had taught Primary School. She would have researched various traditions. Mary tried to relax. She had a complicated journey to make before nightfall.

"Have some more cake, Miss Wandwalker," said Sarah, holding out the pretty plate. Mary shook her head. Sarah was nervous. Ah, she's picked up on how snappy I'm feeling. Mary tried to smile at the young woman. She took the plate, cut the slice in half, and returned the other half to the cake plate. Sarah's tea was darker than Mary normally tolerated, but she kept sipping.

Caroline was finishing her second slice of parkin when she noticed Sarah staring at the wallpaper. It was unlikely to be the brown leaves that worried her.

"Sarah?"

The dark head stayed where it was, her expression invisible.

"Anything you need to tell us, Sarah. My taxi is in eight minutes." Mary did not like the strained sound of her own voice.

"So sad. All those cakes," Sarah whispered. Her cheek glittered. Mary's response spilled out before she could stop herself.

"Rhiannon always went First Class."

"First Class, and not enough love," echoed Caroline. She gasped, giving a start to both Mary and Sarah. Caroline locked her gaze on Mary. Her eyes were green in sunshine. Caroline was surfacing from a long time underwater.

Mary pushed her chair back. Had Sarah put whisky in the tea? She was about to ask when a strangled sound drew her back to Caroline.

"Mary!" she got out. "I. . .you. . ."

Mary stood up. "She's having a fit. Sarah, water!"

The girl gave a sob and lunged for the door.

"No, no, I'm fine," croaked Caroline, struggling to be calm. "Stay, Sarah. This is *good.* It's what I need to do. What *we* need to do, Mary."

"Caroline, sit back on the sofa, you're sweating."

Mary was alarmed. What if Caroline was ill? Could she leave her here safely? Sarah was so young, even if hardly inexperienced.

"*Listen*, Mary," Caroline stood up, and enunciated slowly. "You are not going on the field trip. I. . . won't let you. You haven't recovered. It's me. I must go. Let me borrow your suitcase. The zipper is stuck on mine."

Relief shot through Mary only to be instantly dismissed. Not with Caroline's history, I can't possibly let her go. She drew on her resources.

"Don't be foolish, Caroline. Of course, I'm going. You of all people know I owe Rhiannon."

There, I've said it aloud. To the person who was too kind to tell me. I'm a woman in my sixties, with a lot of experience being in charge. Yet I let down Rhiannon North, the girl with all the cake in the world. And no head.

Mary could see Caroline shaking her head. Sarah had left the room and now reappeared with Mary's elderly suitcase. Ignoring Mary, Caroline fell on her knees, flipped the case open and began tossing the neatly packed belongings onto the sofa. She looked up to address Sarah.

"Sarah, I need my underwear, my clean jeans, and anything of mine in the bathroom."

The girl ran for the stairs. "And my spare cash is in the bedside cupboard!" shouted Caroline after her. "Thank goodness I visited the hole in the wall days ago." She was too preoccupied to pay attention to Mary.

"Caroline, you're being ridiculous. The taxi at Reading is booked in my name. . .So's the first-class train ticket."

"You can re-book the taxi into my name very easily. It'll be over an hour before I arrive at Reading. The first-class thing is silly. It's not like flying. I'll buy another ticket." Caroline sat back on her heels.

"This is not happening. Put my clothes back *right now*. You've messed them all up."

Mary attempted to grab the case from Caroline, who hung on. Mary lost her footing and ended up sprawled on the crumb-strewn carpet. She glared at Caroline, the empty suitcase between them. Other people might laugh at the situation. Not Mary Wandwalker.

"Now look what you. . ." the crack in her voice stopped Mary. She levered herself onto the sofa and put her hands over her face. *I can't do this.* Her shoulders shook.

"Have a good cry." Caroline put an arm around her.

"I *never* cry," Mary said, affronted. I don't care if I sound ridiculous, she thought. She felt for her handkerchief in the tangled pile of underwear and toiletries on the sofa.

There was a rapping at the front door just as Sarah returned with arm full of un-ironed laundry. Five pill bottles balanced on top. Sarah had a wallet between her teeth. Caroline pointed to the empty suitcase, and Sarah filled it with remarkable speed. She was almost as neat as Mary in folding blouses and finding pockets for small items.

"I'll tell the taxi five minutes," Caroline got up. Mary waited, too stunned to do anything else.

"You've had a terrible shock," said Caroline, returning. She'd retrieved her best jacket from the coat rack, secondhand— but good quality. Its sober rust supported what was left of the copper in her curls.

"Face it Mary, I know you feel you've let Rhiannon down. That's your way of caring. But you're not fit to travel. You know I'm right."

Mary nodded. I feel defeated, she thought. I *am* defeated. At least for now.

"Unfinished business, you and Rhiannon," said Caroline. "You have to stay here, near the body in the morgue, as they put her back. . .together."

Mary shuddered. Resist it as she tried, Caroline was right. Flashes of the head, the blue eyes, the twists of gold in the torc. . .and the water flowing beneath perfect white limbs. Pink tendons of the neck hung like worms. Rhiannon was showing her this. Even in this sunny room, the girl was calling her.

"What about. . ." Mary was reluctant to be too explicit, "your health?"

"Is variable. As always. But I'm tough. You know that, Mary. It's only for a few days. You know why I have to go." Caroline twisted her lips into a weary smile. "It sounds crazy, I know, what with severed heads and mad Celts, and Anna under Joe's spell. Dearest Mary, somehow, even for me, love is involved. I thought I could leave it, leave her. I can't."

Mary remembered this dignity in Caroline. Remembered, too, why she had felt her necessary to the Depth Enquiry Agency. Two weeks ago, when Anna's desertion was new, Caroline sank down. Now, for the first time since that painful exchange, Mary could see that she was back as a woman with ideas and actions. At least two of the DEA were a family again. She nodded. She could trust Caroline. It was a new thought; a good one.

"It's just for a few days," Mary repeated, as much to persuade herself. Her voice sounded more human. Now what did she need to tell Caroline?

"Although the field trip began before. . .Rhiannon was discovered, the Oxford Police got statements from the Reborn Celts at the camp. Reading Police knew where to find them. That's what I tried to explain to Mr. North's lawyer on the phone. Can you believe that Mer-Corp has an *Oxford* lawyer? Well, never mind. I offered to talk to the Celts when they got back. No good, Mr. North must have one of us on the field trip to collect evidence. He doesn't trust our police."

Mary's voice faded. Caroline nodded. The rapping at the door returned, insistent.

"I'll take the suitcase out," Sarah reassured Mary.

"Thanks." Mary and Caroline spoke at once. Their eyes met. Neither felt like laughing. Caroline pulled Mary to her feet, hugged her, then dashed for the door.

Left alone, Mary listened to three voices ripple into Caroline getting into the car, saying goodbye to Sarah, and the click of the closing door. The vehicle, a little tugboat in Mary's musing, nosed out of Norham Gardens and into Oxford's currents. Mary found herself bereft, yet not alone.

"Shall I fetch your phone, Miss Wandwalker?"

"Don't worry, Sarah. I'll call the lawyer about Caroline going instead of me."

"Will she be OK?"

Mary didn't see Sarah's concern. Her mind followed the flow of traffic. Oxford has so many channels, she thought. The city of learning clasps the young Thames until it becomes a mature river at Reading. From there the Thames launches curves and sinews towards London, the city of the ancient Celts. Caroline has embarked on a journey to an unknown shore.

"Caroline is the strongest person I know," she said, into the tides between Oxford and the sea.

CHAPTER 13
CELTIC SUMMER SCHOOL
DOES A FIELD TRIP

Of the bizarre and bloody events during the Summer School's Celtic field trip, Mary received accounts from two people whom she trusted. Each had a different perspective. In their own way, both Caroline and Wiseman, tried and failed to control the torrent that led to the second murder. Much later, Mary made a cursory attempt to question Anna. As usual, the young woman offered little by means of 'normal' conversation.

"It was a time of. . .of unclarity."

Angling her back to Mary, she bent further over her enhanced computer. "After all, it was just before the solstice," she added.

Mary grimaced. "Yes, I know." It was wiser to leave Anna alone.

For those long June days of the Celtic field trip, Mary was in the unusual position of waiting for news. Much later she decided to compile a detailed report. She clicked on the file of those first soundings. The transcribed phone messages, texts and other data started a trickle that became a flood. It all began with phone messages after the best sleep she had had in months, the night after Caroline's departure.

"Miss Wandwalker, we gotta talk. Right away. Call me." Wiseman sounded strained. They were close to the solstice, the longest day of the year, and Wiseman phoned from the dark when she was asleep. She pressed for the next message.

"Mary, you haven't got back to me. I'm real disappointed you didn't come. I know, I know, Mrs. Jones is a kind lady, but she's not you. She stares like I'm crazy when I try to talk to her about Joe. To my mind he is sick. . . He looks… feverish."

Mary pursed her lips. She would have words with Jez Wiseman. She had a flash of Joe Griffith flushed and perspiring as he pulled Anna towards the train. Hmm.

"Mary. . .Miss Wandwalker, I apologize for being so sharp. I meant no disrespect. When I get riled up, I fall into California time. Mrs. Jones sat me down and went over finding the body, that poor girl. When I saw her at Exmoor, I never thought. . .the head too. People like me, vets that is, never forget. . .Ah, snakes alive, read your email."

The dial tone clicked in again.

Wiseman's long email began with him asking her to increase the message time on her phone:

I keep getting cut off.

At that point, Mary put a second pot of coffee on to drip. Even after so many years, she did not like mobile phones. Yes, she thought, I know I'm being ridiculous. Guarding my personal space like a dragon, but these devices are an intrusion.

Of course, she reflected, I do see that phones are magical for young people, connecting them to an ocean of images. For me, computers are a sore point. After all, I got fired from the Archive when it went digital. Mary growled. She missed Caroline. She would say that in exchange for the job I did for far too long I got Caroline and Anna. Well, for that I am grateful, really, I am. Despite Anna's attempts to teach me smartphone lore. I admit that I am a woman from another century. To whit, I am not comfortable with my phone switched on. No, I am not going to increase the message length to suit Dr. Wiseman.

Mary sipped fresh coffee at the kitchen window. She was building up to Wiseman's unread email (and three later from Caroline), trying to loosen the knots in her stomach. Another delaying tactic was gazing at the dry garden. Yes, I can imagine it during midterms with slouching students avoiding their essays. In that I am kin to modern young people.

During the Oxford term, eight Exmoor undergraduates shared the rackety Victorian house. Mary remembered her own after-exam parties forty years ago; the fizzy wine shared with a few souls, who, like her, could not afford champagne. One year there was a fashion for mead in paper cups, so the scent of honeysuckle wafted over the College lawn. Toasts and libations splashed on gowns as much as they trickled down the throats of students.

Mary heard a step behind her.

"Hello Sarah," she said without moving. "Did you sleep well?"

"Sort of, Miss Wandwalker. Yourself?"

"Bad dreams," Mary muttered into her coffee. She reached for the pot with an unsteady hand.

"Um. . .Miss Wandwalker. . ."

"It's alright, Sarah. I know."

Mary turned to look at the girl. She was standing on one foot by the door, her eyes huge. There were food stains on her yellow T shirt.

"Don't worry, Sarah. I'm getting to the emails. Right now. I've checked the phone, and there's no news in the messages."

Mary forced a smile. She could tell it wasn't working for Sarah, whose expression remained unchanged.

"I want to speak to Caroline too, as you do, so as soon as I've caught up, we'll call her together."

Sarah nodded. When her face brightened her dark skin glowed. She stayed where she was, leaving Mary no choice but to return to her laptop.

++++

Later, Mary would paste chunks of those initial emails into her brisk report. On the first day of the field trip, they came from Wiseman with only brief notes from Caroline.

Wiseman wrote:

I would like your opinion, now that the field trip is starting in earnest. I have a bad feeling it is going to be drums in the woods. I'm not against that sort of thing, except they want to do it at night. I'm sure there will be drugs. We have a strict no drugs policy back in California.

Out amongst farms and chalk downs, we are too isolated. Our field includes a crescent shaped lake with woods above. Since the site is miles from the main road, there's no distraction, no relief from whatever the Celts are planning. No one will tell me what the last day "immersion" rite involves. Meanwhile we bivouac in a barn divided into classrooms and dorms. As you can imagine, it's compost toilets and unstable Wi-Fi. At night I can hear owls and screams I don't want to think about. Foxes, said Colin Morrigan, hunting, scenting blood. Did I mention that I don't like it here?

Mary bit her lip, remembering the crunch when she trod on syringes in the Exmoor Well Garden. Wiseman was just getting started.

Don't get me started on the food! Americans know how to barbecue. Clearly you Brits don't. Yeah, I am putting off getting to the point. You see, my bad feeling got worse when Joe started his prep for the rituals. Too intense, he's making a pressure cooker for my guys. Did I mention that your Dr Barin Morrigan insisted on screening everyone? At first, I thought that was a good idea. You know, weed out the fragile vets. But now I'm not so sure. For one thing, Morrigan and Joe turned down all the women. I don't like that.

Don't they get that men are more dangerous with no women around? Even enlisted women have that effect. Yeah, you three DEA women are – were – invited. Maybe you, Miss Wandwalker, could quell this rising tide. Now Joe says the Oxford students can only observe. They get to join in at the end of the field trip with the immersion rite, whatever that is.

Turns out the lake is sacred because it is a lost bit of the Thames. Centuries ago, there was a great flood and the river changed course. The lake was originally a great curve in the unstoppable flow to London and the sea. The field trip is all about re-consecrating it, or so I gather.

Mary, I don't like the secrecy. Ten minutes ago, I saw Barin shut the classroom door in Caroline's face. She looked real upset.

From the email sent two hours later:

". . .Young Colin let slip they've chosen equal numbers of whites and ethnic minorities (he used another word I will not repeat) to make up ten. I smell something rotten here. In Army speak, we could have one helluva snafu! What makes these Celts think they know US vets? One of the so-called African Americans is actually African, not American. He was recruited straight from South Africa, because of some software he developed. Now he's awaiting a green card.

When I agreed to this, I thought it would be Joe Griffith, survivor of horrors, leading a calming workshop. I imagined Joe was the man I fought alongside, my buddy for life. Now that the field trip has gone full Celtic, Joe's got the jitters. His neck is so red his scars have lit up. Anyone can see he's too wound up.

A good CO would be marching him to the company shrink. Not here. The Morrigans have taken over. Even that whitehaired kid is giving orders. He announced in the evening briefing that he's the Son of Light. His full rising will be at the summer solstice. WTF! His mom, Simmy (what kind of name is that?), is the one woman invited to whatever's going on tonight in the woods. She was introduced as the High Priestess of the Ceremonies. Didn't you tell me she is a climate scientist?

There was more, but Mary went straight to the notes on the Celtic Pantheon put together by Anna. . .before Joe. And before she'd abandoned the DEA. "Son of Light, Mabon," she read, "a solar god of Spring, youth and. . .virility." Hmm.

As for Simmy, didn't I tell Wiseman about her? Yet come to think of it, Simmy is a bit of an enigma. What do I really know about the woman?

Mary recalled noticing Sarah and Colin one day in the quad.

"Sarah!" she shouted. "You still in? Can I ask you something about the Morrigans?"

Sarah materialized at once.

"Read this." Mary moved out of her chair.

Sarah began immediately. An intelligent girl thought Mary. Sarah's shrewd expression reminded Mary of Caroline on Holywell's trafficked women. Constantly around violent men, those teenagers developed heightened skills of survival. I can see that ruminated Mary. Staying afloat meant knowing what was beneath. Finished reading, Sarah raised her head with a silent question.

"Simmy and Colin: I was wondering about them," said Mary. "Didn't you talk to Colin in the quad that day?"

Sarah put her palms to her forehead as she recollected her exchange with Colin. Her concentration was total.

"I made sure to be careful asking questions. Caroline told me why we were doing the Summer School. I mean as well as teaching me like Janet wanted," Sarah finally said.

She shot a nervous glance at Mary, who nodded. Mary and Caroline had agreed that protecting Sarah included telling her of their suspicions of the Reborn Celts.

Reassured, Sarah warmed to her task.

"Caroline said I could be useful; that it's an honor to be trusted." She took a big breath.

"Colin's strange. To begin with, he was too polite. I mean, like he's a bit racist. When he stopped staring, he seemed kinda sad." She paused then began again.

"Oh, he likes Simmy, even though he says she doesn't know how to be a mother. As for Joe, he gets him, that's what he said, 'gets' him. He wishes Joe was family. That's when he said his parents died of overdoses. They were Reborn Celts too."

Mary nodded. Sarah risked a tiny smile.

"That's right, Colin relaxed when we chatted about Mums and Dads. Mine and my brother were killed in the Congo by the men who took me."

Mary blinked at Sarah's matter of fact tone. The young woman was absorbed in her task for the hard-to-read Miss Wandwalker. Sarah continued.

"When I was hanging with Colin, I said that Simmy's climate science sounded way off the Celts religion. And then Colin said. . .Now what was it? Oh, yeah. He said I couldn't be more wrong. You see, Simmy believes she's the first of many climate scientists who'll join the Reborn Celts."

Mary choked.

"Well, it's like this," Sarah said, keen to explain. "You see, Miss Wandwalker, Simmy insists they're in despair, the scientists. They've been warning governments and the public about global warming for. . .for heaps of years, and nothing's been done. So Simmy says science can't do it alone. Science must be folded into religion. The Celtic religion is the right one because the land and water are their sacred source of life."

She paused, dredging up more memories. "Colin said people today believe in money like a god. As if money can be eaten, drunk and breathed. Simmy swears that an old religion is better than a new one because old beliefs don't die; they just go underground."

"Into hidden springs and lost rivers," mused Mary. She was thoughtful, seeing Sarah watching for her response.

"Even with her family connection, going from scientist to Reborn Celt is a big leap."

"Caroline said that there was more to Simmy joining the Reborn Celts than her job. Caroline feels it's because she lost her family. Her lover left and took their baby. It happened days before her father jumped off Waterloo Bridge."

"The Reborn Celts were also Simmy's only remaining family in Barinthus," noted Mary. "You know, Sarah, I don't think the Professor likes Colin."

"Sarah agreed. "I saw his evil looks. Colin hates him back."

Mary sighed. "I wish I'd spent more time with Caroline, especially since classes began. This whole Reborn Celts thing is crying out for both of us."

"Perhaps all three of you?" asked Sarah. That was a hint.

Mary's jaw tightened. She did not want to talk about Anna.

"Caroline thinks so. And me too. I want to help."

"Thank you, Sarah," said Mary to the serious girl. "Don't forget that we are supposed to be taking care of *you*. Not the other way round. I forgot that about. . .well, you know who." She trailed off. Time to get a grip, Mary, she told herself.

"Sarah, do you think I should stop underestimating Caroline?

Sarah's eyes opened wide. Mary's mouth twitched.

"Alright then, did you get any more from Colin?"

"He saved her. Simmy, I mean."

"What? Oh, that's *his* opinion," replied Mary skeptically. "Colin's out to be the next Joe Griffith. The fighting Celt as warrior-savior."

"Yeah, that's Colin. He says he's proud of his actual parents. To him they are heroes who went to the old gods, not victims of drugs."

Sarah rubbed the carpet with her white sandal, open to deep bronze toes.

"What is it, Sarah?"

There was a pregnant pause before Sarah spoke quickly.

"Colin. . .he almost said the Reborn Celts must be white. He looked at me that way, you know."

Mary nodded. Her mind went to Mr. Jeffreys. He would know what to say.

"Stupid boy," she said.

Sarah tried not to laugh.

"Anyhow, the way Colin tells it, as soon as he was fostered, he went on to Simmy about the Celts holding water sacred. He got Simmy hooked, he said. The climate crisis is because we're no longer Celts – just like she explained in class. Modern folk don't have a sacred bond to the land. The Reborn Celts exist to change that. You remember that lecture when she kept saying. . ."

"That we live in Celtic times. Yes, I heard; Joe said it too. It's true. Except we don't."

Sarah raised her eyebrows. "I don't understand you, Miss Wandwalker."

"To tell you the truth, there's a lot here I don't understand, Sarah. However, let's consider what Simmy was doing in that class."

Mary could do lecture mode. It was her usual response to the young people she used to manage in the Archive.

"Simmy told us that we're in Climate Emergency because we've lost the Celtic earth-based religion. Those gods kept the people from exploiting nature. Then she proclaims we live in Celtic times. She and they can't have it both ways."

"I suppose the Reborn Celts are trying to change us back to what we were. By saying that we still are them, underneath," Sarah said.

Mary started walking up and down.

"Don't you see that you can't shift people, a whole society, back thousands of years. It is not as if we even *know* the Celts, the real ones. There's no writing. All we have are stories mangled by the Christians, plus Roman propaganda. It was the Romans who said the Celts practiced human sacrifice."

"You mean the Celts did not cut off heads and put them down wells?" Sarah seemed shocked.

Mary froze. "We don't know for sure," she admitted. "However, today historians say no. True, the Celts killed prisoners of war, but so did the Romans. As for severed heads, yes, the Celts did that a thing about heads. They thought the head contained the spirit. In fact, the head of a Celtic king is said to be buried under the Tower of London."

Mary recalled Mr. Jeffreys seated outside the National Theatre. The sunshine glinting off the Thames behind him made his figure stand out black as night. She spoke as if also to him.

"The Reborn Celts *imagine* the past, like we all have the tendency to do. The problem is, they are trying to save the world through a vision warped by. . ." Rhiannon dangling the torc floated back into her mind, ". . .by some very modern problems. Like the way war kills the mind and heart, and young people like you not feeling safe from the future."

Mary drummed her fingers on the table. Sarah was frowning. Mary had more to say.

"The Reborn Celts offer simple certainties in exchange for today's terror of the unknown. But don't you see, Sarah, their indisputable conviction is a way of *avoiding* the real work of facing the climate emergency? Their rituals make anxiety worse because they are bent on sanctifying with blood. Violence petrifies; we become frozen. You saw what happened to Rhiannon."

Sarah was trying to understand. "You don't think that we are Celts, Miss Wandwalker? I mean, that you white people are? At Holywell. . ."

Again, Mary was jolted by Sarah's mention of race. This time she was ready for the unhealed wound.

"Sarah, stop this! There's one thing I'm sure of, and it is that if the Reborn Celts believe it's about being white, then they are part of the world's problems, not the solution. You and I could be more related than Caroline and I."

Sarah looked doubtful.

"I'll get you a book on it."

"But Holywell. . ." Sarah started.

". . .Is nothing like the Reborn Celts," Mary finished.

She'd had her doubts about the counselor-witches. Well, yes, she remained skeptical about what they called magic. Yet the witches were trustworthy in their service. She could even sympathize with Caroline's enthusiasm. Now she had to find a way of putting it to Sarah that would not infuriate Janet.

Mary knew that the witches included the planet as a living partner in their therapies. It even made a sort of sense. When it came down to it, Holywell helped Caroline. Their herbs and training offered Caroline support that helped with her depression.

"You see, Sarah, Holywell's witches are better Celts than the Reborn Celts. They *do,* they don't just read sensational stories and let their emotions run riot. And by the way, this is Caroline speaking. We have talked a bit, you know. "

Mary lowered her voice, seeing Sarah edging away.

"Alright, don't worry about all this. You can see for yourself that Holywell is about helping people. They're not forcing you to change through dubious means like drugs. You of all people know they keep their spirituality to themselves to protect you. After all, you're here because they would not risk indoctrinating you young girls, I mean, women."

Mary gave a dry smile. "Thank you for saying you want to help. You already have, and I should have told you before. Which reminds me, with Caroline away, have you phoned Janet?"

Sarah nodded. "I have to call her every morning with a full account."

"She's looking out for you." Mary continued. "Holywell keeps up to date. Your witches train as counselors because they see how complex people are, and how fragile. They know about not having simple answers or resorting to violence."

"Caroline would say that Holywell is founded on love."

"So she would," agreed Mary, as she put her glasses back on to return to the screen.

Wiseman had sent a third email.

They are off to the woods with drums and their priestess. I don't like it, Mary. None of the vets have had time to get to know each other. Most have traces of PTSD, and that Morrigan kid looks like he's brewing full blown mania. Caroline whispered that she is going after them. I don't think she is in danger. My concern is psychological harm to the vets. If I could hike through the bushes like I used to, I'd be right there.

Oh God, thought Mary. Caroline, no, no, please don't. Hang on, her email is later. Gripped by unease, she clicked on Caroline's emails before remembering to switch her phone back on. The initial email from Caroline was a day old, and surprisingly reassuring.

> Dearest Mary, the journey was not at all bad. Even if First Class on a train is a letdown, the minibus is quite comfortable apart from the bit on the farm track. Will call or write after I've spoken with Anna.

....

Mary opened today's second and longer email from Caroline.

> Oh, Mary, I am so useless. She wouldn't say a word to me nor look me in the eye. Not even to return a 'hello.' She was sitting by Joe on one of the picnic tables outside and yet they didn't talk to each other, either. They left separately. I'm confused. None of the Reborn Celts spoke to Anna. It is as if they have put her in a glass box. I'm typing this on my phone and in my camp bed. Jez is waving to me...
>
> ... he says Joe went behind his back to make the field trip a men's thing, apart from Simmy. I knew that because Barin barred me from the session. His version was those of us from Oxford must wait to be invited into the ceremonies. I have a feeling it's not worth waiting for that call. Anna has gone off on her own. Poor Jez stresses so much that I volunteered to 'scout out' the secret in the woods, as Anna might say, if she were still our Anna. Mary, I must keep trying to reach her. I've never seen her so lost and that is without leaving the camp.
>
> An hour later: Emotional exhaustion set in as I was following them into the woods. Very tired. Sorry, Mary. Will try again tomorrow.

CHAPTER 14
CAROLINE AND ANNA

"So did you?" asked Mary of the white face on the screen. "Did you try again to reach Anna?"

"Let me tell you in my own way," Caroline appealed. Either the connection was poor, or the appearance of being underwater reflected her state. It was Mary who'd worn the carpet in her hours of waiting. Contacted at last, she wanted to shake everything out of Caroline. No one was hurt— yet— even though Anna had screamed.

"Anna?" said Mary, her words tight. "Yelling and screaming? Just tell me what's happened."

"A row," said Caroline. "Worse than a row. With Joe Griffith. I heard them this morning." She gave a shuddering sigh. "I was hiding round the corner trying to overhear. Don't say anything. I hate myself for it. I just had to know what was going on. Anna's been so strange. Strange even for her, I mean." She paused and continued quietly.

"After the shouting stopped, I met Jez Wiseman. He was nice, said he'd be listening too, if his wheelchair didn't squeak. You know, he's so upset about Joe."

"CAROLINE. Stop avoiding and tell me."

"Sorry. Sorry. Yes, you must be frantic. Well, breakfast was almost done. With no sign of Anna and Joe, I went to find them. I could hear a man, Joe angry, then pleading. No, Mary, I couldn't make out the words. Anna was low and fierce. You know how she gets. I was terrified she'd sense me listening. We have. . .had. . .a connection. And then. . ."

111

Caroline swallowed. Bleakness infused her image.

"Then there was this. . .well, howl. Horrible, inhuman, almost a. . .a dog howling." Caroline pressed her lips together before continuing.

"I knew it was Anna. She rushed past me. Then she swerved to take the path up the hill. Joe started to follow, then he stopped because he noticed the vets staring. He made a face for them as if to say 'women' then herded everyone into the classroom. Paid no attention to me, of course. Caroline paused for a wan smile.

"You found her then? Anna?" Mary felt better. Things might not be too serious.

"Yes, she was sitting high up on the edge of the wood. There is a wild area, full of rabbits in the early morning. There was Anna sitting amongst rabbits and little birds who were not afraid of her. They scattered for me, however. Her black hair flew in the wind. She was looking up. talking to crows passing overhead, as if, she wanted to leap into the air and join them. When I got close, she. . ."

Caroline's voice caught. "Oh, Mary, she wouldn't talk to me."

"She said nothing at all?"

"At first. Then, when I tried to touch her, she said:

"'Not yet. It's not over yet. Something's coming. It's not over.'"

"Typical Anna."

"Yes," said Caroline. She was chewing on her middle two fingernails. "What worries me, Mary, no, it terrifies me, is that then I knew. I know, for sure Mary, that she is drowning. Whatever this is, she's lost in it. That's new. That's not Anna. I'm scared."

Mary clamped down her dismay. "Did Anna say anything else?"

"Just that I must leave her with the wild." 'It quiets me,' she said. I could see it was true, so I left. You see, I haven't forgotten our case." Caroline managed a tiny smile. "With Anna safe for the moment, I went to keep an eye on Joe Griffith and the other Celts."

"And have you?"

"Sort of. When I arrived back, there was an even worse row beginning. At first it was Jez arguing with Joe. Jez asked Joe for an itinerary, a sort of lesson plan. Then he wanted Joe to keep all the ritual work near the lodging where Jez could see it from his wheelchair. No disappearing into woods, where Jez could not follow.

Joe laughed. He said something like— hang on, I took notes: 'The wild Celts are beginning to burst out of the vets. It is imperative that they roam the woods tonight. Together the men will drum the impotence out of each other. Soaked in nature, they will find their goddess and their warrior souls.'

At that rejection, Jez totally lost it. The row got so loud that the walls shook. Then Simmy, Colin, and Barin all burst in. Then it was Colin and Barin going at it; Colin shouting at Barin to stop influencing his mother. You'd think it would be the other way around. It ended with all of them yelling, until Jez wheeled out of the office and saw me."

"I don't like this," said Mary. "If Jez, a veteran himself, thinks it is in danger of getting out of control. . ."

Caroline sighed. "That was this morning. I just saw Jez, Barin, and Simmy having lunch together. Not as friends, but at least calmed down. Jez waved me over after the Morrigans walked off. He told me that he's been reassured by Barin and Simmy that they are really in charge.

"Joe is so romantic," they told him. "So passionate. He wants to go too fast. We've sent him and Colin to do a special meditation under oak trees. In short, the Morrigans promised to slow it down and ease the atmosphere."

Mary coughed, one of her wary responses.

"What do *you* think, Caroline? You're the one on site." Even though Caroline appeared to be underwater, Mary could see her pleasure at being consulted. I must remember that, she said to herself.

"Joe's unstable," said Caroline, after a pause. She knew what she was talking about. "Yes, he's unstable. . .And I think I agree with Jez. Joe's not in charge. It's Barin and the other two, Simmy and Colin. Joe's the star, but they are running the show."

"Let's hope it is a show," said Mary, grimly. "Over where you are," she emphasized. "It was more than a show here."

"Do you believe one of them killed Rhiannon?"

Mary paused. "It must have been. If not one of them, then one of the students acting under their direction. What's the alternative?"

"Although the police said they rule out someone breaking into the college, it still leaves a rogue student *not* under the Celts direction."

"How likely is that? Given that the Reborn Celts, OK Joe really, keeps going on about blood and sacrifice. Think about it, Caroline. Rhiannon arrived here right before the summer school. She saw no one outside it. We know because she was with us. It has to be about the Reborn Celts."

My responsibility, though Mary didn't say it out loud. Caroline heard it anyway.

"You know Mary, it's not. . ."

"Don't say it."

Each summoned their recollections of the other summer school students, mostly elderly stalwarts of Oxford extra-mural courses. These women and men sought a bit of excitement in an otherwise dull summer. Their prim figures slipped away from the Waking of the Well before it got too interesting. One glass of wine and a slice of quiche and they were off to bed.

This online call was the first time Mary and Caroline had a chance to talk over the murder since Caroline's departure. Mary was convinced that Joe, or Simmy, or Barin, maybe even Colin, had killed Rhiannon. The murderer thrust the torc on her severed head before shoving her down the well. The next night Rhiannon's torso was placed where the river Eponia met the Thames.

The Oxford police had let slip that the four Reborn Celts supplied alibis for each other for the entire fatal night. As a result, the police continued to seek trace evidence to break the case.

Mary bit her lips on the curious fact that Anna had no alibi for the murder. She claimed that she'd left the Waking of the Well before Mary arrived. The remainder of the night she'd spent wandering the streets, a habit Mary recognized, while the police found it unsatisfactory. They planned to re-interview her, as well as Joe and the Morrigans on their return from the field trip. Meanwhile, there was the puzzle of the heated exchanges between Joe and Anna.

"Perhaps she and Joe are going to break up," said Mary, trying to remember her impression of Anna at the train station. "At least, I certainly hope so."

Caroline's image on the screen seemed to get a little more focused. Mary found herself unable to speculate further. She needed to *see* Anna to judge her behavior. Damn it, she should have gone. After all, the field trip should be just a matter of getting through this ghastly immersion rite.

"I'm so glad you didn't come here," said Caroline. "I'm exhausted, and it will be worse when I get home. One of us has to stay strong."

Mary gave Caroline a tight smile. The younger woman knew her too well.

She had a plan and proceeded to share it with Caroline. Once the field trip was done, the Reborn Celts would be swept up by the police. At that moment, she and Caroline would intercept Anna and keep her from Joe until she explained everything. Caroline grinned at that.

Mary checked the date. Only tonight's occult activities for Caroline to endure, followed by the so-called immersion rite. Probably it referred to pagan baptism in that remnant of the Thames. How bad could that be?

In the days to come, Mary bitterly regretted her blithe assumption. On the other hand, even if she could have persuaded

Caroline to leave early, it would not have changed the bloody events of the night. Mary went to bed to the whispers of owls from her open window. Just suppose, she thought sleepily, they call to one another across the country. Like me, Caroline, and Anna swim under a net of owls hooting.

CHAPTER 15
SECOND RITE: IMMERSION

The following morning, Mary woke to find that her voicemail was crammed with messages—all of which told her to ring the number for Reading Police Station. There had been an 'incident' at the Celtic field trip.

Mary dropped her phone on the bed and yelled for Sarah. It was early, so the young woman might still be asleep. She shouted again. Horror filled the house as if it had rained indoors all night. Her hand was shaking as she picked up the phone and pressed her email app. The message headers from Caroline were:

I must follow them.
Joe's Meltdown.
Don't look at this alone. Another beheading!

And the most recent, Mary made sure: Bringing Anna home as soon as I can.

Relief flooded Mary: it wasn't Anna. It wasn't Caroline.

A soft knock, and the door opened on a dark head with fearful eyes. Mary screamed. Instantly Sarah was at her bedside.

"Miss Wandwalker, what is it? Are you hurt? Tell me what I can do."

"You. . .you put your head round the door," Mary managed. "I could see. . . your head."

"My head? What do you mean?"

Mary reached for Sarah's arm. "Messages about another beheading. On the field trip."

Sarah gasped. The dark patina of her skin turned chalky.

Mary was contrite. "No, no. Not Caroline. Or Anna."

"The Goddess be blessed." Sarah sat on the bed. "That's what Janet would say. Oh, Miss Wandwalker. Who is it then?"

"Don't know." Mary's mouth had dried. "I have to look."

"I'll look with you."

Mary nodded.

Sarah's T-shirt and shorts were even more stained than usual. Probably cocoa, guessed Mary. The previous night, sleepless Mary had descended to the kitchen (after checking for news) and found Sarah with a pan of hot milk.

Now in the shattered morning, she and Sarah stared at one another across the bed. Mary held her phone away from her as if it were about to explode. I must ask Sarah about the washing machine, thought Mary. No that's silly, avoiding what we must do. As if she could hear her, Sarah retrieved Mary's laptop from the dressing table.

"We can see better on this," she said, bringing it over. Sitting by Mary on the bed, Sarah pointed to the last message first.

> Bringing Anna home as soon as I can. Together
they read:
> Anna's stunned, out of it. The police say we can
> leave in a couple of hours. Sorry. I'll let you know
> when we'll arrive in Oxford. It would be great if
> you could meet us at the station. What with bags
> and Anna, so strange, I'll need help.

"They're all right," murmured Mary. "And on their way home." There was a choking sound from Sarah.

"Look here," said Mary indicating the rest of the message. They both read:

> It's thanks to Jez Wiseman that they're letting
> us go at all. Of course, the crucial fact is that the
> police are convinced that one of the veterans did

this terrible thing. I don't think so, and nor does Jez, because of what happened to Rhiannon. The murders must be connected. Jez got on to Frederic North who called the American Ambassador. Anyway, we're all being released for now until the police forces sort out jurisdiction.

"Who's dead?" whispered Sarah. She was a lot calmer now.

"I don't know," said Mary. "However," she said slowly, I'm getting an idea. Sarah, you don't have to do this, but I should look at the photograph of the body, or bits of it. The third email is a picture file. Sarah. . .perhaps you?

"I'm not going anywhere until we know what's happened."

"Not even to put the coffee on, I suppose," muttered Mary. "Oh, well," and she clicked the image open. It was a huge file that loaded with excruciating slowness. Both women gulped.

Don't look at this alone. Another beheading! Caroline had warned.

This time the eyes were closed. The head with shorter, darker, and wet curls lay in the shallows of the lake. Cloudy crimson water failed to cover the hair, lapping an unshaven chin. It trickled out of the colorless lips. Suntan on the cheeks now appeared painted on to blue-white skin. Mary's eyes could not linger on the face, so she turned to the axe blade, partly visible at the extreme edge. It was like the wood chopper that the Oxford police had found in the Exmoor well garden.

"So much blood," whispered Sarah.

"Not really," rasped Mary, then cleared her throat.

"It's water; water colored by blood. See there's another file. Caroline attached a picture of the whole scene."

This one opened faster. Mary kept talking; it reminded her to keep breathing.

"The lake is a sort of crescent. That must be the head, that blob, just on the inner curve. There is a long thing in the reeds.

Oh, I thought it a log. It isn't. Immersion, they called it. Second rite. Those bastards."

"Rhiannon," said Sarah.

"Yes, Rhiannon. This murder is much the same," agreed Mary. "Another axe, for example."

"Joe." Sarah breathed his name as if taking the stopper from a bottle. The reality of the severed head bubbled from the screen.

Mary shut the computer with a snap. She reached for her bedside water glass, then noticed Sarah had moved.

"Sarah?"

The girl was looking out of the window. She swung back to face Mary.

"It's all right, Miss Wandwalker. I've seen bad things before. But if you don't mind, I'll put the coffee on and make toast before you tell me about the other messages."

"Well, yes, that would be most helpful."

"I liked him," said Sarah, her face stony. "Even though he had a race thing, I still liked him. He. . .wasn't like the men. . .the men in that house in London."

Mary did not know what to say. Sarah was one of seven trafficked teenagers rescued from a brothel in London. The trauma of abduction and forced sex had been compounded testifying in court in return for 'exceptional leave to remain' in the UK. Holywell's counselor-witches volunteered to care for the scarred young women. That Joe Griffith wasn't "like the men in London," meant something from a young woman to whom men had been predators.

"Would you care to do a load of washing, Sarah?"

The words were out before Mary could bite them back. Her cheeks flared. I could kick myself. Why do I do that? Why not consider what Caroline would do? Even Anna would be better. Sarah was staring at her.

Months ago, at Holywell, she, Caroline, and Anna had been with the trafficked women who were slumped over mugs of tea. Their attitudes spelled a preference for more intoxicating liquids. One girl sat on a sofa staring into space. Too thin, Sarah was scratching at the track marks on her left arm, making them raw again. Anna watched from a corner. At the call for dinner, she'd taken the girl's ravaged arm. Together they went arm and arm into the communal dining room. Now in Oxford, Sarah's expression had become sorrowful.

"I'm really sorry," Mary whispered. "I am so sorry. I didn't mean to suggest. . ." Her voice trailed away because she had, of course, meant to suggest that Sarah's clothes were dirty. What a reaction to Sarah noticing— no, *caring* about, an attractive man, who didn't treat her like a bit of meat. Mary had no words, so Sarah spoke.

"He smiled at me; you know. Just once. Really smiled at me. It was like. . .special." Sarah's tone was wondering. There were possibilities in that one smile. Things she'd not expected for herself.

Mary swallowed the retort that Joe Griffith smiled at everyone. He even grinned at an old woman whose name he mangled. Right now, she thought, even I can see that this smile is valuable. Whatever Joe Griffith was, this fleeting drop in the river of his life would be remembered.

"I'm glad he smiled at you," she said.

Sarah looked at her, absorbing their exchange.

"Coffee," she said. "And yes, I do know how to use the washing machine."

"I'll be down as soon as I've read the last emails. And Sarah. . ."

"Yes."

"He should have smiled at you more often."

CHAPTER 16
EMAILS FROM THE SECOND
RITE OF IMMERSION

Opening her computer again to the image of Joe Griffith's severed head, Mary caught sight of a third file, smaller than the others. This photo the back of an envelope with a few scrawled words. Some of the letters had gone fuzzy in Caroline's phone. To be sure Mary hit zoom and read the message in stark capitals: "THE BLOOD WILL RISE AT THE SOLSTICE." Below that, someone, presumably Caroline, had typed: "Note found by lake near body."

Mary felt a stirring at 'rise.' She fumbled for her notebook. "So 'old school,'" Anna had mocked. That's it, the third and final rite is about rising. Mary's insides tightened as she recollected that Joe Griffith proclaiming that the summer solstice would see a 'Blood Rising.' She shivered, despite the intensifying heat. Seven days to the solstice, and they had no idea where this ominous 'Blood Rising,' would be staged. They had no information that could stop the Reborn Celts.

Mary would not give up, however.

Perhaps Rhiannon's body at the confluence of the Thames and the lost Celtic river was a clue. And this note from Caroline was a confirmation she realized. The murders of Rhiannon and Joe are connected. Now to that first letter from Caroline. She could see it was a long one, written in stages.

I must follow them...

5pm.

Everyone's talking about the rain. It started twenty minutes ago and is such a relief from the heat even if only a shower. Barin watched the Americans with a superior expression, until Joe started whispering in his ear. They went off together. Colin tried to follow and Simmy called him back.

Mary, the real surprise is Simmy. The rain revived her; she is buoyed up, like she might start dancing. I forgot she's a water scientist. As soon as the rain began (it is drizzle right now) she ran outside and began taking photographs of the sky. I called after her, but I don't think she heard.

Colin heard me and said that she was taking pictures of clouds to assess their water capacity. I think he wanted to go with Joe and is angry about being left behind. He's particularly mad that Joe went off with Barin. No love lost there. Colin started to say something about Simmy's research connecting sky patterns with underground water. That was when she shouted at him to fetch her equipment.

It's one hour later.

Some of the vets want to go and drum outside; to start the night ceremony early. They are joshing about rain spirits, even though none of them knows what this means.

Oh, a few minutes ago Joe Griffith came back to forbid it. He said the right moment was under the new moon tonight, rain or no rain. Some of the guys are irked. Then Barin steps forward and says that to honor the gods of water and sky, free time for all until dinner. The vets start to relax and melt away. Colin tried to whisper to Joe, who brushed him off. The boy is sulking.

I went over to where Jez has been watching all this. He said that the vets will gather in the common room to drink beer and tell combat stories. Jez looks less stressed, with the rain. Even though he appears very tired. This can't be good for him, all the strain with his buddy Joe.

5.35pm

Simmy just passed by looking quite extraordinary. She's wrapped in a burgundy cloak that is too long, dragging and getting muddy. I couldn't take my eyes off her head, where she has a wreath of ivy, real ivy.

Then I remembered seeing Colin collecting ivy this morning from where it grows up one side of the barn. He must have made the wreath for her. Simmy's also carrying string bags with glass tubes and retorts. Since she seems to be alone, I will go after her and see if she'll talk to me this time.

5.55pm

They're all in dinner now. I did follow Simmy and saw her set up the glass instruments near trees. I notice she chose beech, sycamore, and oak. They are all suffering from the drought, even I can tell. Simmy was quite talkative to start with. She plans to measure the amount of rain that the trees will receive tonight.

Simmy is... a scientist in a robe. I started to ask her about being a priestess, and she shut down as if slamming a lid on a well. I'll give her exact words, because I remember them (I did have my phone on record, like you said, Mary, but there was too much pattering of rain). She said:

"Tonight, we have a very important ceremony. Secret and sanctified. Just for men and the Priestess. You initiates, you and Anna, are to observe from the outside, to absorb the resonances. Wait until the solstice. Everything will become clear then."

"But why is tonight only for men?"

"Because of the nature of their wounds," she said.

Then she stalked off. The rain got harder and dripped down the neck of my anorak, so I'm writing this over dinner. It's beef stew boiled on the BBQ, and I don't like the look of it. Either the meat is underdone, or they've included those very hot peppers that dissolve. Anyway, it is far too red for me. I'm sticking to the salad bowls and the desserts.

Between you and I, I'm hoping to entice Anna away from Joe for a few minutes. They are drinking a bottle of red wine handed to them by Barin. Colin was furious when Barin refused to pour him a glass. He appealed to Joe, who just laughed and kissed

Anna. As we know, alcohol has no effect on Anna. I am dying for her, Mary. For a smile, a touch, a kind word.

6.40pm

The rain's so heavy that I got soaked running to the main building. The lights were on in Jez's office, so I planned to have a word with him since – you've guessed it - Anna turned me away. She looked unhappy as she ducked outside. To me she muttered she was exhausted and going straight to bed. It's not like Anna to be so tired. I'm worried, and not just about her. Thank the goddess of Holywell there is not much more of this hellish event.

6.50pm

Jez wouldn't say much to me either. I think he feels he ought not to upset me. Mary, you'd know how to get these people to talk.

You see, I am braver than people think. Not like Anna, whose courage is baked into her bones. Not like you, who will face down any authority. My courage is of the creeping around in the dark kind. I've done it before. Storm or no storm, tonight's the night I am going to follow Joe and his merry men. Plus Simmy. With the rain and the wind rising over the hills, no one sees beyond the pool of light of their torches.

There's a lighting ceremony before they all go into the woods to a fireplace they built. When the fire is starting to produce white ash, they form the circle for the drumming. That boy Colin lets things slip. Fortunately, I know where they keep electric torches. I'm British, after all Continuous rain doesn't scare me.

No, Caroline, no, groaned Mary. It would be unbearable to read of her friend's risk taking had she not known her to be— at this very moment—f about to board a train at Reading Station. Even so, the next section smelled of exhaustion, and fear. What had happened at the secret ceremony? The title of the final message filled her with foreboding despite her knowledge of the bloody climax of the ritual.

Joe's meltdown.

2am

Dearest concerned Mary. You must not worry, as I am back, whole, except for a few scratches. My feet are bloody. I've bandaged them and they don't hurt – much. Couldn't sleep after my hot shower so I am writing this and will send it straight away. I'm not risking the phone. Too many are awake and might hear me.

Yes, it *was* a storm, a real one, with wind, thunder, and lightning. The sky lit up as if the moon itself had exploded. So wet was it that when I caught up with the Celts, their smoky fire made everyone cough.

Mary, I'll never forget the sight of the men crouched in a circle with Joe standing silvered by rain. When lightning struck, I could see tremendous detail like a photo flash. Joe, oh god, he had a thing on his head with deer antlers – he was the horned god. For a second, he *was* the storm

Joe ordered the men to keep drumming. Wet trees hung over the clearing. At any moment lightning could strike or branches be blown onto the men. Every few seconds electricity bounced off the tops of the hills several miles away.

A little closer, I could see they'd taken off the top half of their clothes; not Simmy, the men. So, in addition to the Celts, there were ten bare chested men, water streaming down unshaven faces and muscled chests as they banged the drums. Water poured off their heads; rain jumped off the drums at every beat. Joe was dancing in the center of the circle, whirling, and yelling.

At equidistant points among the drummers, Simmy, Barin and Colin were taking turns to chant something. Colin made himself up to look like a skull, menacing. I wasn't near enough to get the words or even tell if they were in English. Together with the falling rain it sounded like they were growing a river. Perhaps they were.

Because then I saw the ground was liquefying in the mud. So feverish were the drums they made ripples in the pools at their feet. Mary, we were just halfway up the hill. There is a spot where the slope pauses into a sort of platform. Well, it's not there anymore. I started to get scared when I saw what was happening to the rising ground above the chanting and dancing.

I'd moved closer, but there was no chance of making out any of the words with the sound of water and stamping on the earth. Above the platform, streams running down the hillside were enlarging and collecting leaves and sticks. Neither the Reborn Celts, nor the vets, noticed. I tried to shout a warning. Nothing got through to them, they were so enraptured.

It is impossible to explain, except to say that the ceremony was as big as the storm. Or it was a part of the storm. I knew that I could not stop what they were doing, Simmy stood up, went to Joe, and kissed him on the mouth. It wasn't until then that I realized that he was naked, and so was she under her cloak.

Ah, said Mary to herself: the sacred marriage ritual. She'd read about it. The Celts enacted the sacred bond to the land via sexual union between King and Priestess. In fact, it had crossed her mind that it could explain Joe's urgent grabbing of Anna at the train station. His lover would be a better vehicle for divine sexuality than Simmy. What happened to change his partner in the ceremony? Hoping for answers, Mary read on.

Mary, I know you think I'm a prude. I'm not, but I must admit that I was so astonished that I covered my face. A mistake because it made me miss something, some disruption to the plan. A wild noise made me look up. The rain and dark were filled with figures yelling and trying to escape. It was too late to find out what came first: the vets breaking the circle, or the mudslide onto the platform. Anyway, water, clogged with dead leaves and stones were pouring down.

Drums went flying, and I saw two vets fighting with Joe, or trying to restrain him. There were shouts about the mountain falling and Joe trying to kill them by exposing them to the storm. At last, a couple of men started dragging others in the direction they'd come. Simmy was looking back at Joe while Colin dragged her by one arm. He was screaming obscenities at Joe. I couldn't see Barin at all. That man seems to be able to disappear at will.

Get out of there, muttered Mary while reading. Even though she knew that Caroline was OK, she could smell the danger in the rain and muddy water.

I got away before the main mudslide engulfed what was left of the platform. I'd held back with foolish ideas of tracking the erupting anger. With all the shouting, I thought I heard something from Joe about Rhiannon. Maybe I imagined it. Mary,

129

do you think she was supposed to be in this... this ceremony?

I think she wanted to, thought Mary, flooded with sadness. She thought it would make her a goddess. If she'd known about the sacred marriage, she would have offered herself. I can see her, ecstatic, hair streaming like yellow fire, embracing any kind of storm.

Too late to find the safe path, I held onto a tree, embracing it with both arms. Soon I felt my feet slide away from me. The whole hillside was becoming a streambed with rivulets of mud everywhere. My shoes just weren't gripping so I had to take them off. Half-naked mud men streamed past me. I heard shouts of 'Get the bastard. No, later! Get out of here! The whole hillside's going..."

Someone howled, or perhaps it was a shriek. I let go of the tree and crawled until I found firmer footing. My socks had torn open on sharp stones, so I was barefoot. (Yes, I know, silly of me to take off my shoes in the hope of being quiet). I ran, Mary. And then, of course, I fell and slid with the mud until I grabbed a tree root.

Thank goodness one of the last vets heard my scream. I waved what was left of my torch. He grabbed my hand, hauled me up and then helped me to the path. As soon as we were in sight of the Barn, he just said, "You'll be safe now Ma'am," and saluted, trotting off to the dorm. I was too stunned to utter a word. So relieved was I that I didn't feel my feet. Water ran down my back, and my jacket weighed a ton from being soaked through.

When I got to the women's shower, I just fell on the floor and waited for warm water. It hurt my feet so much, as if knives were being thrust into each sole. I watched the mud and blood find the drain everywhere. It was a relief to see just a few minor cuts.

Mary, afterwards I didn't even want to eat. Me? I was so cold, so hollowed out. Like I said, I almost phoned you, then decided to write instead. You know, I don't think this field trip is a success. Don't laugh. You know what I mean. The vets are furious. Something's going on with Joe Griffith, that's for sure. Worst of all there's no sign of Anna.

In the morning, if morning ever comes, I will try again to get Anna home. Yours forever, Caroline.

Mary stared at the screen. She could smell the liquid earth; she could smell the dark; she could hear shouts, even screams. Something was indeed going on with Joe, his body now in a hospital morgue. It's almost here, the summer solstice. *Oh Caroline, I'm so glad you're coming home.*

CHAPTER 17
OXFORD AND A CONFESSION

Mary told herself that it was foolish to have a bad feeling about going to meet Caroline and Anna. Perhaps it was because when last at the train station, she'd discovered Rhiannon missing. Mary swallowed. While she'd been floundering, Rhiannon wore the golden torc as a crown. Her neck had been sliced by a simple woodcutting axe, or so the police said. Those terrible eyes.

In a bit of a daze Mary launched herself up the steps that led into the station. Usually striding ahead, today, she let herself sink into the crowd. She did not weave around sleek businessmen like speedboats racing ahead of youths of indeterminate gender, with gritty hair and lobster backpacks

Vaguely, Mary noted that there was no one like herself: older, not aged; distinctive, yet not fashionable. And of course, no one else was carrying a handbag popular in the 1950's. Anna would mock. She began to pace the tight waiting area. After all, her linen suit was impeccable. She'd pressed it herself after Sarah had tried and failed. Mary had found it hard to credit that the young woman had never used an iron before.

Soon, very soon, Caroline and Anna would flow through the ticket barriers with the magisterial calm of old Father Thames. Stop Mary, don't think of the Thames, of London, of standing on the river's beach again and smelling the sea and sewage lapping at the tent. That tent was sacred, for it held a young body without a head.

Concentrate on spotting Caroline and Anna, Mary told herself. She barely noticed time passing until she glanced at her phone. Yes, the train had arrived twenty minutes ago. What could be taking so long on the platform? Could she persuade the bored youth guarding the barrier to let her go and find out?

Mary had drifted to the station as if moving underwater. It was Rhiannon's fault. Water, rivers, wells were not an escape from the murder victim. They were movement, an irrigation of Mary's viscera.

After all, we're made of water, came Rhiannon's self-important tones. Mary knew the voice was one only she could hear.

Yes, Rhiannon, muttered Mary, scanning again for Caroline's curves and Anna's flowing black hair. But she grunted to the girl speaking inside her, you must let me go— enough of me at least— so I can find out who killed you. A petulant sniff, and then she—

"Mary! Mary, over here." Caroline was waving, instead of presenting her ticket to the tight mouth of the electronic gate. The bored youth sighed and let her through. Caroline had been weeping. That can't be good. Where is Anna?

"Miss Wandwalker, I've been looking for you." The male voice came from behind Mary. She spun round to find a grim Inspector Walbrook. He had on that be-ready-for-bad-news face that Mary recognized.

"Inspector Walbrook, what are you doing here? I'm meeting. . ."

"Miss Vronsky and Mrs. Jones. Yes, we know. My Sergeant is bringing Mrs. Jones over to you now."

And indeed, a familiar young officer in a ponytail, the one with the Hindu mark, was steering Caroline by the elbow. Caroline's freckles stood out like a disease. She lunged forward to Mary, shaking off the restraining arm.

"Mary, it's Anna," she gasped. "Oh, Mary, you've got to help her." She fell onto Mary's shoulder, chest heaving with dry sobs. Mary, embarrassed in front of the police, awkwardly patted Caroline's back.

"Caroline, whatever's the matter? Come over and sit down. Please." Out of the corner of an eye she could see that Walbrook, and his Sergeant had already pulled a table and chairs out of the nearby café and into neutral territory. Caroline moaned as Mary put her in a seat.

Sensing that Rhiannon was watching from inside her, the police from outside, Mary found it harder than usual to deal with Caroline's strong emotions. She turned to Walbrook.

"Inspector, what's going on?" Yes, she could still summon her authoritative voice.

"Miss Vronsky. . ."

"Anna confessed to killing Rhiannon." Caroline sputtered out. Her tone was despairing. She would not look at Mary.

Rhiannon, *wait*, Mary silently said to the creature inside her. She could hear a distant laughter and then suddenly Rhiannon was gone.

"Oh." Mary had to think fast. "When, Inspector? Just when did Anna make this remarkable confession? Not today, surely? Caroline, drink the water the Sergeant is offering you."

Caroline took a swig from the open bottle, coughed, was slapped on the back by the expressionless woman, and drank again. Walbrook watched Mary and Caroline with a sardonic expression. He suspects us, realized Mary. This is some sort of test. No, it's a trial. She placed both feet on either side of her handbag. Right, we're not moving until I know what Walbrook is up to.

"Caroline?" said Mary.

"Everyone keeps giving me water!" said Caroline. "Well, I 'spose, it's time for my pills." She started fumbling in her carrier bag.

"Caroline." said Mary, louder.

"OK, I'll find them in a minute. It was awful, Mary. She wouldn't talk to me. Not in the police station, not on the train. Then as we approached Oxford she started crying. Crying Anna! She never cries. And if she did. . .hurt anyone, it would not be silent tears dripping all over her dress. She wouldn't let me touch her. I got her to eat a piece of chocolate, nothing else. She wouldn't speak."

"Go on," said Mary.

"When we got off the train, she kind of woke up— got that fixed look on her face. I couldn't keep up with her as she raced for the uniformed policeman on the platform. You know how Anna feels about the police. Yet she grabbed his arm and said. . .she said. . ." Caroline froze.

Mary wanted to shake her. She sat on her hands. Finally, Caroline forced out the words:

"She said she cut the head off Rhiannon North. Then she said, 'I'm telling you I'm a murderer.'"

Mary's jaw hurt. "What happened then?" She itched to put her chair in front of Walbrook. Instead, he edged closer to Caroline. His Sergeant was entering notes on some sort of iPad.

"He put us in a waiting room," said Caroline. "I suppose he called you," she said looking at Walbrook. She went back to rummaging in her bag, extracted some pills, and took them with the rest of the water.

Walbrook intervened. "Miss Vronsky was taken into custody," he said. "She's already on her way to be processed. We're taking you two to be interviewed. The Sergeant will drive us. You should know, Miss Wandwalker, that I have taken overall control of the case. For now, my team will be based in Oxford."

"I see you do think the death of Joe Griffith is connected."

"Given that he was a prime suspect in the North beheading *and* suffered the same fate, well, there is a distinct possibility. You should know that the Police keep open minds."

"Ha," said Mary, skeptical as ever.

"What was that, Miss Wandwalker?"

"The two murders," said Mary, "were not exactly the same."

"Mary!" wailed Caroline. "It's *Anna* they've arrested! Don't you care at all?"

"Yes, of course I do," Mary snapped. She glared at Caroline and saw something she had not expected. Mary swung away to make sure that Walbrook did not see how taken aback she was by Caroline's reaction.

Outside the station, the unhappy foursome bathed in waves of heat. They dashed for the air conditioned police vehicle.

Mary now understood what troubled her about Caroline's distress. It wasn't despair from her chronic depression. Right now, there was something different. She was hurting because she thought that Anna could be guilty. Working through this, Mary stumbled across something even more surprising. It was an instinct she could not explain, a conviction that Anna wasn't guilty of either of these murders.

Whence came that extraordinary notion in the face of Anna's confession? Well, it had something to do with Rhiannon, thought a rueful Mary, as they drew into an underground car park, a dark cave choked with petrol fumes. Nothing from Rhiannon's talkative ghost corroborates the startling news from Anna. If Rhiannon, who'd disliked and feared Anna, does not trust the confession, well perhaps it is time to put my skepticism to good use.

CHAPTER 18
MR. JEFFREYS IS FURIOUS

It must be after midnight, Mary estimated. She was astounded to discover it was only 7:00 p.m. She sat in the police canteen contemplating a cold cheese and potato pie. Next to it sat her sixth polystyrene cup of vending machine coffee, half drunk. It was remarkable for milk powder surfacing in blobs like cultures grown in petri dishes. Her attention wandered to the buzzing phone. She ignored it. She tapped an unpainted fingernail on the sticky Formica table. It's not fair that Caroline is facing that police officer alone.

Immediately after their arrival at the now familiar Oxford police station, Mary and Caroline were interrogated together. Incensed by Walbrook and his team's prejudices about victims of trafficking, such as Anna, after an hour of heated argument Mary stopped, temporarily, she promised Caroline, mutely. To Mary and Caroline, it appeared that the police had too many interrogators. They could work in relays.

Mary was aware of Caroline's vulnerability, and so, tried to get them away from the pressure of describing Anna's dark past. Such details could be used against her. Mary folded her arms and demanded they were to be let go. No, Mrs. Jones would now be questioned, alone. Miss Wandwalker could wait for her in the canteen. Mary insisted that Caroline was not robust enough to be questioned without herself present. In response, Walbrook summoned a doctor.

Smelling of hospital disinfectant, the elderly physician spent five minutes with Caroline, and then pronounced her fit

139

for interviews. Mary scowled at the old man. In reply, he stuck out his tongue.

"Dr. Sung is about to retire," commented a young Sergeant. "Now Miss Wandwalker, let me show you where you can wait for Mrs. Jones. The Detective Inspector will want another word."

Mary rose with all the dignity she could muster and swept from the tiny interview room. Hours later she woke up in the Waiting Area to find figures in uniform frowning over her. They plonked Mary in another bare windowless room. There she had to repeat her account of discovering Rhiannon's head for at least the sixth time. Afterwards, she was escorted to the grubby canteen, which only served coffee from a sister machine to the Coke dispenser. The brown liquid was stale and harsh, like the questions had been.

Mary knew that making witnesses repeat stories was standard police procedure. Complex lies might dissolve in the face of dogged questioning. Nevertheless, she was tempted to shout her frustration. She and Caroline had been made to talk without being heard. They knew Anna; the police did not. Only determination to understand Anna's strange behavior stopped Mary from demanding a lawyer.

There was always a chance they could get to see Anna tonight. Although unwilling to take her confession at face value, Mary reflected that Anna had no alibi for Rhiannon's murder (nor for the killing of Joe, if Caroline was right). On the other hand, apart from the oddly timed admission of guilt, there was no real evidence against her.

When she and Caroline were finally reunited, Mary lost no opportunity to make that point. Walbrook changed his response.

"That's not quite true," he said, deadpan. "Miss Vronsky's fingerprint is on the murder weapon."

Caroline put her head down on the desk with a moan. Mary guessed she was wiped out.

"The weapon? What weapon?" inquired Mary.

"The axe that was found half buried in the Well Garden. Every used blade has a unique pattern of minute nicks. Forensics confirms this one matches the actual wound. On the shaft there is a partial print that belongs to Miss Vronsky."

"Partial?"

"A *big* part of her right thumb," Walbrook snapped back.

"How interesting, Inspector," Mary was not too tired to drive in her own kind of blade. "Anna Vronsky is left-handed. I would have expected her hold the axe in it to remove a human head. Given the state of the actual er. . .remains. Quite a neat job, I thought. You'll recall that Mrs. Jones and I had some minutes with. . .with the head before the police arrived."

Inspector Walbrook's jaw tightened. His Sergeant was tapping furiously into his iPad. Caroline sat up. She gripped Mary's arm. That was when Mary was sent back to the canteen for a second time.

Mary was not as sangfroid about the decapitation as she appeared to be. Talking about it, she could sense a stirring from the Rhiannon in her. That made her very nervous. Her inner companion was unpredictable. In the outer world, Mary was at the mercy of Walbrook, who represented the machinery of law and order. How I loathe these interminable repetitions, she thought. It's as if we're in an endless loop.

Charge Anna or not, Mary thought. Let her go home with us or put her in a cell for the night. Caroline and I need sleep. Do the police expect us to go on the run? Right now we could not stumble to the nearest bus stop. Mary had given up on access to Anna. That too was backed up by the doctor. He'd popped in on Anna to confirm that she could stay overnight. She had spoken no words since being placed in police custody.

In the eternity of waiting, Mary forgot about her phone. Her brain was stuck playing scenes of red blood splattered on green grass, people weeping, running by the Thames, the sun on an Oxford pavement, and, yes, those mocking eyes within her. Mary found herself slipping from the plastic chair. To stay awake, she required stimulation. Walking over to a dispensing machine was too much. On the table a greasy pie and a half inch of vile coffee stared back at her. The scum on the surface was vibrating. Oh, it is— the juddering my phone under the wrap. I must have put it on silent.

Eleven messages from Mr. Jeffreys. Ah, Mr. Jeffreys. Too tired to do anything else, she pressed the reply button.

"Don't tell me you couldn't have got back to me before now," Mr. Jeffreys snapped. Mary checked around her. No one.

"Mr. Jeffreys, how are you?" She was too tired to care what he said.

"Bloody furious, that's how I am, Miss Wandwalker. How could you have let things get this far?"

"I. . .*we* joined the Reborn Celts, as you said. I warned you that the third rite is planned for the solstice and. . ."

"Rhiannon North."

It hit Mary hard. I guess I still care what he says. No words. I have no words.

Mr. Jeffreys did. "She was your responsibility. Have you any idea how important her father is? To this country? I've even had the PM on the phone. . ."

"She was eighteen years old." Mary yelled before she could stop herself. She pictured Jeffreys surrounded by his files, his screens, massive bookcases, all the signs of security and political cronies. Jeffreys did not reply. He understood Mary too well to require her elaboration. She did it anyway.

"Eighteen. A child. Not a political or economic pawn."

Inside Mary, Rhiannon was listening. Mary could feel her intensity.

Mr. Jeffreys cleared his throat. His words bit. "I was going to refer you to the perilous position of Anna Vronsky. As her legal guardian, was it wise to let her go off with a bunch of homicidal Celts?"

He had her there. Anna's criminal past had not been forgiven. She was on parole for ten years, with Mary as guarantor that she would stick to the regime of model citizen and valuable employee of the Depth Enquiry Agency. Yes, Mary was compromised. Damn it Jeffreys. Can't you see I'm sinking, sinking into the dark where Rhiannon waits for me. Mistakes have been made; I admit. True, but is it fair to blame me for Anna's position? Just how much foresight do you expect?

"Mr. Jeffreys," she finally said, weary beyond measure. "We don't know, for sure, that they are homicidal Celts. So far there is no definitive evidence to tie the Morrigan family to either murder. Am I assuming correctly that Anna's partial print is all that links her to the axe?"

She waited, knowing that Jeffreys would appreciate her expectation that the police evidence would be shared with him.

"You are right, Miss Wandwalker." He was stiff.

Progress.

"I did plan to go on the wretched field trip, you know. Caroline convinced me to let her take my place. All things considering, I think she did a good job of keeping an eye on Anna."

"That would be the good job that included the beheading of Griffith?" Jeffreys was not relenting. Mary was hoping for the sense of irony they both shared.

"Unfortunate."

"And Vronsky's confession?"

"I don't believe it." Mary was surprised to hear herself say this out loud.

"Nonsense! You're dreaming, Mary. A pipe dream of making a family out of a depressed woman and a criminal."

Jeffreys stopped. He was not callous as a rule. The pressure on him must be acute. He ploughed on. "Vronsky was always on a knife edge between usefulness and liability. Looks to me like the worst of her took over. It's cuckoo to think otherwise. With her conviction you can stop playing at being Enquiry agents. As a result of your incompetence the DEA will be dissolved. I will see to it myself."

There was a click, and Mr. Jeffreys was gone. Mary put down the phone with a shaking hand. Dissolve the DEA? It would be the end of everything she'd worked for. Mr. Jeffreys had never spoken that brutally before. Could he be serious? He can't do that.

Forget it, Mary. He's right. Mary's neck colored with shame, like an indelible stain on one of Anna's designer dresses. She swallowed the last of the disgusting coffee. It's over, she admitted. Really. Over. My grand idea to make a family out of a professional agency; one that worked in depth with problems too personal for most detectives. Oh yes, I've gone deep indeed.

A sour taste rose in Mary's throat. The Rhiannon inside her was infectious with poisonous glee. Mary stared down at sticky table. She wanted to put her head in her arms and sleep forever.

Caroline would be here any minute, she thought. After that journey, and five hours of interrogation, I can't abandon her now. Time to grasp my responsibilities. I let Rhiannon down, fatally. The very least I can do is stick by Caroline and Anna to the end. Even if it means the end of everything we've worked for.

With Mary's failure to keep Rhiannon safe, the teenager's death alone was enough to destroy the DEA, even if Anna was innocent. And rightly so, realized Mary. I should have thought of this before. My mistakes doom the Agency. Anna will go to prison. Caroline would go to pieces. I'll be alone and reviled. Mary heard a bitter laugh and could not tell if it was herself or Rhiannon's ghost.

At last, a door swung in the opposite corner of the dead canteen. It was Caroline, wobbling around tables and chairs as if in physical pain. Before her friend reached the chair opposite her, Mary could tell from her expression of relief that they were allowed to leave. They could drown this endless day in food or wine or the hope of dreamless sleep. When Caroline opened her mouth to say this, the older woman put up a hand to stop her.

To Caroline's bleached pallor, Mary had an instinctive reaction. She hit redial and spoke before she could think better of it.

"Mr. Jeffreys? Yes, it's Mary Wandwalker. Now, listen to me if you please. I'm telling you that Anna Vronsky is innocent. She did not commit these murders. We know our Anna. The

DEA will clear her, and we will get to the bottom of the Reborn Celts too. You have my word. Goodnight."

She hung up before he could reply. Returning the phone to her handbag, she stood up taking Caroline's elbow.

"Let's go. We've a lot to do tomorrow."

Caroline's chin lifted to meet Mary's. She nodded, a slight smile spreading across her cracked lips as they made their way to the street, where Mary hailed a cab to take them to Norham Gardens and their beds. Caroline slumped in the vehicle and had to be woken. Mary had time to make a couple of entries into her notebook. Back in her bedroom she stared at out of the window as the evening stars revealed their ancient stories across the city.

CHAPTER 19
ANNA

The following morning began with a thundering at the front door. Caroline got up to answer it. She had been lying awake, too miserable to get out of bed. Mary must be deeply asleep not to be stirring by now. The banging was followed by a scraping sound. Was someone trying to get in?

"Mary, wake up," yelled Caroline. "Stop," she continued halfway down the stairs:. "Wait, I'm coming." She flung open the door, then gasped at the looming figure with the rising sun behind him.

"Good morning, Mrs. Jones. I've brought back your companion." Mr. Jeffreys stepped aside to reveal a figure wrapped in a white towel from head to toe. Matted strands of long dark hair covered most of her face.

"Anna!"

Caroline leapt to gather Anna in her arms.

"What have you done to her?" Mary wore her dressing gown like a general's uniform. Her eyes never wavered from Mr. Jeffreys. Conscious of her own tatty pajamas, Caroline guided Anna up the stairs.

"Put her to bed," called Mr. Jeffreys, then turned to Mary. "She's released into your custody until she is sufficiently recovered for more questioning. You should be grateful, Miss Wandwalker. Walbrook wanted her kept under guard in hospital."

"What have you done?" Mr. Jeffreys raised an eyebrow. Mary wasn't in the mood. "Stop playing games. She looks terrible."

"It's all in the email I sent an hour ago," grunted Jeffreys. "Given the circumstances, I want you to have everything in writing. I must get back to London." He turned and made for a bullet shaped car that matched his grey suit: large, expensive, and customized.

Mr. Jeffreys thought better of his exit line and turned back to Mary.

"This changes nothing." He was sober. "Your competence, as guardian for Vronsky and as an Enquiry agent, is fatally compromised. The DEA cannot go on like this. Today the Morrigans will be questioned by the authorities. There's nothing left for you to do."

"What about Anna?" said Mary, stubbornly. "What happened?"

Mr. Jeffreys glanced at his driver. Taking a couple of steps back to Mary, he took note of her defiance.

"Vronsky collapsed late last night. She was rushed to hospital and tested for the usual poisons. When they found unidentifiable toxins, she was transferred to the John Whitcliffe Research Center. They have a lab that treats over-enthusiastic research students." He scowled at Mary while she waited for him to finish. "By this morning, they'd taken enough vials of her blood to test, so I had her discharged. It's only temporary, while enquiries continue. I have explained all this in the email. Read it." He looked after Anna, frowning. "No doubt, Miss Wandwalker, no doubt your homicidal Celts are responsible."

Then he was gone. Mary stiffened at '*your* homicidal Celts.' Infuriated not to have the last word, she followed his car with her eyes until it turned out of Norham Gardens and entered the metallic soup of Oxford. There was something different about the car. That's it. No smell of petrol fumes. What lingered in the rising warmth was steam. A hydrogen car, of course, thought Mary to herself as she shut the door. A hydrogen car emits water vapor. There're not on the market yet. Just like Mr. Jeffreys to secure a prototype.

Checking that Anna was asleep in Caroline's bed, Mary opened her email, also making sure that Sarah had started brewing coffee.

"Thank you," she said to the mug placed beside her. Sipping the chocolate-colored brew from Kenya she'd discovered at the Covered Market, Mary began to think more clearly. She'd have to read Mr. Jeffreys' email before checking out Anna's condition for herself. After the bare bones information in his message, she found a couple of ominous notes.

A mixture of heroin, cocaine, and various standard hallucinogens were found by the initial tests. They also retrieved a vegetable substance that they could not identify. Given her condition, permission was granted to send her to the research unit at the John Whitcliffe. Vronsky regained consciousness briefly, and so after they have taken sufficient blood, and provided they consider her condition is stable, I will bring her to you.

Miss Wandwalker, I cannot stress too much the severity of the situation for Vronsky and yourself. Walbrook is convinced of her guilt. I agree that the case against her is compelling when you consider the tortuous relationships. There is also the question of the Griffith death. Initial enquiries are concentrating on the veterans because of their history of traumatic stress disorder. Most of the Americans have records of arrests for drunken brawls or assault. However, they have also begun considering sex as a possible motive. Some mumbo jumbo about beheading and Freud, I believe.

Mary winced at the mention of Freud. Give her C. G. Jung's more creative fantasies any day. Freud had linked sex and death as streams merging into an unstoppable river. Was that what had happened to Joe Griffith? She recalled the fog of longing that had surrounded him at Exmoor. What about lonely Rhiannon? For Rhiannon had been lonely, Mary could see now.

Not just me, came mutinous words. Oh Rhiannon, do go away, Mary muttered. I must concentrate. Mr. Jeffreys is telling me about Anna. I must try to see the whole investigation.

> There will be no more sleuthing for you. Forgive me for being so blunt after our long association at the Archives, but I must tell you that your DEA is incompetent. All you can do now is concentrate on saving Miss Vronsky. Whatever you may think, I take seriously your conviction that she is innocent. The police will find the evidence. You must get into her mind.

Get into Anna's mind, she repeated. You mean, as well as dealing with Rhiannon? Mary sighed.

Yes, came back the irrepressible imp in her head. You must enter Anna's spirit-world. It won't be anything like you expect. Anna is far far away. The Otherworld has claimed her.

Mary drank the rest of the coffee. She was prepared to ask some very piercing questions of 'her' Rhiannon. Yet later, when she tried to find the dead girl, the waters were opaque. Rhiannon had dived deep. She wasn't talking to Mary anymore.

CHAPTER 20
NO MORE DEPTH
ENQUIRY AGENCY?

Anna slept all that day and the next. On the third morning Caroline remained beside her bed, flowing from anxiety to relief and back again. At least Anna was home. They were together again, at last. Mary would know what to do. Every so often, Mary appeared with cups of tea, or pieces of toast prepared by Sarah. Without registering, Caroline consumed everything. Her every sinew concentrated on the sleeping woman. Anna's breath was as regular as waves.

Meanwhile, Mary worked the phone. She alternated between trying to get information from Inspector Walbrook's team and from the research department at the John Whitcliffe. The police weren't divulging anything, and the hospital just said that they were consulting a local expert on vegetable poisons. In short, Mary was to let the professionals do their jobs.

After a couple of days, Mary was ready to hammer her computer screen with her fists. She could not reach anyone useful on the phone. The internet provided over a hundred nasty conditions to which Anna's symptoms could be correlated. Instead of attacking the computer Mary made an unladylike sound. She was surprised when a concerned voice responded.

"Go outside, Miss Wandwalker. Get some fresh air. It's what you would tell Caroline." Sarah stood in the doorway. Savory steam accompanied her from the kitchen.

Mary noted Sarah's bolder approach. Caroline would appreciate it, and so she pushed down her habit of dignified rejection. But even so...

"Why all this cooking, Sarah? It's far too hot today."

"Digestion," said Sarah, with quiet assurance. "Cooking enables more nutrients to be digested if people are sick. From the look of Anna, she hasn't eaten much in the last few days. You don't when you're on drugs."

Mary blinked. She'd forgotten those track marks on the young woman's arm.

"Good idea," she said.

Sarah risked a quick smile. "Get away from the computer, Miss Wandwalker. At least for a few minutes. It will do you good."

Mary found herself shutting her laptop and standing up. Well, there is a garden. She may as well sit in it. Even though it was far too muggy outside to linger.

Planted to mimic all other gardens on the street, this garden cupped a too bright sun. In places that might have had flowers in better years, Mary noted withered sticks and straw-like stalks. A brown leaf glided down to join a scattering on the grass. Yes, the horse chestnut trees were beginning to shed their leaves— in June. This cannot be good, Mary thought.

She knew nothing about horticulture. Her suburban childhood was buried with her parents, who had died unexpectedly of flu when she was seventeen. Miss Wandwalker spent her adulthood in a London apartment with no plants whatsoever. Nothing to care for. Nothing that could die or otherwise abandon her.

Glad that the trees provided shade, Mary sat down on the garden's bench and rose at once. That iron arm rest was *hot*. She moved to the middle, facing the rented house. There was the bedroom window through which Caroline and Anna waited for her to save them. Mary dropped her eyes to the kitchen, where a dark head moved to and fro: Sarah, a strong young woman with a painful past. Mary Wandwalker could do nothing for her either.

No longer can I avoid Mr. Jeffreys' condemnation. He is right. I should have done better, particularly by Rhiannon. As if it needed confirmation, a lawsuit from Mr. North would arrive any day. Given their parlous financial state, the DEA would have no choice except to file for bankruptcy. We will be forced to sell the house in Surrey, our actual home. That will seal the breakup of the DEA. Ending the business will dissolve the family. Anna would be taken by the authorities and go to prison if convicted; Caroline would blame Mary. Don't forget about me, came a whisper in her head.

Yes, said Mary. Yelling at the phantom won't make her go away. I've tried that. Might as well be honest, and start with the voice inside, the essence of Rhiannon, or whatever it is.

"Okay. You too, Rhiannon," she said aloud. "I also let *you* down. Now give it a rest while I tackle the bigger picture."

Along with Rhiannon, Joe Griffith was dead. Anna was accused of the first murder. No, not just accused. Mary winced, *confessed*. While a motive could be stitched together from Rhiannon's infatuation with Joe, but why confess when no one had accused her? And why do I feel that the confession is so wrong?

She remembered shouting Anna's innocence to Mr. Jeffreys in that dreadful phone call. He'd been impressed, as he has admitted. So, Mary enquired of the fears and bafflement that constituted her relationship with Anna, why do I feel that you did not kill anyone? After all, logic says you are guilty. Your confession confirms it. Yet Mary's instinct was that that Anna did not kill either Rhiannon or Joe. That instinct felt like a rope thrown over a raging torrent. Wildly risky, in fact, crazily dangerous, yet it was all she had. What now?

Mary applied her mind. Anna was, no, *is still* poisoned. She could have been controlled by drugs and done things she would never do otherwise. Why else load her up with so many narcotics and exotic toxins? This was Caroline's great fear. Caroline believed that Anna had been drugged into a state of hallucination and forced to kill Rhiannon. She was relying on

Mary to convince the police that such undue influence amounted to innocence.

There was more to the convoluted path of the drugs. Mary was beginning to see that, manipulated by chemicals, Anna could have participated in the killing of Joe Griffith. I must think like the police. After all, Joe and Anna's mutual infatuation was melting. Lovers' quarrels could turn violent. Mary recalled when Anna had seemed to reach out to her at the train station. Had it been a cry for help? Had Anna feared she might not be in control?

Mary had long recognized the aggression that was the legacy of Anna's traumatic past in sex trafficking. All Mary could be sure of was that Anna had been rescued from her captors by George Jones, a policeman and Mary's long-lost son. His passion for Anna had cost him his life. The bond between his widow, Caroline, and Anna often puzzled Mary. Yet she could not deny that their love had been a life raft for both. It had saved Anna and Caroline from drowning in pain and loss of the same man.

Just what had been awoken in Anna by Joe Griffith? He was the warrior who declared killing to be a sacred duty. Shedding blood was his route to the gods. Had the unrestrained sexuality of his affair with Anna let loose demons in her? After all, they were alike, Mary realized. Burned into their souls was a savagery inflicted when they were defenseless. With the addition of powerful narcotics, how hard would it be to turn Anna into an instrument of murder?

Such a road to Anna's guilt would be taken by the police. It was Inspector Walbrook's position, even after the tests on Anna's blood. Unless the mystery toxins could be deciphered in a way to exonerate Anna, Walbrook would pursue criminal charges. Caroline would say that Anna was innocent because of what had been put into her body. Walbrook would insist that she was still responsible for the crime. Both perspectives would be argued in court.

After twenty minutes of absentmindedly watching leaves drift down, Mary found that she didn't buy either version. Yes, Mr. Jeffreys' rational appraisal was devastating. Her inexperience *had* left the Depth Enquiry Agency floundering. For a moment Mary felt swamped by failure. It is so easy to drown, to give up. Yet a glance up at the windows was enough to remind her that giving up was not an option.

Alright, Mr. Jeffreys, Mary said to herself. Alright, I accept your word for my responsibility: "Incompetence." But not the guilt of Anna. *That* I won't accept. Mr. Jeffreys had already conceded to her on that point. The recollection gave Mary a lift. If Anna were innocent, then. . . From within the depths of unknowing that flowed between herself, Caroline, and Anna, Mary felt for other currents, even though nothing so far constituted the kind of evidence that would exonerate Anna and solve the murders.

Just suppose Anna had confessed because of her past, and not these murders? Walbrook was too secure in his own police world. She could hear him dismissing her suggestion that the confession, not the deed, was the product of Anna's drug induced state. Indeed, if Walbrook had access to all the records about Anna (sealed by Mr. Jeffreys), he would be *more* convinced of her guilt. For him the fact that Anna grew up in organized crime opened avenues of suspicion. To Mary it was the reverse.

Mary and Caroline had lived with Anna's iron will for many months. While Caroline had the intimacy of a love affair, Mary pondered the young woman's unusual skills for hunting down elusive information on the internet, along with her aggressive defenses. She'd found the young woman both trustworthy and deceitful, often at the same time. Nothing straightforward worked with Anna. All Mary could do as her legal guardian was to hold onto that complexity and face of the storms in Anna's psyche.

She may think she killed Rhiannon, Mary reasoned, but that is what I don't trust about her. She's lying about her guilt, whether she knows it or not. Anna's dived too deep to be seen.

Her mistake was to get too far within Joe Griffith's torments to swim back. She got caught up in his metaphysical drama and lost her own. Anna needs rescuing, again. The DEA will get her back.

Mary started pacing around the lawn. After a few circuits in the heat, she retreated to the bench. A personal conviction of Anna's innocence was not enough. Anna's fate might depend on finding the true killer, or killers, of Rhiannon and Joe. It meant that Mary and Caroline had to continue with this painful case, if only to save Anna. No matter what Mr. Jeffreys says, we cannot give up, she resolved. I've got to protect Sarah too, she added as an afterthought. *"And yourself,* Mary Wandwalker," came the mermaid voice of Rhiannon.

Mary rose to her feet. The garden was too hot. She would head straight to Anna, if not to shake her awake, then at least to share with Caroline her belief that Anna had killed neither Rhiannon nor Joe. Just as she started towards the back door, it opened. Sarah trotted out to meet her carrying Mary's ringing phone. The chimes of Big Ben, the famous clock used on the BBC, poured over the distant hum of traffic. Rooks cawing overhead began to echo its call.

"I thought it might be news about Anna. From the hospital." said Sarah. She was apologetic.

"Of course, thank you, Sarah."

It wasn't news of Anna's mystery toxins. The poor connection made the male voice sound as if he were shouting from over an ocean, but Mary could still barely make out his words. He was at the British Army Veterans Center, Woolwich Arsenal Barracks; it was the Thames he could see from an office window.

CHAPTER 21
A TORC BETWEEN CELTS

Mary took the phone call. There was a lot of static, but eventually she recognized the voice of Dr Jez Wiseman. So engrossed was she in Anna's plight that she forgot Wiseman had recently lost someone dear to him. However, his call was more about fears for his Graduate School back in California than his own bruised heart.

"Miss Wandwalker, can you hear me? This is very important."

"Is that you, Dr. Wiseman? It's a bad line. Shall I call you back?"

"Never mind that, Miss Wandwalker. Listen to me. The Sacred Well Torc is gone. It's a disaster for my school. The Morrigans stole it during the field trip. I need your help to get it back."

This call was more about fears for his Graduate School back in California than his own bruised heart, Mary realized.

"What do you mean? The torc? What are you talking about?"

Mary frowned at the phone. She must have misheard.

"The torc! The gold torc, Mary! You know. We saw it—with Rhiannon. You took it from her. Two months ago, when we met her at the Exmoor Well. She kept dipping it in the water. Where. . ."

A choking sound came from the phone, and Jez stopped speaking.

Mary remembered being with Wiseman that day. Rhiannon flounced away leaving the torc with Mary. Yes, again she heard the noisy blackbird with shining wings. He'd told her about Joe, the man who. . .Mary bit her lip. Just a couple of days ago Joe's severed head rolled in the shallows of the crescent lake. There would have been a lot of blood. He would have seen it.

"Oh, erm, yes, about Joe Griffith and you. . ."

The words of sorrow would not come. Instead, she gasped.

"Wait a minute, Dr Wiseman, the torc is *here*. Rhiannon retrieved it. I saw it when. . .I mean the police have it, I told you. It was on Rhiannon's. . . head. Like a crown."

"Not *that* torc. Pay attention, Miss Wandwalker. I'm talking about the real one. That torc— I mean, the one Rhiannon showed around the Summer School—that one is a copy. The real torc has vanished from my backpack. Stolen, I'm telling you. And recently."

"Wait, I don't understand. You're saying that Rhiannon never had the real torc? No one told us. How did you get it?"

A huge sigh arrived amid rolling waves of static. Mary had to do something.

"Dr. Wiseman, let me go where the signal may be better," called Mary, starting to walk. "You're breaking up." She thought she heard a muttered "Too right," as she made for the house and better reception. Indoors she sat down hard as if the room might start tossing and turning.

"Tell me please, Dr. Wiseman. Something about Rhiannon and a fake torc? How come you had the real one. . .in a backpack, I mean surely. . ."

"No. Yes. I mean not when we met her, it was real, and then. . . Oh. . .let me tell you the whole story. It's not that complicated."

Mary was sure she heard a groan as Wiseman prepared to explain.

"You see, may I call you Mary?"

He did not wait for her reply. (She preferred Miss Wandwalker.)

"This won't make any sense unless you know that the Norths are mad for their Celtic origins. Goes back generations to when the family used to go hunting for treasures in Europe. Turns out finding Celtic artifacts bonded Rhiannon and her father like nothing else. You see, about a year ago she turned down a place in a top Business School, and denied any interest in her father's business, Mer-Corp. He hoped she'd change her mind, of course; but in the meantime, he gave her the torc, the genuine article. It's pure gold with a trace of silver, a unique alloy according to Albert Edward Morrigan. He sold it to Mr. North to get money for the Reborn Celts."

Mary nodded, then remembered he could not see her. "Yes, I'm with you."

"The next bit is down to Rhiannon. Her father told her to take good care of the real torc. It's worth millions and is way too valuable to leave their heavily protected ranch. So, like any teenager, she ignored her father and brought it to England, to the Summer School."

"Of course, she would," sighed Mary. "Where we saw it. She was planning to use it to seduce Joe Griffith. It was obvious she was besotted."

"Yeah, looks like it," said Wiseman. He sounded even more glum.

The story was clearer now that Wiseman had reached parts that Mary could sketch out for herself. There remained the question of the switch of real for fake torc.

"Months ago, Rhiannon was following Joe on Twitter and all the other social media. The Celtic Summer School even posted clips from his classes on YouTube: Joe, the great warrior, an impressionable youngster's hero. Rhiannon's next step was to persuade her father to pay for the Summer School. He was sensible enough to ask me if I knew anyone who could keep an eye on her. I recommended you, told him the course would be very educational. He had no idea of her feelings for Joe."

"Her obsession," said Mary. It made her sad, digging into what drove Rhiannon to her fate. "It wasn't the normal teenage crush, either. Some part of her believed that she could become Joe's Celtic princess. Or even a goddess."

"Well, you've got to see that she was a kind of princess already," said Jez. "America has never gotten over ditching your monarchy. Now we have CEOs of corporations like Mer-Corp setting up their children like crown princes and princesses. Mr. North was quite open about it. He was horrified when I told him about Rhiannon waving the torc about; FedExed me the copy right away."

"That's when you switched the torc?"

"Yeah, Mr. North was hopping mad with Rhiannon for 'treating it like a toy,' he said. Even so, he could not bear another row. That day she tried it on the neck of the Morrigan kid, Colin, I made the exchange while she bugged Joe about doing a selfie with her. Mr. North insisted I always keep the real torc with me. He planned to have it out with Rhiannon when she got back to the States. Their relationship was too fragile for rows on the phone, he said. It was only after he got the torc for her that she began talking to him again. What a brat."

"She was more than that," said Mary. 'She was a spoiled brat,' had been her own condemnation of Rhiannon. Such opinions left Rhiannon vulnerable. "Rhiannon was lonely," Mary found herself instead saying to Wiseman. It had taken Mary too long to see it. "Some of her. . .her brattishness. . .was a plea. At some level she was asking for help."

"Kind of misfired, didn't it?" said Wiseman. It occurred to Mary that he was angry with Rhiannon on behalf of Joe. Had her adoration contributed to his self-intoxication?

Wiseman was still preoccupied with the torcs.

"I guess Mr. North found it easier to spend money than show affection for the girl. Anyhow, Mr. North said to keep the real one in the safe until he could set up a proper courier. Think of it as guarantor of future donations, he said; joking I think."

Wiseman stopped as his own words pointed to the enormity of the loss. "I *was* hoping that meant the two million he'd mentioned. After satisfying a few creditors, it would pay for our new Indigenous Studies Program. So, I'm in big trouble. No torc. He'll sue, he always does. You gotta help me, Mary. I know it's the Morrigans. They were the ones near my stuff on the field trip. They'll be back in Oxford by now, and I can't leave my guys. Most are re-traumatized by what happened to Joe."

Mary recalled Wiseman's American veterans. They'd need extra rehabilitation now, surely.

"Dr. Wiseman, why are you so certain it was the Morrigans? They didn't know you had the real torc, did they? No one told them about the switch if Rhiannon did not know herself. Mary knew it was a naïve question, yet something is not right in the story, she sensed. Fishing for the exact circumstances, Wiseman's groan rattled her.

"My fault. I did it. Right royally screwed up as you Brits might say. All for Joe. I couldn't give up hope that we might get back our old closeness. I dreamed we could be buddies again. Showing the torc to Joe would bring us together, or so I thought." He paused. Mary had a sinking sensation.

"It killed me, just killed me that he brought along the Morrigans." In the silence Mary could taste his grief, as well as anger. They both contemplated what might have been.

He continued, "Guess I'll tell Mr. North I did it to have more influence over how he was handling the field trip. Mary, Joe was so overjoyed. No, that's not right. He became. . .ecstatic, like in a trance. Said something about the torc Rhiannon showed being a huge disappointment to the Reborn Celts. She insisted he borrow it overnight. I guess he checked it out, found it wasn't authentic."

Mary frowned. Yes, there had been a day when she, Caroline, Sarah, and Rhiannon had stopped at the sandwich shop in the Covered Market. Rhiannon announced she'd left her purse in the classroom. Mary let her run back for it, while they chose their lunch. The girl joined them on the bench in Exmoor quad. She was glowing like the torc itself. So that one was not real. Wiseman kept talking.

". . .I can't get it out of my mind. It's haunting me. When I said I could show Joe the real torc, he jumped like his boots were on fire. I swear the energy just poured off him. He ran over to the Morrigans, shouting for them to come quickly. They're a weird family, Mary. Those crazy blue eyes, even the foster kid has 'em."

"Dr. Wiseman, slow down. When was this?"

"The first evening of the field trip. Most folks were outside because it was starting to get cool. Your Mrs. Jones hadn't arrived. Just the five of us gathered and moved inside to the tiny office. The hairy guy with the creepiest accent, Prof. Barin, had a bottle of Islay whisky."

"Go on," said Mary.

"Thinking back, I reckon they'd decided to hide their excitement. They were all nods and tight lips. I caught significant looks when they thought I was not paying attention. You see, after passing the torc around, we finished that bottle of scotch." He coughed and continued.

"More fool me. There was a lockbox attached to the wall and that's where I put the torc. I know they all saw me put the key in my backpack." He sighed audibly. "I'm not used to so much whisky. We all drank, except the kid, Colin. That Barin snatched the bottle away from him. Simmy would have given him some, but the brother wasn't having it."

"Colin was there too. What about. . ."

"Anna? No, she went to bed early, Joe said. Good thing if you ask me. Why, you sound worried? Is Anna in trouble?"

"You could say that."

"Well, she wasn't in the room. Come to think of it, I got the distinct impression that she was out of their loop. Now about the theft. . ."

"Wait, wait, Dr. Wiseman. . .Jez. This could be important." Mary gripped the phone. "Tell me what gave you the impression that Anna was sidelined? This could help us. For finding the torc as well."

"Ohhh. I get you." There was a pause. "Yeah. Hmm, it could be when we arrived at the lake and Joe said Anna was exhausted. I didn't expect it. At Exmoor she didn't strike me as a sleeper. When she and Joe got together, well, you saw them. They dissolved into one being. Late at night we'd see them walking about the quad; one body and four legs. Yet at the field trip," he mused. "I remember she was strung out, always going to bed. She disappeared earlier each day. I did wonder if she was on something. . .Mary, do you think. . .?

"I do," said Mary. She was grim. "In fact, Dr. Wiseman, they drugged her. She's upstairs asleep right now, won't wake up. The hospital is doing tests. Not everything in her system has been identified."

"Ah."

His tone alerted Mary.

"What do you mean, 'Ah?' If you know what he gave her, tell me. Please, Dr. Wiseman. It could save her life." Mary was shocked at the wobble in her voice.

"Now Mary, you can't be sure it was Joe handing out drugs. Not the way those Celts hung about together. Any of them could have doctored her food or drink."

"Dr. Wiseman, what do you know?"

Mary was back in charge of her emotions. Nothing would stop her getting this information, even if she had to commandeer a taxi and tour every veteran rehab in the country.

"Well, you remember I told you that Joe went to a Native American curing, and it failed."

"He went crazy; had to be restrained, yes."

"Guess that sums it up. Well, he came back with a few of their herbs. In fact, one he wasn't supposed to have. They would not name it— just that Joe raided their restricted stock. I'll forward you the website. Tell the docs treating Anna."

"I will. But how could you let Joe do this?" Mary was stung.

"Hey there, I never knew he stole the stuff until they texted me yesterday. And Anna seemed a big girl to me. Mary, you gotta understand. He saved my life."

Mary bit back a retort. Something had been bothering her. "Joe believed in the Celts— did he ever try to recruit you? I mean you suffered in the war like him. . ."

"Not like him." Jez was very quiet. "He is. . .was the hero. He did the saving. I was blown up. It's taken everything to keep trying with my legs. I got nothing for Joe's gods."

"You weren't alone in being wounded that day."

"Crippled. *Crippled,* Mary." Wiseman flung the word at Mary. He wanted to silence her and succeeded.

"Sorry, I know you mean well. You see, I'd almost finished my PhD before that final tour. It. . .it gave me something to cling to during those nightmare months. Joe didn't have anything to focus his mind. Until the Morrigans. I guess I feel responsible. Didn't try hard enough to offer him some other path. When it all started, I thought the Celts were just his Welsh heritage, you know, roots. It didn't occur to me that those bastard white supremacists would latch on to him."

Mary recalled her initial conversation with Mr. Jeffreys. She too had once dismissed these Celts as over enthusiastic historians.

"Don't feel too responsible, Dr. Wiseman. When I saw Joe first. . .He had gone into his world of gods. No one could compete with that. We tried to detach Anna from him. We didn't try hard enough. Well, I didn't."

Neither of them mentioned Rhiannon out loud. No evidence singled out her killer. Yet Mary could not dislodge an image of Joe Griffith throttling her by the light of flaming torches. So far, she had not risked asking Rhiannon's ghost. Mary's silent, I feel responsible for what happened to Rhiannon too, crossed the miles between them.

She heard a sound like a clearing throat. "I guess that's where we came in, Mary. Rhiannon's torc. You should not feel bad. You're not responsible for who she was— that's on her family."

Mary felt better. She was grateful for his thoughtfulness. Wiseman didn't know that Rhiannon was still with her, waiting for the right moment to rise. She should focus on what she could do something about— like why he phoned.

"Thank you, Dr. Wiseman. You are kind. So, about the torc, the real one. You're sure that the Morrigans took it."

"Gotta be them. I showed it to no one else. Plus, my American vets have all heard of Mer-Corp. If Mr. North is worried about theft, he'll have his own security detail. Those creeps will go after thieves themselves. Too much stress for my guys in rehab."

"OK. We can accept that the Morrigans took the torc," said Mary. "What does Mr. North say about it? You've informed the police, of course."

This time the silence was pregnant. Gotcha, thought Mary. Wiseman would have to spell it out.

"Erm, you see, Mary, you are the first person I've told. Client confidentiality covers this, I'm hoping. I'm still a DEA client, aren't I?"

Mary said nothing.

"Please Mary, you know I have to keep Mr. North and Mer-Corp happy. Hey, it's not just the donation. Mer-Corp are real bad juju. My Graduate School doesn't stand a chance against their lawyers." He sighed, sounding weary. "North is said to be prostrate with grief. I'm betting that at any moment he's gonna remember the torc. Mary, please find the Morrigans and get it back."

CHAPTER 22
LOCAL EXPERTS AND
INCOMPETENT DETECTIVES

It struck Mary that she and Caroline were caught between two clients with opposite agendas. While Mr. Jeffreys wanted to shut down the DEA, Wiseman was desperate that they expand the case.

"Finding the real torc would be a big clue in catching Joe's killer," he'd said, hopefully. "And whatever Mr. J. says he wants, you'll be looking out for Anna. That's who you are. Searching for the torc's gotta help her. After all, she may know more than you think."

Mary agreed to pursue the torc while making it clear that Anna's future would be their priority. She was keen to end the phone call after Wiseman's suggestive remark. The last thing they needed was for Anna to be accused of yet another crime. Time to see if the young woman could be roused. And if not that, at least she could update Caroline with the morning's news.

As Mary climbed the stairs, she had a moment of lightheadedness. She grabbed the banister with both hands, noticing a twinge in her back. Getting old? Certainly not. Mary quickened her pace and swung open the bedroom door. A picture of affection greeted her in the rising and falling of breaths. Anna was snoring under the covers; Caroline was curled up next to her, also sound asleep.

Mary hesitated. Both women had undergone more strain than she could imagine. Best to let them sleep. She could use the time to track the Morrigans. They'll not be hard to find, she concluded. Minus Joe, Simmy and Barin will have to teach on the Summer School. Wait, didn't the College shut it down? I must check on that too.

She turned from the sleeping women and tiptoed to the top of the stairs. A knocking sounded from the front door. Oh, surely not the police again, she fumed: enough. As she descended to the hallway, Mary composed some choice remarks for Inspector Walbrook. She would *not* let the police have Anna while she was in this drugged sleep. When she wakes up the three of us will talk before anyone goes anywhere, she promised herself.

Before Mary reached the door, the knocking had graduated to banging. Sarah appeared from the kitchen, sweaty and alarmed.

"Do you want to take Anna out the back," she whispered to Mary. "I can get you an Uber."

Mary smiled at her. "Thank you, dear. I won't let them take Anna. Even if they have a warrant, she's too ill to be moved."

Taking a deep breath, Mary flung open the front door. Instead of Walbrook fronting an array of cars and unsmiling officers, she found a short old woman with improbable red hair. The woman scowled, sticking her chin up at Mary.

After taking in the basket of dried herbs, and a laptop under the other arm, Mary caught sight of boots with metal toecaps. So that accounts for the flakes on the step, poisonous snow, she thought in rising anger. Mary opened her mouth to protest as the woman pushed past her.

"About time," Janet grumbled. "Sarah, dear, take these herbs and brew my Chinese Willow Tea— the one with the extra ingredients I showed you. Wandwalker, you can take the laptop."

The machine, sticky with what Mary hoped was jam, was thrust into Mary's unwilling arms.

"Janet," said Mary between her teeth. She shut the door. "What are you doing here?"

The old woman let loose a cackle that Mary was sure she used to mock the stereotype of witches.

"Come to see Anna, of course," she said over her shoulder. She stamped up the stairs as if intending to wake any sleepers. The bannisters shook. "Didn't you hear that I'm the local expert on vegetable toxins?" she flung back at Mary.

Mary opened her mouth, then closed it. That's right, Mr. Jeffreys mentioned that the unit at the John Whitcliffe Hospital was calling in an expert; Janet, the local witch. She followed Janet to Anna's room, where Caroline was rubbing her eyes.

Hazy fragments surfaced about Janet's unique education. At Holywell she'd gone from foster child to authority on all things magical from the earth. This included a Ph.D. in Plant Pharmacology, as well as training with a visiting African shaman. Naturally, she'd delved into Holywell's own long history with herbs. Janet was the local expert, all right. Given her achievements, perhaps, just perhaps, she could wake Anna up.

Janet began trying to do just that. She had taken Caroline's place on the bed and was pulling up Anna's eyelids.

"Don't hurt her!" squeaked Caroline. Janet gave her a look. Caroline backed away while Janet pulled a strand of Anna's midnight hair to her nose.

"What are you doing?" said Mary.

"Waiting for the tea," snapped Janet. She grasped one of Anna's hands and pulled the fingers, as if checking for stiffness. After letting the hand drop, she scooted to the bottom of the bed, pushing Mary aside. Pulling up the covers, Janet exposed Anna's bare feet. They were sun tanned and rather dirty. Scarlet-black nail polish was flaking off. Two adjacent toes were purplish with cracked nails, as if someone had stood on them.

"Hum," said Janet. She took a blackened spoon from her herb basket and began tapping the soles of each foot, alternating three taps on one, then the other.

"Janet," pleaded Caroline. "We trust you, we do, but. . ."

"Wandwalker doesn't," said the old woman with a grin. "Trust me, that is."

"I'm sure you think you know what you're doing," said Mary.

She felt absurd. They were letting Janet do her tricks because they were too desperate to refuse her help. And she knew it.

"Ha!" barked Janet. "That's what I don't. Know, that is. Not until I've been to the hospital lab and tried her blood spectrum against a few of my herbs. What I'm *doing*, however," she said with exaggerated condescension, "is calling Anna home. Silver," she tapped the spoon again, "is moon and fire, Anna's elements. Ah, the tea, at last."

Sarah arrived with a tray, a teapot, and one cup. "No waterwort, Janet. Did you bring some?"

"Yes. Put this in and it will be ready to pour." Janet bent over her basket to pick out a scrunched up brown leaf, which she handed over. Not unlike those on the lawn, Mary reflected. Probably bitter, this tea.

"How are you going to get her to drink it?"

"Oh, the tea's not for Anna. It's for you, all three of you. For clarity of mind with a touch of divination. Take the tray away, Sarah. Make sure you share the tea. It's also a joining spell."

Janet's malicious grin included everyone not asleep. "Wandwalker, Caroline, follow her down and wait for me."

Off balance, as so often with Janet, Mary searched for words to refuse. The old witch's red hair caught a ray of sun from a gap in the closed curtains. Circling the spoon over Anna's ankles, a reflected glow touched naked flesh, and Mary saw. . .or did she? She held her breath. The tiniest of movements, a twitch, a shiver in the leg.

Caroline saw it too. She clutched Mary's arm, holding her breath. Mary stared, willing Anna to move again, to make a noise, do anything.

"Go!" ordered Janet.

"Come on, Mary," whispered Caroline. "Janet is taking care of her."

Mary let Caroline pull her down to the kitchen where three cups of brilliant yellow tea were steaming. Drowning the smell of Sarah's vegetable soup, the tea's vinegary-mustard odor did not appeal. Sarah was sitting at the kitchen table, her attention divided between the bubbling soup and the trio of cups. She glanced at Caroline.

"I think Janet wants us to drink it together. That is, all of us at once," said Caroline. Mary could tell she was torn between Janet, as her Holywell mentor, and the awful smell.

"You've had this before?" inquired Mary.

"Well. . .erm, not this recipe," said Sarah with less confidence. "It never smelled this way. Not exactly."

Mary took a big breath, sat down, and drew the cup and saucer to her. The other two did the same. Peering at the yellow fluid, Mary felt the steam deposit drops onto her nose. She guessed she was not alone in trying to dismiss the idea of urine. Three pairs of eyes met.

"I wouldn't even consider this if it wasn't for Anna," said Mary, after a pause.

"For Anna," echoed Caroline and Sarah. All three of them raised cups and downed the tea, in several swallows.

"Aargh!" Mary spewed half of her tea onto the table. Sarah leapt to get a tea towel and flung it over the spill.

"Mary, dear. . ." Caroline croaked as she got to her feet. The tea must have made her hoarse. She grabbed Mary's shoulders.

"Strong, sort of soapy," muttered Sarah, wiping up the mess. She was using the new towel with the Exmoor College crest. How appropriate, thought Mary, forcing down her nausea. She rose to grab a glass and fill it at the tap.

Janet appeared in the doorway. "You've drunk the tea, that's good," she said. Taking in Sarah wringing out the stained cloth and their wan expressions, she grinned again. "I'm off to the hospital. In the meantime," she handed Sarah several paper bags from which desiccated leaves poked in various colors, "Soak these in warm water. Then make a poultice for Anna's feet and head. She should come round in a couple of hours."

"Do you have a clue? About what they gave her?" Caroline was hopeful.

"I don't make guesses, Caroline. You should know better."

171

"Sure, yes. Sorry, Janet."

"But if I did. . ." Janet paused, relishing the instant attention. After the pause she sighed. "I'd say some fool mixed an herbal psychedelic. Could include Native American herbs. Thanks for the info you sent to the hospital. Plus, Sarah kept me updated me on Anna's recent company. The herbal mixture would have been cut with the coke and heroin found in the tests so far. Insane thing to do. Could easily have killed her."

The kitchen was silent. Mary was too shocked to speak.

"Oh Janet. You will make her better!" Caroline whispered. Her clasped hands were white at the knuckles.

"Aye," said Janet comfortably. "I've treated worse, haven't I Sarah?"

The young woman nodded and unconsciously rubbed the track marks on her bare arm.

Caroline hugged Janet. The old witch tolerated the embrace and met Mary's eyes over Caroline's shoulder.

"Wandwalker needs you, apprentice Caroline," she said, freeing herself.

"That's right," said Mary, finding her voice. "We have several tasks. All connect to the murders. That call I took from President Wiseman has some surprising developments that could affect Anna. No, not her health, Caroline. She cleared her throat. "It seems that to save Anna from the murder charge we may have to find the real Sacred Well Torc. It appears to have been stolen around the time that Joe Griffith was murdered."

Caroline threw up her hands; Sarah looked thoughtful. Janet raised her eyebrows and waved goodbye before heading to the John Whitcliffe Hospital. After the front door clicked shut, Caroline groaned and sank into a kitchen chair. With an automatic hand, Sarah filled the electric kettle. Mary turned off the gas under the bubbling soup and opened a window.

"There are black bits in the soup," she said. "I'll dilute it. While we wait for news from Janet, and for Anna to come round, we'll have lunch and make a plan."

CHAPTER 23
SPELLBOUND

While Sarah scraped out enough of the sticky soup for lunch, Mary related Jez Wiseman's story of the missing torc. She didn't need to enunciate her fears about Anna's role in the theft. Caroline made a face and picked up a spoon. Mary glanced at her own rather solid soup and decided that the first call to Exmoor College couldn't wait.

A few minutes later, she shared the news from the unenthusiastic College Secretary. Yes, pending further enquiries, the police had given permission for the Celtic Summer School to resume. Caroline scraped her bowl in silence. Mary forked in those vegetables still identifiable. Over slices of Rhiannon's stale carrot cake, the depleted DEA team prepared for the afternoon arrival of Inspector Walbrook.

Once he arrived, Walbrook wasted no time in getting to the point.

"If her health permits, I would like to move Miss Vronsky to the Oxford station," the Inspector declared on the doorstep "Our cells are fully equipped with beds, and we have a police doctor standing by. We have further questions for her."

Walbrook's face was impassive. Mary concealed her relief at the shift in Walbrook's attitude towards Anna. A request acknowledging her fragile state Mary could handle. She held open the door.

"Do come in, Inspector. We have wonderful news. Anna's asleep now, but she briefly woke up for a few minutes."

173

Caroline was at her side, panting with shining eyes. She had rushed down the stairs in response to the noise of the two police cars. Their clamor was unmistakable on the quiet residential street. Mary had given up worrying about what the neighbors thought. Meanwhile, Walbrook strode into the living room to loom amongst the furniture.

"Miss Wandwalker. . ."

"Yes, do sit down," said Mary. She indicated the worn sofa, determined to be pleasant. It was where she had retreated when Caroline insisted on taking her place on the ill-fated field trip.

Walbrook's sigh was audible. Accompanied by a different Sergeant than before, he glared at Mary like a general spotting the strengths of his foe.

"Sergeant Cassidy," he said, gesturing to the elderly Sikh taking a chair out of the way. "Mrs. Jones," he turned to Caroline in hope. "What were you saying about Miss Vronsky being fit for questioning?"

"She didn't," jumped in Mary. "Anna is not going to be questioned today. Not by you or anyone. Definitely not until the John Whitcliffe returns my calls about the tests."

"She's far too weak," explained Caroline, clouding.

"You see, Inspector, you are not arresting Anna. That would be the only way you could even think of taking her out of this house." Mary faced Walbrook's brooding dissatisfaction head on.

"We have grounds. . .a warrant," he began.

"No, you don't," countered Mary. "You didn't charge Anna when she confessed at the train station. Your so-called evidence is even weaker now."

For the first time in their acquaintance Walbrook didn't let Mary provoke him. "You don't get to tell me. . ."

"This isn't a personal battle, Inspector." Mary poured molten steel into her tone. Caroline felt her tension drain away. They were safe. Mary had the situation in hand. "I phoned Exmoor College an hour ago. You are aware, of course, that the Celtic Summer School is about to begin again," said Mary as if explaining to an impatient teenager. "In fact, you must have insisted on it, or the College would never go ahead after the second murder."

She slowed. "Let me repeat, the summer school wouldn't be happening if the police, if the *authorities* were convinced of Anna's guilt. You're still investigating Rhiannon's death. Perhaps you don't want to, but you are. Everyone's going back to Exmoor because no killer has been identified."

Walbrook stood up and flexed his hands. He prided himself at revealing no emotions to witnesses. Especially to those who correctly divined his strategy. He decided to retreat without conceding anything to this annoyingly clever woman. He stopped briefly at the door.

"Get Vronsky a solicitor for tomorrow, Miss Wandwalker. She'll need one." He banged the front door in the face of Sergeant Cassidy. The Sergeant reopened the door with elaborate care. At the last moment, he turned and bowed to Mary and Caroline.

Returning to the lounge, they noticed Sarah standing with her hands on her hips.

"The fuzz are. . ."

"Sarah. . ."

"Effing useless." Sarah slammed the door behind her crashing off to the kitchen. The trafficked women of Holywell did not like the police. Caroline grabbed a cushion from the sofa and curled herself into a ball around it. Mary drummed her fingers on the table.

"You will get Anna a lawyer, Mary? I mean, a good one?"

Mary just looked at her.

"Oh. That's right. We have no money. I did look at the DEA bank account. But this is for Anna. Don't we know any. . .er. . .cheap lawyers?"

Mary's lips twitched. Caroline was in no mood to joke. Mary slipped next to her and patted her shoulder. The younger woman ceased biting her knuckles for a few seconds.

Mary chose her next words with care.

"Try not to fret too much, Caroline. No-one's abandoning Anna to Walbrook or his ilk." Mary thought for a moment. Before they consulted lawyers, she should be straight with Caroline about the matter of Anna's guilt, or not. "Caroline, look at me. No, come on, this is important. Think before you speak. You see, I don't think that Anna is guilty of anything criminal on this case."

"Of *course* she's not guilty! The drugs. . ."

"No, not the drugs, Caroline. No, I mean, yes, the drugs. You see. . ."

Keeping the cushion clasped to her chest, Caroline pushed herself to a sitting position. "What are you saying? Anna confessed." A bleak wave shook her, tears not far behind.

Mary's tone was bracing. "Confession isn't always what it seems. Caroline. The drugs could be *why* Anna confessed. Suppose the plan was to get her to believe that she did things when in fact she didn't."

Saying it out loud to Caroline was a comfort. Whereas Walbrook would scoff, then call for all sorts of material evidence before even trying out the idea, Caroline would understand.

"Mary." Caroline jumped and threw down the cushion. The old sofa springs protested. "You're such a genius! That must be it. Anna's innocent. I knew it. We've got to tell her; explain what happened. I'll go up and. . ."

Mary's phone began to buzz. Picking it up, she motioned to Caroline to wait. "It's Janet." Mary mouthed over the phone, "Listen to what she has to say about the plant poisons."

"She's calling you, not me," grumbled Caroline, not meaning it. Delight had brought a flush to her pale cheeks. She kicked the coffee table leg.

"I'll put her on speaker." Mary set the phone on the coffee table. "Janet, yes, this is Mary. Caroline's with me. What's the news?"

"Ahh," was followed by a shuffling of papers. Unusually for her, Janet was hesitating.

"Janet?" Caroline's delight faded a notch.

"Erm, Mary, Caro, calling you because. . .well and Sarah too. . .Look, you have to be very careful with Anna. Her condition is. . .complex."

"Complex. What do you mean?" Mary refused to give in to alarm. "Be specific, Janet. Is Anna going to be alright?" She put out her hand to Caroline.

Now the words came faster. "Alright? Ye. . .es. Probably. Possibly. There's a possibility of long-term changes. We are doing more tests. You see the biggest test here is Anna herself." Janet paused for breath. Neither Mary nor Caroline wanted to interrupt her. "The thing is no one has ever tried this combination on a human being."

The silence was a blanket of snow. Mary could hear a clock ticking.

"Go on," said Mary. Caroline grabbed her hand.

"After the clues from California, I got through to your friend Wiseman. He put me in touch with the Native American healers that Joe Griffith visited. Is it true they threw him out for going crazy?"

It was Caroline who found words. "Yes, that's what Dr. Wiseman told Mary. Hurry up and tell us, Janet. I can't bear it."

A couple of grunts came out of the phone. No, it was some foreign word.

"Better known over here as Danu's Root." Mary's phone twitched on the flat surface. "Extremely rare and highly hallucinogenic. Reputed to have been used by the Celts, or, at any rate, their holy people, the Druids, to tell the future. Danu was their goddess. As I said, no modern research, no records of testing or any trials. We're in the dark with Anna."

Out of nowhere, Mary discovered she was furious. Janet was supposed to know everything about plants and their magic. "In the dark?" Inside her the dark rose. Mary choked; the dark would drown Caroline. Mary had to fight for them both. She struggled for calm, for rationality.

"Janet, how can you. . .how can this drug be so. . .so unknown. I thought Native American medicine integrated safely

177

into alternative remedies in the States," said Mary. "As in tested and written about, if not licensed by the authorities."

"It is," returned Janet with discernible weariness. "Regular, traditional healing from some of the best shamans on the planet is fine when it isn't better than fine. You've not been paying attention to the *name*. Danu's Root is not Native American. It was brought over by the colonists, the ones who kept the old gods of Europe alive. Most probably it was imported by some seventeenth century alchemists."

"We haven't time for a history lesson."

"Yes. I know. It looks like Joe Griffith stole some Danu's Root from the tribe's sacred pouch. The healers weren't using it, as in letting anyone ingest it. Rather, it was kept as a power source." Janet paused.

"A power source? How does that work?" Mary was throwing out questions without much hope for the answers.

"Oh, very straightforward. A healer buries a sample of Danu's Root in sacred soil adjacent to the ritual place. Everyone understands that it must be left alone, never touch naked skin, nor be stored with the healing herbs and cordials. Your Joe Griffith desecrated the ceremony. He dug it up, ate some, then stole the rest.

Of course, he did, Mary thought. Caroline let out a moan loud enough for Janet to hear.

"That must be Caro. Look you gals, keep it together. For Anna's sake, you've got to know about Danu's Root. After getting rediscovered in Connecticut decades ago, it was passed around the tribes. Eventually, Danu's Root reached one of their healers doing plant research at the University of New Mexico. He tried a few things before linking the red dust — the root resembles a yam— to alchemy. Goddess forbid, the fool swallowed it. He barely lived to describe the nightmares. Anyhow, he suggests that the alchemists of Europe were too sensible to use it internally, and so knowledge of its properties drained away."

Caroline opened her mouth. Mary signaled her to let Janet finish.

They heard coughing and sounds of Janet taking a drink. "We got one of the techies here at the John Whitcliffe to do whatever they do. Our preliminary test results fit a couple of Roman apothecary records. It was the Romans who named it Danu's Root; to tell their quacks to stay the hell away, I reckon. Word went round of a Celtic hallucinogenic banned by the Empire. No one was surprised when that madman, Nero, got hold of it for his orgies."

"Fascinating," said Mary, with sarcasm. And terrifying, she did not add in consideration of Caroline, hunched up and paler than ever. "You're saying Joe Griffith heard of the root's Celtic origins. . ."

"Wiseman thinks he stole the rest *after* it made him nuts," said Janet. "Hotline to his gods, I expect. No wonder things got so chaotic at Exmoor."

"And at the field trip, no doubt," reminded Mary, "Joe was murdered with his own medicine. Literally and symbolically."

"What about Anna?" Caroline shouted.

"Jones, Caro, hush now. Wait a mo. . ." Janet's injunction made Caroline lean back into the sofa with a sigh. She kept hold of Mary's hand.

"Give us your best estimate of what this drug might do," rapped Mary, her fury quenched by anxiety for Anna. "We do understand that little is known about it. Never mind, your guesses are better than our fears. Give us *something.*"

She wanted to command. It sounded more like a plea. Caroline squeezed Mary's hand. A long whistle emanated from the phone.

"I see what you're getting at, Wandwalker," said Janet, at last. "OK, I'm trying to synthesize enough of Danu's Root out of Anna's blood to run some real tests. We don't want to take any more out of her unless we must. I'm using a mix of alchemy and spell craft, while a couple of postdocs are tracing the elements in their machines. Plus, we've got IT specialists.

Danu's Root is nowhere in pharmaceutical inventories. Looks like those cultures who knew it banned it. The best person to help us track down Danu's Root is of course—"

"Anna, herself," broke in Caroline. "She can find anything on the web."

"Exactly. And it's just possible that Anna could do that when she wakes."

"Why just possible?" Mary caught the warning note. "Anna opened her eyes earlier. She's coming round."

There was silence.

"Janet?"

"She'll be awake, or close to regular consciousness, but she won't be herself." Janet sounded sorrowful and sure of her prognosis. "Not yet the woman you know, maybe not ever if we cannot make an antidote. She'll be half in this world and half in another. You gotta face it. The woman who wakes in that bed won't be Anna."

"Who is Anna?"

The words spilled from the open door. Mary and Caroline turned heads together. Leaning on the door handle was Anna. Skin a dirty yellow, her hair was so greasy it spread over her shoulders like tar. Caroline let out sob and rushed to embrace her. Anna looked alarmed. Although she tolerated the contact, her eyes were stagnant pools in which nothing stirred. Mary swallowed and picked up the phone.

"Thank you, Janet. We'll call you later."

CHAPTER 24
BACK TO SCHOOL

At 9:02 a.m. the following morning, the students in the Celtic Studies Summer School were bubbling with nervous anticipation. Rhiannon used to sit in the front row, the better to run after Joe during breaks. Someone had placed a pink rosebud on her chair. At the lectern, a subdued Simmy was setting up. Everyone expected an announcement. What would be said about Rhiannon and Joe Griffith? Leaks of Anna's confession were splashed all over social media. No one was prepared for the arrival of all three members of the DEA.

"Anna," gasped Simmy from the lectern. "I didn't. . .I mean, are you. . .recovered?"

The young woman approached Simmy with those stagnant eyes. She, not Simmy, had something public to say.

"I am the wife of Manannan Mac Lir, and I have no name. I come to help Sulis find the springs of life."

Various forms of shock surfaced in Simmy and rippled over the class. Simmy's hands began to shake. She pressed down, leaning on the lectern. The students rushed to their seats, the better to watch her. Also, it felt safer.

"She is Sulis. You have found her," came a loud voice from the back of the room. Colin, of course. Mary spotted him moving to Simmy's side. The lecturer ran her hands through blonde hair showing darker roots. She faced the three women questioningly.

Mary and Caroline stood a little behind Anna. While Caroline was ready to grab Anna, Mary was determined to miss nothing of the Morrigans' reactions. Simmy smoothed down her sand-colored trouser suit and addressed Anna.

"I am called Sulis," she confirmed. "You're right that I am looking for the springs of life, the lost underground rivers that feed the Thames. You can help me, wife of Lir."

Not if I have anything to say about it, thought Mary. When Anna spouted identical words earlier that morning in Norham Gardens, she provoked consternation in the kitchen. Coming to Exmoor like this was hardly what Mr. Jeffreys envisaged for getting into Anna's mind. Yet Mary had convinced Caroline to follow this new person in Anna. They were on a quest for Anna's soul.

Their search for Anna started two hours previously, when she entered the kitchen in Norham Gardens. With hair unkempt and body unwashed, she stood before the three other women in her oldest jeans and a huge aqua t-shirt of Caroline's. Resembling a small tent on Anna, it came to just above the knees. She's lost weight, noted Mary.

Caroline spoke first. "Anna, darling. I thought you were staying in bed."

"Anna gone," said the young woman, to no one in particular. "I am the wife of Manannan Mac Lir, and I have no name. I come to help Sulis find the springs of life."

Caroline dropped her plate of toast. Her eyes sought Mary's in horror.

"How do you spell that?" said Mary, reaching for her laptop. Ignoring her, Anna sat at the table and took a whole loaf of seeded bread in her grubby, hands. She started chewing the crust.

Caroline began to moan. Before she could do anything, Mary pulled her to one side and whispered in her ear. Sarah took the opportunity to retrieve the pieces of the broken plate. The toast, sticky side down, was too close to Anna for Sarah to grab it and not be in reach of a swinging foot.

Meanwhile, Mary reminded Caroline that it was essential that Anna not be forced from wherever she was. She could lash out and someone would get hurt. In a late-night call, Janet had insisted on that. The interaction of Danu's Root and the opiates was far too volatile.

"No stress on Anna's psyche for goddess sake, Wandwalker," reiterated Janet. "She could drown, figuratively. . .permanently."

Now, with Mary's reminders dripping into her ear, Caroline slowly nodded her head. She focused on the dirty woman whose mouth was sunk into the bread, angry black eyes bubbling behind.

"Alright dar. . .I mean, wife of Lir. Let me help you." Caroline eased the loaf from Anna, smiling at the outrage, then quickly cut a slice, and added butter and jam. Anna tensed at the bright red jam before poking it with a finger. After putting her finger to her tongue, she began enthusiastically to lick the jam off the bread, followed by the butter. It gave Mary an idea.

"Drink both of these and we will take you to Sulis." She poured coffee into two large mugs. Janet never said that they could not try the remedies of everyday life. Mary had lived long by what she half believed: a cup of good coffee, and most things can be borne.

"Anna, I mean, the wife of Lir, is coming with us to the summer school," she said to Caroline and Sarah. "You remember, don't you, that Sulis is Simmy's real name. Plus, she mentioned springs of life in her first class, I'm sure of it."

"Erm, springs, energies, yes, watercourses. . .oh, that's it!" Sarah clapped her hands. "Ancient and lost watercourses are the springs of life in the Climate Emergency era," she quoted.

"That's right, and I have Manannan Mac Lir here," said Mary scrolling down the page on WikiEsoterica. "King of the faeries, to the Celts he was Lord of the Otherworld."

"He is risen," said Anna, looking at Sarah. "By Blood Rising and sacrifice, he is risen."

A stunned Caroline made her another slice of bread and jam, and one for herself. By pointing and chewing, she modelled more conventional eating. The wife of Lir proved a quick study.

"Hmm, I wonder if Joe Griffith is the sacrifice she means," muttered Mary. "Could Joe be Mac whoever in the er. . . Otherworld?"

"Manannan Mac Lir," corrected Sarah, working her phone. "There is nothing much about him except he wears a gold torc."

At the word, "torc," Anna flinched, then grabbed the loaf and clutched it to her chest. She looked around at the company with eyes deep as wells. Caroline reached out a hand. Anna moved so fast that Mary barely heard the scape of the chair and a scream from Caroline. Anna hissed at both from where she had gone into a crouch on the floor, hiding the bread with her body.

"Yowee. Anna, please don't!" Caroline cradled her hand. Mary made her uncurl her fingers. The bite drew no blood. "She's gone." Caroline mopped her tears with the tissues that Mary proffered.

"Cheer up, Caroline," said Mary briskly. "We now know something. Don't touch or use the "t" word." She pulled Caroline to the sink to run cold water on her hand. "Try not to worry, Caroline, dear. We'll get her back."

Mary never used endearments.

"Look, we're going to the summer school this morning. It is a chance for clues to Anna's condition and to both murders. No, don't cry, Caroline. If Anna will come with us, it might awaken memories." Caroline began to look thoughtful.

"Not just bad memories," added Mary. "I hope – no, I believe, that solving the crimes will help Anna find her way back. Look how she's reacting to the *gold thing*. We know it means something to her. Locating the real one is bound to help."

Mary wished she was as confident as she sounded. She liked plans. She relished devising projects with measurable and achievable stages. Mary Wandwalker in her Archive days was famous for not letting the unforeseen drown her organizational skills. Those days were past. Mary looked at the wife of Lir crouching in the corner. Time to throw a plank over a raging torrent. What else could they do but go on with the case? Doing nothing would be going along with Mr. Jeffreys wanting to shut down the DEA. It was not an option.

Mary made a wry expression at she who had once been Anna, now ferociously chewing, wiping jam from her mouth, and licking her hands.

Mr. Jeffreys liked life as orderly as the offices he moved between in government circles. But there was nothing neat or ordered about the Reborn Celts. Like Albert Edward Morrigan himself, they were going to have to jump into the river. Unlike him, they had to survive.

Mary murmured, "We'll do more than survive."

Taking Anna to the summer school was practical, as well as dangerous. Given Anna's criminal history as well as her state of radical dissociation (as the medical website put it), Mary decided that Anna could not remain unsupervised in the Otherworld.

"Before we go," said Mary to Anna. "Caroline is going to take the wife of Lir under the shower. No biting."

Anna stared.

Mary was stern. "No biting, or no more food."

Anna's knuckles whitened on the remains of the loaf.

"Leave it on the table and it will be here after the shower."

Anna stood in one graceful curl. Scowling at Mary, she very slowly rested the bread on the table and withdrew her fingers.

"Rain," said Caroline in too bright tones. She reached for Anna's hand, then drew back. Instead, she beckoned Anna to follow her. "Special rain. Warm rain, just for you."

"Put her in some of her best clothes; those designer things she gets online," called Mary after them. Anything to nudge Anna towards herself again.

A shampoo smelling Anna returned in a maroon sleeveless jacket over a white silk shift. Her washed hair was in a damp bun. She would walk between Mary and Caroline if they gave her space. Sarah decided to stay at home.

At Exmoor, Anna's announcement stunned the summer school students, while encouraging Simmy and Colin. Mary tried to conceal her suspicions, watching Simmy accept Anna's new incarnation. Was this because she had collaborated with Joe in drugging the young woman? Mary itched to interrogate Simmy and Colin. Barin too. If only the police could see Anna's predicament as she and Caroline did.

9:11 am. By now, everyone except Mary Wandwalker was seated. Anna accepted Caroline's light touch indicating their seats. The class was very still while Colin moved his chair close to Simmy at the lectern. He was different from before the field trip, Mary noted. As if he'd grown an inch, he was more confident, less the student and more like, well, more like Joe.

Radiating energy, Colin barely breathed while locked on Anna and Simmy. Behind Simmy and projected onto the big screen was the title for this module: "Sacred Waters, Sacrifices, and Solstices". The scarlet lettering glowed over a photograph of a natural pond surrounded by trees and rocks. In small letters was the caption: 'Mabon Sacred Well, In Use Since Celtic times.'

Mary tapped her foot twice. Simmy stopped ignoring her.

"Please take your seat, Miss Wandwalker."

Colin leapt up. Mary ignored him.

"You're not going to say anything to the class? After everything that's happened. Two deaths in this summer school."

"The police requested us not to talk about it."

Simmy's voice lacked full control. Colin snorted at his mother. There was something different about his hair. Oh, he's put golden tips on the white blond, realized Mary. If Anna were herself, I could ask her about it.

"Mother, we want to hear about the sacrifices," said Colin in a stage whisper. "I'll run the slides. Give me the clicker."

"In a minute, Colin. The Reborn Celts," Simmy paused in her address to Mary, quiet and firm, "stress metaphorical sacrifice. It is about renewing the waters by finding the ancient, secret springs, the lost rivers."

"Rivers? Actual lost rivers? They are not metaphors, are they?" Mary was being reasonable. "You're a climate and water scientist." She looked again at the words on the screen then turned back to Simmy. Raising her voice to include the whole room, she said: "I see, you are looking for lost rivers just as the dead Joe Griffith said. Like the lost rivers of London."

Mary put a hand on a chair to steady herself. She was back by the Thames, the shingle beach, murmurs of traffic thundering over the bridge, gulls flying upriver with the early morning tide. The lost river, Eponia, pouring from a rusty pipe, washed the naked torso of a young girl. Desperate to be a member of the Reborn Celts, Rhiannon had truly sacrificed everything. Words flowed from Mary as if from an inner well.

"Who did it, Simmy? Who killed Rhiannon?" The silence in the room smelled of the river. Colin put a reassuring arm around Simmy. He does look older, decided Mary.

"Who gave Anna the Danu's Root?"

That was Caroline. Mary had not noticed her appear beside her. Simmy licked her lips. She was about to speak when the door opened.

"Ah, Miss Wandwalker, Mrs. Jones, please come with me. You are disrupting this important class. It's high time my sister began her lecture."

Barin stood there in a suit too pale for his girth, holding his phone in one hand. Beads of sweat glued strands of hair to his forehead, betraying how rapidly he'd moved across the college. Even though he'd been summoned by Colin texting him, he glared at the young man.

Mary was satisfied at the interruption. Progress, surely, to have rattled the Morrigans. She caught a sliver of movement in the third row. Anna was stroking the silk underneath her jacket. The young woman raised her head to stare back at Mary. Something stirred in those two dark pools.

"Please bring Anna back to the house," Mary Wandwalker instructed Simmy, and got a nod in response. Simmy was not unreachable. Did that make her more or less likely to be a killer? Now to take advantage of Barin's arrival, Mary decided. Just who was this aging Celt who resents Colin's youth.

"Professor Morrigan, how kind of you to make yourself available for our questions. Can I suggest coffee in your study?" Mary swept out, followed by a grinning Caroline. Barin could not answer until the three had gathered at the foot of the stairs.

"Very well, Miss Wandwalker. The police have told me about your so-called Agency. It's time we had a heart to heart."

Heading for his college rooms, Barin strode into the sun, its glare almost consuming his round figure. As they followed him, Mary shielded her eyes, while Caroline put on sunglasses. Mary was in grave doubt that Barin Morrigan had a heart.

CHAPTER 25
THE OTHER/WORLD OF BARIN

Barin's study was. . .well, "expensive," was the first word that came to Mary. Everywhere something was costly and new, or priceless and ancient. A glass case held greenish statuettes, one of a horned male. Behind more glass she could see broken brooches, a few with precious gems. There was a whole shelf of daggers, their iron blades crumbling like dead tissue on a bone. Each one was a Celtic artifact, confirmed the label. Mary planted herself on a newly upholstered armchair. Her shoes sank into a scarlet carpet with a pattern of Celtic knots in purple and silver.

"My own design," murmured Barin as he crossed to what Mary really coveted, the latest coffee storage-grinder-expresso machine. Just on the market, the internet had been trying to sell her one for a week now.

"Welcome to my treasures. Do take a seat, Mrs. Jones. I have something in particular to ask your. . .your Depth Enquiry Agency."

"No coffee for me." Caroline remained at the door. "Dr. Barin, let me return to the class. Anna is. . .isn't well. She needs me."

Barin appeared to be pondering Caroline's request while he pressed switches to start the coffee machine. Then he swiveled to study Caroline. Not for the first time Mary wished her friend would wear something other than old jeans and men's sweaters. But then, Caroline was so defensive about her weight. The amount she ate fluctuated between good days (diet); bad days (binging to mask pain); and terrible days (nothing at all).

"Mrs. Jones. . ." Barin's condescension had an edge, "you're the glue that holds together the rashness of Miss Wandwalker here," he flicked his beard at Mary, a habit she remembered disliking, "and the reckless Miss Vronsky. You want to go back to my sister's class, do you?"

He took a soft chair opposite Mary, shutting Caroline out. "Did you know that my sister showed me your website, your. . .hobby, the so-called Depth Enquiry Agency?"

He's trying to provoke, Mary thought. Was he curious about the DEA, or something else? He keeps saying 'my sister'. What are his feelings for Simmy? Being the son of Albert Edward must have been a hard act to follow.

Caroline jumped in. Marching over, she stood over the seated Celt. She even forgot to pull in her belly.

"Now, pay attention, Dr. Barinthus. I have learned a lot from your Celtic summer school. I've kept up with the reading, followed you on the field trip, and admired the dedication of Simmy." She bit her lip. "Yet, two people have died."

Barin shifted. Caroline was relentless. "They were beheaded just as the Reborn Celts tell us the ancient Celts did." Mary held her breath. "So far, the police have not charged anyone. So far."

Caroline held the pause. "The killer could be you." Barin licked his lips. "As we entered your staircase, I caught sight of Inspector Walbrook. He was making for the Well Garden. So, Dr. Barin, you have chosen to continue the summer school. Now I choose to go back to my class."

Without waiting for a reply, Caroline left, closing the door behind her with a bit of a bang. Mary liked that touch.

Barin's white fingers went to his beard again. Then he put his hands together for three slow claps to the closed door.

"Magnificent, don't you agree, Miss Wandwalker? What a performance!"

"My colleague is indeed remarkable," said Mary. "I believe the coffee is ready."

After receiving a tiny cup of a brew she wished she could enjoy alone, Mary contemplated her antagonist. Barin had surrounded himself with his inheritance, the Celtic treasures gathered by the famously obsessed Albert Edward Morrigan. Simmy, she recalled, had none. No doubt that was because her conversion to the cause postdated Albert Edward writing his will. Mary decided to dig.

"This must be the famous Morrigan collection, Dr Barinthus. Simmy has none of her father's artefacts. You did not care to share?"

Barin's cup trembled. He placed it next to a small stone god sitting on his glass coffee table. The modern world is transparent, thought Mary.

"My sister refused to support our father until the very end," he said.

"She is making up for it now." Barin sniffed.

"Is it because you don't like Colin?"

Barin's hands tensed into fists, then relaxed. He shook his head at Mary.

"My sister is subject to… mistakes," he said in his deliberate way. "That boy is one. I won't let him near anything of my father's. She knows that. Look around, Miss Wandwalker. This was Albert Edward's study and it's much as he left it. We like to think of him as still with us. That's why I want to talk to you."

Mary shivered to think that the dead man, the one who had started this obsession with Celts, might still haunt the treasures he'd pulled from the earth. Barin was waiting for her to be impressed. Well, she would be. She would forbear pointing out his bad taste in stuffing museum quality pieces into a space devoted to himself.

This is hoarding, she thought. She remembered those dragon heads with sharp teeth on the torc. That was Barin; the ancient serpent curled over his gold. Swallowing the last of her coffee, she redoubled her scrutiny

"I think the police enjoyed playing with my collection," he could not resist saying. He swung one silk clad leg over the other. His suit was the perfect fit that comes with bespoke tailoring. Luxuriating in wealth, does this man lust for power as well as money? He sits on his treasures with dragon eyes, while Joe Griffith wanted to save the world. Or change it, through spilling blood.

Barin put down his coffee cup.

"Take a look at the stone carving on the mantlepiece," he said. "It tells you everything that I need from you."

"That small figure…is it local? A kind of god?"

Barin leaned forward. "Yes, indeed, Miss Wandwalker. Oh, yes indeed, local we might say. That stone relief was found in this very college by my father. Right at the bottom of the Celtic well. This god was next to the most amazing pure gold torc ever found!"

"You mean the Sacred Well Torc?"

Barin nodded, transfixed by his recall of the torc. Mary did not add that she knew it, had held the torc in her hands. She also knew it was not pure gold, but rather a unique alloy with a minute amount of silver.

"The sun with a sliver of the moon." Caroline's words, Mary had spoken them aloud. Barin was taken aback.

"Er, yes, perhaps. My father let me hold the torc for a moment. Then he took it away. He wanted money for his Celtic Foundation. It went to some… well-wisher in the United States. I know he really meant the torc for me. Otherwise, why give me the stone god? See here…" He rose and put a white forefinger on the bluish stone. "Here you can see that the male figure has a torc. Astonishing and so rare!"

"And valuable?"

"Beyond price. Any representation of Manannan as sea god – you notice he is riding upon waves, there? To have the sea god wearing a torc, well, as far as we know this is the only such carving in existence. I am writing a monograph on him."

Mary had sat up at the name. "Dr Barinthus, did you say, Manannan? I thought Manannan Mac Lir was king of the Otherworld?" Mary could not keep the urgency from her voice.

Barin noticed. "Why, you're becoming one of us, Miss Wandwalker. These gods took different forms. Perhaps Manannan son of Lir is another incarnation, a terrestrial counterpart to the Lord of the Ocean. Or Manannan could be a local name for another divinity. Our gods are mysterious, Miss Wandwalker. All we can be sure of is that they need feeding."

"Feeding? With blood?" Mary was revolted.

"With torcs," corrected Barin, very cool. "The more precious the better. The Celts loved gold. It was spiritual to them because it could pass through water and remain pure. Water is sacred, the pathway between worlds. You see my dear lady," he paused. Mary pasted on the smile she used to conceal irritation.

"My dear lady, a torc enhances a warrior's spirit; his blood-lust, if you like. The torc consecrates and contains the spirit. It is then handed to the god through watercourses. Gold blesses the water as it becomes a portal to the Otherworld. Our Exmoor sacred well..." he stopped, remembering recent events, then ploughed on. "Our well remains a place of power," he ended with a touch of defiance. "The lost torc must be reunited with his stone god." His voice was brittle now. Mary was getting an impression that gold and the torc drew him like nothing else.

"What about Danu's Root?" said Mary. "Is that to enhance warrior power too? Is that why it was given to Anna?"

"Anna? Oh, Miss Vronsky. I know nothing about her." Barin's dismissive gesture infuriated Mary.

"Danu's Root," she repeated with cold fury.

"Dear lady, I presume you refer to some narcotic. I have nothing to do with the substances some er...student may bring to our rituals. Poor Joe, poor Joe."

Mary was dismayed to find that she believed him. His selfish unconcern was too palpable. If Joe Griffith was the source of Danu's Root, then Barin would be no help in finding an antidote. She swallowed her disappointment. She had a shrewd suspicion of what he wanted from her.

Barin flicked his beard. "Miss Wandwalker, I have twenty-twenty vision, and yet I cannot find something. Something that belongs to me."

"Something made of gold, perhaps?" said Mary. "Belongs to *you*, you say. Not the Reborn Celts?" She was reminded of "my" sister, "my" father. There was a clatter from Barin's chair. A cane with a silver owl top had fallen, striking the glass table. The bird had a cruel beak.

"Not the Reborn Celts," repeated Barin, staring at the silver wings of the owl that were the cane's handle. He continued. "You and your Agency, you find things, don't you?"

"Sometimes we do," said Mary. She was cautious. "Twenty-twenty vision can be a disadvantage, you know. You miss what you do see." She saw his frown.

"Not interested in riddles," muttered Barin. "Here, take these." He flung something from his pocket at Mary, who caught it, to her own surprise. It was a keyring, a disc painted in a Celtic design with a couple of ordinary door keys.

"What…?" she began.

"Door to Simmy's flat and the other one is the key to Colin's bedroom. I want you to search them. She'd do anything for him."

Jealousy thought Mary. Started in childhood no doubt. Albert Edward can't have been a caring father. With the mother dying so soon after giving birth to Simmy, no wonder Barin is so dead set on his father's legacy.

"Search Simmy's apartment? Why now?"

"You haven't asked me what for, Miss Wandwalker."

"I'm guessing it is the Sacred Well Torc, the real one."

"You know it's here? No, don't tell me. Wiseman, it had to be. He's been sending you emails."

"Either this is a double bluff, or you didn't take it?"

"Me? No. It was that guttersnipe, Colin."

"Your nephew? Are you sure?"

"He's *not* my nephew!" shouted Barin, picking up the cane and crashing the beak down on the table. Mary noted several scratches on the glass. Barin had a temper, then.

"That...effing," he scowled at Mary. "That boy is not of Morrigan blood. My father would never countenance...He manipulates Simmy. She won't see it. I've tried opening her eyes. She's so stubborn."

"So how did she. . .?"

"Colin's the son of two of the first members of the Reborn Celts. My father recruited them. When they died."

"Of drugs?"

"Of unfortunate. . .choices, I kept an eye on the boy in foster care. I never expected Simmy to. . .well now she's gone and adopted him. I've seen his room. He's got racist posters my father would return from the dead to burn. Never mind that. She says she didn't take the torc, and I didn't, so it must have been him. Wiseman never showed it to anyone else."

He calmed. "My sister left me a spare set of keys while summer school is in session. I couldn't find a thing in his mess. It's your turn. Colin and Simmy will be here for another couple of hours. Do something to justify your ridiculous agency."

"Now just a minute," said Mary, getting up, which took a bit longer than she'd hoped. Her right foot had gone to sleep. "The DEA is not at your disposal."

Do it. Mary knew that voice. It was Rhiannon from the dark. Without thinking Mary picked up the keys. Rhiannon wanted her to find her killer. Of that she had no doubt.

Alright, said Mary silently, alright. You win. I'll take this chance to investigate Simmy and Colin. But you know, this man here, this Barin, would do anything for gold.

Mary stopped. "Would do anything for gold" wasn't her thought. Or not just hers. She and Rhiannon saw Barin as a dragon guarding his hoard. Was he other than human because of Albert Edward— and Simmy? Mary put the keys in the pocket of her jacket.

"I'll take a look, Dr. Barin," she said aloud. "Not for you. I'm doing it for my friends, for Anna. This isn't over."

With that, Mary Wandwalker left Dr. Barinthus' study and Exmoor College. She dived into the busy currents of Oxford's streets. Walking, preoccupied, she was there, and then she wasn't. She had disappeared. Had some shark snatched her below the surface?

Caroline was so absorbed with Anna's plight that Mary's absence sank below the surface. It was hours before Caroline noticed and then began to worry. After calling several hospitals and checking that Mary had not been grabbed by the police, Caroline, Anna, and Sarah searched the streets in the twilight. Mary Wandwalker was nowhere to be found.

CHAPTER 26
THE DISAPPEARANCE OF
MARY WANDWALKER

By late evening Caroline was distraught and silent. She wanted to run to her bedroom and hide until Mary returned. That she might not return was beyond bearing. She and Sarah collapsed in the kitchen, exhausted. Anna could not be left alone, chewing her last crust of bread in the corner. Nor could she be left with Sarah. The wife of Lir had been scowling at the young woman all through the scrap meal of cheese sandwiches, all Sarah could face making.

"Did we look everywhere?" whispered Sarah, avoiding Anna.

"Everywhere in Oxford? I think so. Mrs. Cram, the Surrey house neighbor, is sure that Mary's not there either. She said she walked right round to the back to check that none of the curtains had moved. Plus, the drive was just the same: no one has swept up those leaves falling too soon."

Sarah looked puzzled at the last remark.

"Mary hates mess," explained Caroline. She put her head in her hands, too weary for anything else.

"She could have gone for a long walk." Sarah was stubborn.

"Sarah, shut the fuck up." Caroline shot back, surprising everyone. Anna coughed up half chewed bread onto the floor beside her, then leaned down to pick it up.

"No Anna! Bad Anna!" That was Sarah, hiding her face as she grabbed the sticky stuff and pulled Anna to the kitchen sink to wash her hands. Her dark cheeks were wet.

"Sarah, I'm sorry," Caroline said, without moving to help. She sat frozen, staring at a table full of plates and crumbs. The block of yellow cheese was only half wrapped in plastic. Mary would never let it begin to dry out like that.

"It's all right," Sarah murmured as she let Anna go. The wife of Lir returned to her corner on the floor. Now Anna glared at Caroline.

Sarah reached out to pat Caroline's arm as she had seen Mary do but pulled back before touching. She was just Sarah, after all. Caroline did not notice.

"I can't do anything; I just can't," said Caroline to the table.

"I'll try her phone again; it's time," said Sarah. Earlier they had agreed to try every twenty minutes, but now Mary's inbox was full. Caroline didn't move not move a muscle, but hung on every sound as Sarah dialed.

"No reply," said Sarah. "Your turn next time."

They needed to talk. Without Mary and Anna sick, Caroline was sure she could not cope. It was up to her now. Caroline never forgot that Sarah had been trafficked. Those bitter waters were closer than ever. However, Caroline had never been this depressed in front of Sarah. And she could not bear to leave the room because it would signal giving up on Mary, at least for tonight. The older woman could not talk, and the younger was too inexperienced.

Sarah tried again. "I was trying to say is that Mary liked to walk by the river. Do you remember when she said she'd heard owls flying down the Thames? Do you remember, Caroline?" Sarah's voice was gentle. She had brushed aside the hurt.

"I'm sorry. I can't right now."

To Caroline, in this state, words were like paving stones heaved out of water. Sarah tried to smile; Caroline did not see. Her eyes followed the flowing and grain of the oak table.

With a sigh, Sarah started to stack the dirty plates. She put the cheese in the fridge when a loud tolling broke out. A scared Anna yelped and made her hands into claws.

"Mary." Caroline's voice cracked. She reached for her phone. They all knew Mary's phone used the chimes of Big Ben. "Yes, it *is* Mary!"

"What does she say? Where is she?"

"Oh, it's just a text," Caroline was not disappointed. Then she read it.

"Aaaarh."

"Here, give it me. The Goddess preserve us." Sarah let the phone slip out of her hands. It fell with a clatter to the floor. Anna leapt on it and appeared to read the stark message:

THE CELTS ARE REBORN. CALL THE POLICE AND WANDWALKER DIES.

Anna sat back on her heels and carefully lifted the phone to the table. Then she crawled into a chair next to Caroline. All three sat stunned.

"Kidnapped! She's been kidnapped!" shrieked Caroline. "We should phone the police."

"Are you nuts?" Sarah snapped. "They'll kill her. Look what they did to Rhiannon."

"And Joe," muttered Caroline. "It's the Reborn Celts who've got her."

"What do they want?" said Sarah. It's usually money or. . ." She stopped, remembering what had been said about the Reborn Celts wanting blood.

"They're going to sacrifice her," gasped Caroline. Certainty shot through her.

"No, they're not." Anna thumped the table with both fists. "We won't let them."

"Darling Anna, you're back."

The young woman pushed her chair back and frowned at her companions in the lamplight.

"I am Anna." She put a hand up. "Sometimes. Sometimes I am wife of Lir. She says we must dream. We must dream Mary by the sacred well." Anna's eyes watered.

Caroline enfolded her in an embrace. Sarah was scrolling through her phone.

"I knew I saved the site. Got it!"

"What site? Is it about Anna?"

"Yes. Sort of. It's about dreaming. The Celts used dreams to foretell the future. They had a particular thing about dreams near water. You know. . ."

"Their portals to the Otherworld, yes, I get it. We. . ."

"We have to sleep at Exmoor. By the sacred well. Our dreams will lead us to Mary."

CHAPTER 27
GOING TO COLLEGE?

"I did my best, I tried. No good. They won't give us rooms. Not tonight." Caroline switched off her phone. Her drained look was back. Tripping over one of three small overnight bags didn't help. Sarah was twisting the damp tea towel she seemed to be using for comfort. Anna slept soundly on the sofa. It was so unlike the vigorous young woman that Caroline feared the wife of Lir was in charge again. She did not want to inquire.

"Why not? Is it too late?" said Sarah, at last.

Caroline looked at the clock on the sitting room wall. "It's not yet 11:00 p.m. We cannot be alone in arriving so late. They *say* they are fully booked. Yet I'm sure a lot of the conference delegates cancelled."

"After the murder? Yes. Not surprising. Oh," Sarah stopped. "Caroline, I've got an idea." She left the room and through the half open door Caroline heard her speaking into her phone, quiet and intense. Caroline sighed and rested her eyes on the woman she loved. Wedging herself next to the sleeping form, she stroked Anna's bare arm.

What would Anna be doing if she was herself? Hmm, it was a dangerous speculation. Well, for a start, she would have broken into Exmoor's online booking and got them the best rooms for divination; those looking onto the sacred well garden. The smell of watered grass seeped into Caroline's nose. Then Anna would. . .

Mary's laptop! It was on the dining table, a sealed hoard. Passwords were a game to Anna, whose cyber skills

201

were boundless. By now she would have all Mary's precious information at her fingertips. Anna would be gleeful. She would pour it all out for Caroline. Oh, Mary would be so cross.

Anxiety pulled Caroline's attention from the computer. There was something else they should be doing. Try as she might, Caroline could not remember what. It was like fishing by hand. Every time something swam into reach, her arms came up empty and dripping. What was so slippery, and so vital?

The missing idea was not about informing the police. Not yet, anyway. Much too dangerous. Anna? Well Anna would be planning drastic measures. Maybe dangerous to Mary, Caroline thought. Caroline would be arguing for caution, while Anna would try to win her over with kisses. Caroline smiled, kissing Anna's wild hair. There she was, a Celtic warrior bunching up Caroline's T-shirt on the shabby sofa.

Caroline felt relieved that *her* Anna was not awake in her dangerous incarnation. Anna was not rattling the sharpest knives in the kitchen, not claiming that she could locate an illegal gun in Oxford in sixty seconds.

An abrupt knock broke into Caroline's reverie. She leapt up.

"At last, Mary! Thank the Goddess and all the witches." Caroline ran for the front door. At that moment Anna stirred, then jumped up. Eyes darting about, she felt her empty pockets. No weapon. The young woman dived for the curtains. Wrapping herself in camouflage, she became as stone. She barely breathed.

Out in the hall, Caroline was having trouble with the front door.

"Mary. . .wait!" Caroline's hand shook on the chain. "Mary. . .where. . ."

The door fell open. A shorter, older woman than Mary pushed past Caroline and nodded at Sarah, who was putting her phone away.

"Hello Sarah, Caro. Let me sit down. I've had a hell of a day."

"Janet." Caroline whispered. "Oh, Janet, come in," she added, wishing her emotions were not so obvious. Then Janet was a witch; she read people as if their souls had the transparency of pure water.

"What's up Caro? Mary not about?" Janet marched into the sitting room and put down her basket on the table. It was empty. "That lab's too crowded for my best work. I had to stick it out because my spells needed the air conditioning. The rest of the John Whitcliffe is too stuffy for words. Ah." Janet spotted the bulge at the window with one set of dirty toes peeking out. "Anna's behind the curtains, I see. Must be feeling scared. Who is she, by the way? I've been wondering. Do get me something to drink, Caro. Whisky if you have it."

"Janet, this isn't a good time. Could you come back. . .I mean, what about the antidote for Anna? Do you have it?"

"Not yet." Janet frowned; her suspicions aroused. She threw herself onto the sofa that Anna had vacated. "Why are you so uptight? Don't tell me there's no whisky?" She gave a bark of laughter.

"*Tell* her," hissed Sarah in Caroline's left ear.

"Tell me what?" Janet sat forward and ran her hand through her flaming tufts. "Caro, this is no time for games. For Anna's sake I need to know what's going on."

Caroline opened her mouth, but no words gushed forth. For Anna's sake? Could the kidnap of Mary affect Janet's work to save Anna? Mary was her rock; Anna her everything. Caroline was mute.

Sarah took a seat opposite Janet, cutting off the witch's glare.

"Janet, Miss Wandwalker's been kidnapped. The text said no police, or they'll kill her." She swallowed, her face grave

"They'll kill her anyway." Janet's response was automatic, even while she looked shocked. "Ah, that's it," she said. "They mean to sacrifice her. She is the crone sacrifice at the summer solstice."

A strangled sound came from Caroline. She put her face in her hands.

Janet counted on her fingers. "Today's the 16th. That gives us five days. Whisky," she said. The witch was brisk. "For all three, no, four of us." She turned to the bulge in the curtains.

"WHO ARE YOU WHO HIDES IN OUR HOME?" Janet didn't shout. She had a way of making her voice flow through walls. After a few seconds, Anna stepped out. Sarah had disappeared, in search of whisky.

"I am the wife of Manannan Mac Lir, and I have no name."

Anna's voice betrayed no expression. Her eyes were flickering, and she stood with her hands moving on her waist as if feeling for weapons. Caroline groaned. "You were Anna a few minutes ago."

"Ah, yes, quite," said Janet. "I hope Sarah finds that whisky. I thought Wandwalker kept some."

"MR. JEFFREYS!" shouted Caroline. "I knew it. I found it. Mr. Jeffreys."

"What about that old coot?" Janet looked suspicious. Mr. Jeffreys was from the world of officialdom she despised.

"That's what I was trying to remember." Caroline was flushed. "What we should be doing. We can't call the police, far too dangerous, but Mary would want us to tell Mr. Jeffreys that she's been kidnapped."

"Well, I didn't think you wanted to tell him that she's taken to spell craft," said a tart Janet. "That one will never turn to the Goddess. As for the kidnapping, well, perhaps she would want him to know," said Janet. "Those two go back to the Dark Ages. But is it the right thing to do? Isn't contacting Jeffreys the same as calling the police? Won't he just hand it over to them and their kidnapping-whatever squad."

"I suppose so," said Caroline, crestfallen. "But we have to do something."

"We *are* doing something. We're going to dream," said Sarah, returning with a tray. Next to four wine glasses, a dusty bottle was wobbling. Bowmore Single Malt graced the label in blue letters above a sketch of a beach.

"Here, I've got it," said Caroline, saving the bottle from tipping over. "The talk of whisky is what made me remember. Mary had bought this Single Malt because she always keeps something for Mr. Jeffreys. We haven't tried it because I don't like spirits. Not this kind, anyway," she added with trace of Mary's irony.

"And the gels are told not to drink," said Janet. "As part of the treatment. That means at Holywell we don't imbibe. Well, not in front of the gels, anyway. Now give it here, Caro. I take it you don't want any?"

Caroline held out a glass. Janet winked and put a large measure of amber liquid in all four. Caroline and Sarah sipped bravely, exchanging grimaces. Janet drank hers and poured another. Anna stepped up to the table, seized the remaining glass and knocked back the spirit in one long gulp.

"Anna," she said and fell backwards onto the sofa. She was unconscious.

Caroline was at her side in a heartbeat.

"No, no. Leave her be." That was Janet. Pushing away Caroline, she grabbed hold of Anna. She sat her up with her head resting on the back of the sofa and then started pulling at her eyelids. "As I thought, she's gone under again. Good news— not so much as at first. More like a deep sleep. We should let her wake in her own time. Won't be before the morning."

Janet stood to one side as Caroline made Anna comfortable on the sofa again. "Don't be disappointed, Caro, this is improvement. Anna needs time, and she needs the antidote. Which is coming, I promise."

"I thought you said you'd had a hell of a day."

"So I did. A helluva day making slow, real, progress. We've almost isolated the right herbs. That's the science techies calling their weird colleagues from all over. India and Sub-Saharan Africa have given us some good leads. I've been working on how to combine the active ingredients to cure without killing. It is coming. You have to be patient."

Caroline gulped at the reiteration of the dangers Anna faced. Janet was pacing the room and did not notice.

"Now, for the Wandwalker problem I recommend divination. Like I said before. The most effective will be. . ."

"Dreams. Best of all dreams from a sacred place, we know, Janet." Caroline was firm. "We did dream magic at Holywell."

"You wouldn't let me in that class," reproached Sarah to Janet. "Caroline's been teaching me while we've been at the Celtic Summer School."

Janet pursed her lips. Caroline did not turn away. "Mary said. . ."

"Oh yes? What did Mary say?" Janet looked stern.

"She said better white magic than black magic."

"She said that the Reborn Celts specialized in recruiting people like me."

Janet and Caroline stared at Sarah. "No, not trafficked women, but people looking for. . . for guidance, spirituality a way of. . ."

"'Of simplifying this scary century to a grotesque religion of beauty in violence,'" Caroline quoted. Mary's determined clarity was refreshing. Janet grinned.

"That's our Wandwalker. So tonight, you will invite Lady Moon to direct your souls?"

"Yes, we're trying to get rooms above the sacred well. To find Mary we are trying to follow the craziness," said Caroline. She stood up, a little woozy from the unaccustomed alcohol.

"Hmm," said Janet. "Let me think this through with the Goddess." She went to the window and pulled back curtains to a street of black shadows and city lights. "Turn off the lamps, Caro."

In the dark, the nearest streetlight bathed the room in an orange glow. Sarah stood by the light switch at the door. Caroline stroked Anna's hair while watching the figure at the window.

"I see her." Janet threw her arms wide. Between them and above her head Caroline glimpsed the sickle moon. It was almost drowned by Oxford's illuminated spires.

"Enough. Put on the lights, Sarah." Everyone blinked.

Janet was brisk. "The Goddess sees what's been going on. These Reborn Celts are perverting her wisdom and the magic of the sacred earth. So far, you three," Janet nodded at the sleeping Anna, "or rather you and Mary," to Caroline, "have tried to investigate in the normal way. Anna here— well, maybe she fell too deep into the well. You would know why, or how, Caro."

"Yes, of course. Anna tried too hard. She. . ." Caroline choked.

"I see," said Janet. "They took Wandwalker, and you can't go to the law. I agree that it's too dangerous right now. In these circumstances. . .well, I see Wandwalker's point about white magic against black. The compassion of the Goddess is rising. When the law is powerless, She will find a way. You, Caro," Janet leaned over and touched her cheek. "Because of your great love for Anna *and* for Wandwalker— you are protected against the wickedness of blood magic. We'll make a witch of you yet!"

"You understand," Caroline was relieved.

"But not Sarah. Sarah stays here with me and Anna. No, don't look at me like that, Sarah. You are in the care of Holywell. That means something. No sleeping in the places of death." Caroline knew Janet was right. She felt calm. She was ready to go it alone. Sarah shot her a tormented glance and then nodded.

Caroline groaned. "The problem is that Exmoor won't let us in. Is there anymore whisky?"

Just then a car horn sounded on the street. Sarah picked up one of the packed bags and handed it to Caroline.

"That's your taxi for Exmoor. Come on. He won't wait. I'll look after Anna."

"B. . .but."

"I called Olga," said Sarah. "She confirmed all those rooms are empty. No one wanted to watch the police at work, and it will take days to clean all the blood and needles and such. Olga knows how to open the delivery entrance to Exmoor. She'll get you into the room closest to the sacred well with her master key. They gave it to her to turf out the lazy students. You are meeting her in ten minutes at the back gate."

"Go!" said Janet, pushing Caroline to the door and handing her the wrong bag. Caroline accepted her own from Sarah. "I'll stay the night with Anna. Sarah can get some proper sleep. Be back by eight A.M., Caro. With a few hours' sleep, I can get back to the antidote. I can feel the drops distilling in my bones. As soon as Anna is herself again, you two can use your dreams to find Wandwalker."

Caroline responded to the hearty tone of Janet just as she always warmed to the decisive intelligence of Mary.

"Olga, backdoor, divination, alright," she muttered. She gave Anna a longing look and let herself be hustled out. "OK Sarah, tell the taxi I'm coming. If that's what it takes to find Mary, I'll be a Celt."

CHAPTER 28
KIDNAPPED

Mary was under water. She'd been under water for a long time. Rhiannon was there. No, it was just her severed head talking. The murdered girl's hair billowed out from under the torc. Hair and metal sucked sparks of sunlight from above. The torc flashed, and Mary blinked.

Wake up, Mary. The owl flies down the river.

"Whaaa. . ." Mary groaned. Her head was throbbing and there was a revolting taste in her mouth. Why was it so dark? Why was Rhiannon back?

Wake up. I will sing to you.

"No, don't," grunted Mary. "No singing. No noise." She realized that the voice she was hearing was in her head. A head within her head. No need to force her parched tongue around words. Go away, Rhiannon, she said to that grotesque head. No, wait a minute. Tell me why I can't see.

You've been kidnapped, came the mocking voice. Your hands are tied. The dark is because you're blind-folded.

Rhiannon was gleeful. It alarmed Mary in her current state. Was she going mad? No, no, such thoughts were no good. An image of Caroline swam up beside the head. You are not going mad, Mary, said Caroline, very steady. That's my job.

Caroline vanished just as Mary started to investigate the stiffness of her arms. Her wrists were bound in front, tied far too tight. She brought her hands up to her mouth to discover that she was unable to loosen the plastic ties. Her teeth and tongue felt around each wrist. No, this won't work.

Mary told herself not to panic. She was not afraid of the dark. She would not be. Right now, she had no idea how long she'd been kept tethered. It could be hours. Caroline and Sarah must be frantic. Leaning over, she confirmed that her phone was gone from her skirt pocket. They were not *that* stupid.

The Celts. It must be the Reborn Celts who were responsible for this. . .this outrage. Mary fed her anger. Anything was better than imagining what else might be in this blackness. This was too much. Sternness flowed into her body. Pushing herself more upright, something big and cold came out of the wall at the small of her back. Oh, so the rope around her middle tied her to the thing that was digging into her back! She twisted so that one hand could touch the metal. It was a big smooth ring, about an inch thick.

She tugged. Nothing. It must be anchored in the stone wall. For the wall *was* stone, she could tell by the cold seeping into her body through her linen suit. She could even find the edges of the slabs by turning and using her fingers again. Blood was returning to them with a pricking sensation, but neither the metal ring nor the wall itself would yield in the slightest. Mary kicked the wall in experimentation, no, exasperation. The kick served to increase the pain in her ankles and knock off one of her sandals. She was too dispirited to find out if she had enough rope to recover it.

Could she yell for help?

"Unhmn. Help. Aaaaaargh" No, she could not. She couldn't move her tongue; it was so heavy. They must have drugged her. Anyway, she was now sure that she was in a building with thick walls. From the reverberation it sounded as if she was alone. Well, alone—apart from Rhiannon's ghost. There was a movement and the head bobbed up again. Rhiannon stuck her tongue out, then disappeared.

Mary began to sniff. Apart from the grit that she could feel all around, she detected damp, mold, and something sweetish at the root of the pervading odor. Now, what else could she do to stave off panic?

You have a choice. Choose. Choose quickly. Mary started. She had not expected those tones. Rhiannon? No. This voice was not playing games, although it was that of a woman. Caroline? No, too imperative: Anna. Mary was astonished. Anna was telling her to choose, but choose what?

Whether to survive. Mary answered her own question. Go on, Mary. Choose to give up, or to survive. Panic, crying, being paralyzed with fear, fainting: these were luxuries. Anna knew about being denied freedom of the body. Heat bubbled in Mary's mouth. She had a sudden visceral sense of Anna. Just for a millisecond she felt Anna's unhealed wounds *from inside.*

That jolt of Anna was a tonic for Mary's aching body; a tot of whisky for the soul, she reflected. Treading in dangerous waters, Mary was a survivor too. There had been a night, oh, many nights forty years ago, when an abandoned, pregnant Mary had contemplated such existential questions. Nights of bleeding, and tears after the baby had gone for adoption. It had been her choice, a choice that still hurt, her wound that would not heal. Trapped in her own defeat, she'd survived. Back then she had decided to survive. She could do so again.

If only there was some water, or even better, coffee. This horrible taste must come from the stuff on the cloth that had been thrust onto her face. She wasn't ready to think about that yet.

Something, there was something, cool, slippery: a plastic bottle. It must be water left for her. Mary wanted to sing! Water is the liquid of life, of hope. Even her stone tongue started to sweat in joyful anticipation. She stretched and stretched, trying to make her tethered hands into a claw to retrieve the bottle. She was almost there.

With a tiny thud, the bottle fell over and rolled out of reach.

Aaaaarh! Mary threw herself in its direction until the rope at her middle dug like a knife. It was no use. The bottle of sweet water was gone.

Mary recalled "Kidnapping 101": give the captive a drink. Just her luck to be taken by amateurs. What would Anna do?

Huh, Anna would get the water whatever the cost in torn flesh. Mary's head ached. A sign of dehydration, no doubt.

This is vile, said Mary Wandwalker to herself. She rested her head back on the stone wall, fighting nausea. I won't do this. This is ridiculous, and vile. I'm going to get out of here.

CHAPTER 29
CAROLINE HAS TROUBLE SLEEPING

So depleted was Caroline, that on reaching the room above the sacred well she could barely pull her pajamas from the tangle in her bag. Dropping clothes on the floor, she fell on the bed. In five minutes, she was snoring. Yet, her sleeping mind brimmed with anxieties. Tossing and moaning, images of Anna's damaged brain and Mary's dead body kept her in the shallows of sleep. At two A.M., she awoke, irrevocably locked out of slumber. No chance then of the helpful dream she was counting on.

After thumping Exmoor College's thin pillow, Caroline threw back the sheet and sat up. She did not put on the light. There was too much in the room already. The illuminated city streamed through cheap curtains. What had Janet said about the goddess providing?

Caroline went to the window and stared at slumbering Oxford. A car alarm hooted in the distance, stopping after a couple of minutes. A late reveler, or an unskillful thief? she wondered. The thought of carjackers made her smile because it brought back a mischievously healthy Anna. Six months ago, it took the combined efforts of Mary and herself to dissuade Anna from stealing an expensive car for the DEA.

Caroline smiled again. She recalled Anna's novel way of calming her when her depression was at its worst. Already a night walker, Anna instituted a ritual of leading Caroline through the streets. A wordless rhythm of striding hand in hand, these nocturnal ramblings loosened her body and soothed her soul. It was like the whole neighborhood was rocking her to sleep.

Anna never stopped until Caroline said "home," even if they stayed out until sunrise.

When the night walking began, Mary had frowned. She preferred brisk exercise in daylight. Nevertheless, she refrained from commenting. Mary soon grasped that the ritual was part of what worked between the overweight middle-aged depressive and the lean wild warrior. Tonight, at Exmoor, Caroline hugged her ample body at the window. Mary could accept what she did not understand. Caroline loved her for that.

She gazed down to the garden, craning her neck against the glass to spot the pitch black well. Perhaps the dream she needed was there, trapped in the old well, like. . .no, don't think of Rhiannon. It was Mary and Anna she was searching for. The window had been painted shut. After a lot of scraping and rattling, Caroline got it open and leaned out. By resting her heavy bosoms on the windowsill, she could make out a faint ring below. Like shortbread, she thought. Or those biscuits with jam in the hole in the middle.

For the first time since Mary's disappearance, she wanted biscuits, a lot of biscuits. Good thing she'd decided not to bring food to the college. Caroline was no dream expert, but she guessed that comfort eating blocked the spirits. Or locked in the bad ones. Comfort eating left her submerged. Living with Anna and Mary she managed to use food less to mop up her demons. As Mary had said in her succinct way: "It makes the demons fat along with you, Caroline."

Caroline slammed the window shut. Then she opened it again, looking up not down. Janet once told her that too much moonlight made her afraid. Yet tonight, Janet had made a point of seeking Lady Moon. Here at Exmoor Caroline saw no moon. She could not tell if it was the direction, or just too much light from the city. Mary would know, she concluded, feeling glum. In her right mind, Anna would conjure up the moon by hacking into the street cameras.

Repressing another smile, she turned back toward the bed. There was a crunch under her slippers. This time she leapt for the light switch and saw a paper bag in her jeans pocket that contained dry leaves and twigs. Janet! She'd pressed this into my hands, thought Caroline, while I directed the taxi driver to Exmoor. Caroline sat on the bed and spread out the contents. One herb was bay; she also got a whiff of sage. With the ingredients was a box of matches. Ah, thought Caroline. It must be a fire spell. Well, here goes.

To begin conjuring Janet would draw a circle around herself with chalk. Sometimes she addressed the four cardinal points of the compass by their elemental affinities: Earth, Air, Fire and Water. Not sure of directions, Caroline pushed the bed to the wall, then spun around the room with her arms extended to carve a circle in the air. She then placed an item of her clothing at four equidistant points. Caroline thought she heard a distant cackle as she held the lighted match to the bundle.

At first the herbs were slow to ignite. Then with smoke came a pungent smell. After a minute and without warning, the bundle ignited. Caroline gasped, dropping the flaming twigs onto the carpet.

Oh, goddess, please, no!

Caroline hopped from one bare foot to the other, shaking her singed hand. When the pain did not stop, she dived for the wash basin. Water soothed her scorched skin. On the carpet the fire formed a fountain, no more than a foot high. Caroline screamed, remembered the water glass, and used it to throw tumblerfuls on the flames in quick succession. The fire spat like a golden serpent, then died. Caroline coughed up a tiny grains of burnt carpet from the smoke.

What had been on fire was now a soggy black hole. Caroline held onto the sink behind her. Her heart dropped to her feet, no further, she sensed. Feeling blindly for chairs and wall, she eased herself around the room, collapsing on the bed.

After a few minutes a more delicate smell permeated Caroline's nostrils. The foliage had released elements of sage, violets, a woody cinnamon smell, and something sweet like toffee.

"Smoke," muttered Caroline, calmer. She should kick herself. "Yes, of course. That's it. A smoke spell. Thank you, Janet."

Janet must have told her to light the herbal charm over the sink so she could add water safely. Then she should have purified the room by wafting the smoke into every corner, and at entrances and exits.

Sorry, Janet, Caroline muttered as she got under the covers again. She heard chuckling, far away. Caroline twisted her lips. It was rather funny. Comedy was good medicine; that had been one of Mary's sayings. All at once Caroline was back asleep.

CHAPTER 30
RETURN OF THE GOLDEN TORC

Not again, Olga thought. She stuck her arms akimbo at the second oversleeping member of the DEA at Exmoor.

"*Caroline wake up.*" Olga whispered and shook Caroline's shoulder. "You've got to go, before the Chief Scout comes round. You promised." Olga started pulling at her bedcovers. "And I see I have to do something about that hole in the carpet."

Caroline was awake and flushed with guilt. "Oh, Olga..."

"Never mind. Get dressed. I'll bring the rug from Room 16 to hide it. And some extra air freshener.

Just before 9 a.m., Janet opened the front door to the house in Norham Gardens. Her scowl shrieked reproach. "Really, Caro. We said 8 am! You're what. . .almost an hour late!"

Caroline was out of breath. "S-Sorry." She dodged past Janet to check on Anna, who was still sleeping on the sofa. Then she turned to the annoyed witch.

"I'm so sorry, Janet. Forgot to take my alarm. Olga just woke me."

"Dammit, Caro, I wanted to talk over your dream. Now I must go. We've had some good news back at the lab. A package arrived from the Turkish border."

"Where? What sort of package?" Caroline wasn't paying the bustling Janet much attention. Anna turned in her sleep. She looks younger than ever, Caroline thought.

"Danu Root," said Janet, grabbing the last piece of toast. Sarah was nowhere to be seen. "Or rather for the first time, the whole plant, not just the root. The leaves could have what I need to complete the antidote. Now Caro, write down everything you can remember about the dream. I'll be back." Janet banged the front door behind her.

"But there was nothing, nothing at all," a sad Caroline said to Janet's retreating figure.

With Janet gone, so was the optimism in the room. Caroline was wretched. With Mary missing, the imminent solstice was dragging them towards something terrible. Another day and they were no nearer finding her. Caroline damped down her fear. She'd slept for hours in the smoke infused room. On waking her dreams dissolved like water into sand.

"You. Must. Try." When had Anna moved? She was sitting up, her eyes screwed up as if trying to remember Caroline.

"Darling. . ." Anna stopped her with her eyes. Then she pointed at the table with biros and Mary's laptop.

"Try. Write," she commanded. Caroline looked around the room for paper.

"I wish we had Mary's notebook," she muttered. "She keeps it in her handbag." Mentioning Mary returned Caroline to her task. There was a biro and an old-fashioned cheque book in her bag. Won't it have blank pages at the back? Taking pen and book, Caroline placed them next to the plate with crumbs. Breakfast would be nice. Anna's face was uncompromising.

Caroline sighed, feeling that crushing sense of failure again. Creeping down the staircase at Exmoor, the stink of smoke and charred carpet seeped into Caroline's muddled recall. Nothing, nothing useful. Oh Mary, Caroline picked up a pen. Perhaps holding it would help words gush from the dark.

"Drink this, both of you." A mug of something fragrant appeared beside the empty checkbook. Another was placed nearer Anna.

"Sarah?"

"I heard you come in. Janet sent me to make the tea. Chinese willow bark and something extra for memory. And I put honey in it for you, Caroline."

A smile eased Caroline's pinched features. Sarah sat next to Anna and handed her the tea. Anna sipped. Caroline sipped. After a minute's silence, she put down the mug and scrawled a few words.

"That's all I've got," she said putting down the pen. "Maybe Janet can find more."

"Can I see?" Sarah was trying not to be eager. Caroline was sorry to disappoint her faith in anything prescribed by Holywell.

"Read. To me." Anna sounded far away. Sarah took the mug from her and shared a worried look with Caroline.

No help for it, thought Caroline. "OK, it's not much. I wrote: 'A river, the sound of a big river. Horses plunge into the river. A flash of something in the water. Yellow, no, gold. I guess it could be a torc. My eyes filled with blood.'"

She looked up. "Next thing I knew, Olga was shaking me. Some memory of what happened to Rhiannon, I guess. I can't see it helping us to find Mary."

"A. Night. Mare." Anna's mouth twisted.

"What is it? What did you say?"

"Night. Mare." Anna frowned at Caroline. It took a moment.

"Night... mare? Oh, yes! Yes," said Caroline, fascinated. "Horses. It was a nightmare. But how does it help us find Mary?"

"The torc. The gold torc. A ransom." Anna drooped.

"Lie down, Anna. Don't tax yourself."

"Listen to her, Caroline."

Caroline was shocked to see that Sarah was grinning. "She means we can use the torc to get Mary back. The Reborn Celts are desperate for it."

"Oh Sarah, you're getting confused! They already have the real torc! Don't you remember what Jez Wiseman told Mary? One of them stole it from his backpack."

"Must sleep." Crouching in a ball, Anna put her arm over her eyes. Her breathing became regular. How Caroline longed to lie beside her and forget their fears for Mary.

Sarah was rooting in the cloth bag she'd carried to classes. "You mean this torc?"

She held out a torc with both hands as if it were an offering. Morning light made the facets sparkle on Sarah's brown arms and face. She shone like an African princess.

Caroline's mouth fell open. The torc looked exactly like the one that Caroline last saw on Rhiannon's severed head. She gagged. Hang on, no. That one had been a fake, Mary had said. She put up a hand to her aching brow. All these torcs. Please let me go to bed until it is all over, she longed to say. Well, at least until Mary gets home and takes charge. Caroline swallowed hard.

"Where did you get *that*?"

Since the coffee table was crowded with mugs and pens, Sarah put the torc on the plate with the crumbs. She shook both her wrists. Of course, gold is heavy. Caroline stretched out and picked it up the torc. Then she placed it back down. With that heft, it must be real gold. Was it the genuine torc? How could it appear in their sitting room? She gazed at Sarah.

"Explain, Sarah, please."

"Joe Griffith's suitcase was delivered early this morning. Anna's name and this address was written on the label; by her, I think. The man said that it had never been picked up at the Left Luggage counter in Reading. I signed as Anna for the suitcase. I thought you wouldn't mind. When I opened it and saw the torc, I decided to wait for you. I didn't show it to Janet."

"Good work, Sarah," said Caroline. "I don't know how Janet feels about ancient artifacts, but the fewer people who know we have it the better."

"Are we going to use it to get Mary back?"

"You bet," said Caroline, feeling a lot better. "We are going to do what Mary would do. Take the initiative. In fact, Sarah, can you make me a pot of Mary's favorite coffee?"

CHAPTER 31
BY THE BOATHOUSES, OXFORD

The phone call was brief and to the point. Caroline decided to try Barin first, then move on to Simmy if he claimed no knowledge of Mary's confinement. It wasn't a summer school day, so she found him at home. Despite his obvious excitement, he neither confirmed nor denied the kidnapping. However, he did agree to produce Mary in return for the real Sacred Well Torc. The arrangement must remain confidential, he specified. No contacting Simmy, and above all, nothing was to be said to Colin. Caroline assumed he wanted to be in sole control of the operation.

The exchange was set for two p.m. on the towpath next to the College Boathouses. Caroline was buoyed by further improvement in Anna. After she woke up around noon, a skinny student in a lab coat arrived with an envelope from Janet. Inside they found instructions and a tiny amount of green powder to be given to Anna in milk.

She'd not come herself, the note said, because the brewing process was delicate, and she wanted to distill a couple more doses before some crucial ingredient disintegrated. After making a face at the milk, Anna drank it down in one gulp. She listened while Caroline was negotiating.

"I come," she said, before Caroline could say anything.

"Not this time, Anna. He said I was to come alone with the torc. Why don't you rest until Janet gets here with the second dose?"

221

Anna grunted and settled back on the sofa. Relieved, Caroline went to discuss an early lunch with Sarah. When she returned, Anna spoke again.

"The wife of Lir will go with you."

"Whaaat? Oh no." Caroline was aghast. She'd hoped that the wife of Lir was long gone.

Anna chuckled from the sofa.

"Don't *do* that!" Caroline ran from the room, jumping up and down in the hall. She dare not show her delight in Anna's recovered spirits.

Just before Tom Tower at Cardinal College struck two p.m., Caroline carried a supermarket shopping bag onto the tow path. Barin had promised to take her to where Mary was "residing comfortably." Caroline gritted her teeth at those odious Oxford tones. Naturally he wanted to see the torc first. And the deal was "null and void" if the police had been notified.

It was another sweltering afternoon. Summer had come too soon, and it felt as if the solstice ought to be long past. Yet her weighty emotions pulled Caroline under in the lofty plane trees planted by the path. She told herself keep her head above the surface this afternoon. Her palm on the bag was sweaty. Too hot for her preferred jeans, she had to wear a light cotton frock. Anna told her it added ten pounds. That was before she'd become ill, before Joe Griffith. Caroline wished she could jump back in time and hug Anna for that brutal honesty.

It was too hot for most of the tourists who took over from the student runners and rowers of term. Ahead, Caroline spotted a round bearded figure with the boathouses framing him from behind. Heat rising from the tarmac made his image shiver like a mirage. Only a few dog walkers were within shouting distance. No one was paying attention to Caroline because both humans and dogs gazed at the lazy river with longing.

Time slowed. Caroline could hear her steps echoing. Barin gleamed in the sun's dazzle. Must be in one of his expensive suits. Her legs felt weighed down, her thighs slippery under the awful dress. Eyes pressed on her from all around, from high college windows, from behind tree trunks, even from the single punt on the river. Caroline noticed that the boat was slowly spinning instead of going straight. At least those people had troubles of their own, and so were not spying on her.

Laughter wafted from the three would-be punters. One young man struggled to stab the river bottom with the pole. He was trying to thrust the shallow boat forward. An echo of heavy boots from behind made Caroline realize that she'd become distracted. Much worse, she now knew what Anna meant by smelling danger. Her skin prickled all over. It was too late.

Beguiled by the laughter on the river, she did not see them coming. The joggers put on ski masks, then came up on either side of her. The one on the left grabbed the bag; the one on the right her arms. Despite her grip on the bag's straps, they slipped from her damp fingers. She wailed, but something fast and fierce suddenly interrupted the mugging.

Caroline felt a visceral joy in her terror. It was Anna, clawing at the shopping bag in the grasp of a masked man all in black. Two sets of arms and legs struggled on the tow path while Caroline was dragged backwards onto the grass by the other assailant. She could not free herself from the bruising hold.

"Owwww! Hel. . ." A glove was clamped over her mouth. Yet the attack was attracting notice: the young men in the punt stood aghast.

One of them fell into the water. Diverted by the struggle on land, he'd made the rookie mistake of leaning on the pole as the punt slid away.

Caroline's jogger released her suddenly. She saw the black figure dive for the bag. He dragged it away from the fight between the other attacker and Anna. Before Caroline could stagger over, the bag was gone. Caroline looked in the direction of Barin. He too had disappeared. A second, louder splash was followed by a wave onto the path. Anna and the assailant had fallen into the river.

"ANNA" screamed Caroline. "She can't swim!" she heard herself yell.

In fact, she had no idea whether Anna could swim. She was about to jump in the water herself, when she saw that the other two punters were already helping Anna out. They were both athletic young men in American baseball caps. Anna's opponent rolled onto the bank and ran off, shedding water everywhere. Rescuers and rescued collapsed onto the dry grass.

"Thank you, thank you," gasped Caroline at the three soaked men. Below their similar buzz haircuts, they flashed dazzling white teeth.

"No problem, Ma'am," one said.

"Sure didn't expect to see that kind of assault, here in Oxford," said another. "Seems like such a quiet town." The one with brown curly hair was dialing his phone.

"No, no!" Caroline realized what he must be doing. "No, no police. Let me and my. . . my. . ."

"Girlfriend?" said Curls with a smile.

"Yeah, let me and my girlfriend handle it."

There was a pause. Caroline stood straighter. She wished she was Mary. Young men like these— were they from a sports team? Mary had a tone they would obey.

"Are you sure that's what you want Ma'am?"

That could have been any of them. They exchanged glances that said weird women, strange country.

"Police detain you. Go now." That was Anna, loud and imperious. She was combing water from her long hair with her fingers. She picked a bit of slimy weed from the back of her neck and held it out to Caroline.

"How horrible. Let me get you home to a shower." Caroline took a deep breath and faced their rescuers. "Thank you, guys, for what you've done. We will never forget it. But involving the police will interrupt your. . .your holiday. Plus, I need to get Anna home. She's been sick. We'll deal with matters from here."

"Well, y'all, I guess we better find that boat." All three gazed past the boathouses. Coiling like a snake swallowing its prey, the river had carried the punt out of sight. The young men jogged off in pursuit of their hired boat.

Caroline shook out her dress, damp from embracing Anna, and put her arm around the wet woman. Knowing it was hopeless, she took a last look around.

"We've lost the torc, haven't we?"

"Ambush," said Anna. "Wife of Lir say go home."

"Anna, please say you are here too."

Anna sniffed. Then she nodded.

Caroline decided not to push her luck. Plus, even in this record summer heat the river Thames at Oxford was notorious for its low temperature. Anna had suffered a shock. Herself too. They should get back to the house and regroup with Sarah and Janet. In fact, Caroline would call Janet about the rest of the antidote. Sarah would be desperate for news. Caroline had lost their one bargaining chip to get Mary back. She wondered which of her companions would be first to say, "I told you so."

CHAPTER 32
THE DREAM

"I told you so. Dream divination is what you need. Not silly heroics." Janet stirred the milk with the same blackened silver spoon she had used to tap Anna's feet days ago. With Anna asleep on the sofa, Janet, Caroline, and Sarah had gathered in the kitchen.

"Shouldn't that spoon be cleaned first?" Caroline was grabbing at details. She did not want to think of Mary in a prison. Nor of the proximity of the summer solstice, and what that might mean for the Reborn Celts predilection for beheadings.

"There's some metal cleaner under the sink," muttered Sarah from the kitchen corner. "I'll just. . ."

"Leave it," snapped Janet. "Caro, get a grip."

She held up the blackened spoon and made a circle over the greenish milk, then placed the spoon on the saucer beneath the glass. Janet scrutinized the Danu's Root antidote for a few moments. Then she put her tongue between her front teeth.

Caroline realized that Janet was looking worn. Her hair's white roots were longer than the scarlet dye she was so fond of. Janet eased her chair back. "Hmm. Good idea to rest the mixture." She was ready for another bite at Caroline.

"So, today you lost the torc. Oh, Caro, why didn't you wait for me to help you with that dream? Taking risks. . .no good."

"Please don't upset Caroline." Sarah's voice was husky. Unlike Janet, who was focused on the concoction, Sarah studied Caroline. She had been the one to receive the wet and dispirited duo a couple of hours ago. Sarah continued. "We had to try something! The torc was a chance, a chance for. . ."

"A chance squandered," retorted Janet. "An effing wasted opportunity. Your jaunt to the river, Caroline, lost a valuable advantage. Quite apart from the damage to Anna's recovery, Wandwalker would never have fallen for such a trick. . ."

"Stop it." Caroline banged the kitchen table, making the green milk bounce in the glass. Sarah flinched. "Sorry," she continued. "Look, Janet, don't start in about Mary. You don't know her like I. . .like we do!"

She got a sniff.

"Stop telling us what to do. Please." Caroline's calm threatened to dissolve. She had thought she couldn't cry anymore. "I can't bear it," hovered on her tongue.

Sarah brought Caroline a cup of water.

"Shall I make tea?" she whispered.

Caroline wished she could smile. "No more tea," she managed to say. She forced herself to pick up the glass of green milk, using both hands to stop the glass trembling. It was time for Anna's medicine.

"We are going to get Anna well," she croaked in the direction of Janet. "And then we're going find Mary. I don't know how, but we will."

Sarah followed Caroline out with the milk. Left alone in the kitchen, Janet drummed her fingers on the table. That arthritis in her right knee always got worse when she was overtired. Pain washed away her patience. She'd be ratty with the gals back at Holywell. Dorothy, the manager, had spoken to her about it more than once. Even so, there was no question of abandoning her charge, Sarah, to the craziness in this house.

Janet pursed her lips. She'd been sharp with Caro, too sharp. Well, darn it, she supposed she could call the DEA trio her friends. Testing her leg by carefully putting weight on it, she rose and hobbled to join the others in the lounge. Her grim expression became more thoughtful.

"No, no, no." That was Anna from the sofa, awake, and not cooperative. "Bad. Milk bad. Moldy. Green bits, not grass."

"Darling, that's just the medicine. Take a sip. . .please."

"Wife of Lir not like."

"Yes, but we want *Anna* back!" Despite exhaustion, Caroline was determined to get Anna to take the second dose.

"Anna does not like."

"Yes, I know. It will make you better, I promise."

"Anna is not good enough?" There was a flicker in Anna's expression that caused Caroline to pause. The young woman on the sofa folded her arms. Her stance made defiance physical. Caroline opened her mouth, glanced at Janet, and shut it again. Why wasn't Janet insisting?

"What about Mary? Won't you take this medicine for Mary? She's been kidnapped, remember?"

After those words, Caroline had a strange sensation, as if a kind of test was being administered. What would any of them do for Mary's safe return?

Anna said nothing. She acquired a remote expression. The Anna they knew had vanished into a distant pool like a sprite.

"Perhaps the wife of Lir knows where Mary is?" Janet's intervention made Caroline gasp.

"Anna?" Caroline whispered.

Anna's folded arms acquired fists. She scowled. Janet put her hand on Caroline's arm to make her wait. It's a spell, thought Caroline. Right now, in this room, we're in a spell.

When it came, the voice was not Anna's. It spoke slow with a rich depth.

"Wife. Of. Lir. See. Mary. Dream. Go dream."

Depleted by the utterance that was not her, Anna curled up again on the sofa.

"Take it away," she pointed at the green milk in a normal tone. "Anna and wife of Lir. Both must stay."

"Alright," said Janet.

A wail escaped from Caroline.

229

"Don't say it, Caro. Listen to me on this at least. Here Sarah, take it, and make sure you pour it away. The antidote must be made fresh every time. Back at the lab, I have enough herbs and essences for one more try. The time is not now."

Sarah removed the milk then reappeared, watchful as an owl.

"Janet, you can't just leave her," Caroline whispered, agonized.

"Face it, Caro. You can't force Anna. And I don't think you've got the picture. If the wife of Lir wants to be here, it is not for us to send her away. She's just as real as any dream."

Caroline stared at Janet, and then at Anna. She had nothing to say.

"Let it play out." Janet was compassionate but firm. "Like I said, I have another dose. Let Anna decide whether to take it or not. She is walking between worlds now."

"The Otherworld of Manannan Mac Lir," said Sarah from the corner.

"No doubt," said Janet. "Now Caro, you heard Anna. What about that dream?"

With reluctance, Caroline took her checkbook from her handbag. She looked at her dream notes. Hopeless.

"Are you ready to be serious about your dream?"

"Mary wouldn't," muttered Caroline.

"You do her a disservice," said Janet, with one of her grim smiles. "Yes, she'd play it by the book if she could. But as you well know, Mary was, *is*, I mean, prepared to read some strange books. Hand over those notes. Ah ha."

She read out: 'A river, the sound of a big river. Horses plunge into the river. A flash of something in the water. Yellow, no gold. I guess it could be a torc. My eyes filled with blood.' Hmm. OK, I take it back, Caro. I was too hasty. Blasted knee! That attempt with the torc could well be foreshadowed. Given these dream images, I don't blame you for trying it."

"I just assumed the torc and the blood was a memory of finding Rhiannon." Caroline felt better.

"Could well be," Janet sighed, took out a pair of spectacles, and put them on. "Memories can be helpful for divination. We miss how often reality is on a repeat cycle."

"You mean criminals have a pattern, a style?"

"That too."

"Well, we *are* dealing with the Reborn Celts. They believe we can relive ancient lives," Caroline mused.

"Exactly. Now what about those horses? Try to jump back into that dream. Were you a horse? Could the horse be Anna falling into the river today?"

"No." That was Anna. Her eyes were open. "Anna not beast. Anna run, not gallop."

"No, indeed."

"You should have seen her, Janet, trying to rescue the torc. Anna grabbed the bag. She held it so tight that she was forced into the river." Caroline leant over and kissed Anna's head.

"That's not being a horse," contributed Sarah.

"No," muttered Janet. "So where in this hellish case do we have horses? Celtic horses no doubt."

They sat pondering. Slowly Caroline began to sniff. Yes, it was the smell of spring grass when she did a school trip to the chalk downs. Janet picked up her excitement and waited.

"I got it! Horses on the hillside," Caroline said, opening a laptop in haste. "You know, Janet. That horse cut into the chalk that can be seen for miles. I took the first graders. Maybe it is where they've got Mary. I'm looking it up now!"

"Hmm, maybe." Janet did not sound convinced.

Caroline held up her laptop so Sarah too could see the grassy hillside with the horse design in the exposed chalk. "Suggested to be tribal marking of territory," she read out from the notes. "It's near here, in Oxfordshire."

"No, that's not our horse." Sarah was jumping and waving her phone. "Ours is a river!"

"Horse. Runs. London." That was Anna nodding at Sarah and propping her head up on a cushion.

"Of course!" Caroline slapped her computer shut and tossed it onto an empty armchair. "The river Eponia is linked to the horse goddess. It's the lost Celtic river in London. I've been there. I mean, Mary and I were where it meets the Thames."

"Calm down. Let's take this a step at a time." For once Janet was approving. "Now why do we think this horse is a river, not a hillside?"

"Because Epona with no 'I' is a Celtic horse goddess and Eponia with an 'I' is the name of a lost river in London. The river is thought to be a road for the goddess." Sarah was reading from her phone.

"The place where we, well, the police found Rhiannon's body," said Caroline.

"Minus her head." That was Janet, a stickler for exactitude, learned from spell-making, Caroline realized.

"Minus her head," she echoed. "And that's it, I see it now. The body on the bank of the Thames was washed by water from the Eponia. All that's left of the river is water from a pipe."

"You mean, all that's visible, not all that's left," corrected Janet. "London's lost rivers are still there, underground. They were sacred to the people. Many feed wells that could be Celtic in origin."

"The Rising. The Blood Rising." That was Anna, more awake.

"What? Oh, yes. The third rite is Uprising, also Blood Rising. There's a theme, waking, rising. . ."

"Finding lost rivers." Caroline recalled from Simmy's lecture.

"And beheading." They all went quiet at Janet's brutal uttering of what they were all thinking.

"Mary," said Caroline.

"Do you think they've found the lost river Eponia?" Sarah sounded a bit lost herself.

Anna reached out and took Caroline's hand. The conclusion was too horrifying.

"Mary," said Anna, as if to stamp home what was at stake.

"Yes, Mary," agreed Caroline, seeing Janet nod. "You see, Sarah, they are not finding the river; they are releasing it. Blood Rising and Uprising indicates a sacrifice to bring the river back."

It was left to Janet to spell it out. "These terrorists have no notion of the real Celts. Instead of protecting the sacred waters, they plan to. . .to behead Mary. She is the crone sacrifice whose life-blood will be poured into the source of the Eponia as they release it."

"Somewhere in London." Sarah was daunted.

"Time to get cracking," said Janet. "It's three days until the solstice. We've got to find the riverhead and Mary before the sun sets on the shortest night of the year.

CHAPTER 33
THE PRISONER

In Mary's nightmare, she was transported to Exmoor College. She was walking towards the well in the pre-dawn hours after the Waking party. A syringe scrunched under one of her sensible shoes. This time she knew what was coming. Rhiannon was calling her from the water at the bottom of the well. Helpless to stop, Mary moved nearer and nearer.

The dead girl sounded far away. The water underneath Oxford was taking them on a long journey. Even though she could not make out the words, Mary could tell that the tinny voice was mocking her. With every fiber of her being she wanted to turn around. She longed to call Caroline. The sky was a peculiar red, neither dark nor light.

I am alone, Mary thought. Revulsion choked her as she saw her fingers reach for the clammy stones. Her neck was bending forwards, she could not close her eyes. A wave of odors, sweat, rust, and blood filled her lungs. The severed head was pulling her down.

Rhiannon, please stop doing this. Mary would give anything not to be dragged into the water with that bobbing head. She glimpsed its hair spreading out, greenish weeds stuck to a bald skull. Mary could taste the slime; her fingers were covered with gobs of dissolving flesh. Despite retching, she could not stop. The well rim was *so* slippery, she was going to fall! There was no appeal to the dead. Down there Rhiannon was ghoul and goddess. The only way out was through those staring eyes.

Those eyes were spouts of water without a source.

Mary ceased fighting. That thing, waiting in the well, was her death.

I EAT THE DARK.

Those words blazed as she launched herself headfirst down the well. She expected an instant collision with the decaying head. The well grew darker, giving Mary the sensation of a vertical tunnel. Above her the well's mouth lost its stars, shrinking to the size of a plate, a dot. . .then it was gone. Bathed in its own eerie glow, the head swam up to meet her.

It was not Rhiannon, but Mary's dead son, George, who had been Caroline's husband and Anna's lover. He was what made their bond indissoluble.

Mary sank down and down, far below the head. She was spinning in the waters beneath Oxford, without light, without breath.

She woke painfully to the darkness. Her body was pressed onto cold stone and there was grit under her cheek. Oh, that's right, I'm lying on a dirty floor, trussed up, she thought. A noise had roused her: a door in need of oiling was being unlocked. Someone's coming, she realized. Trying to lift her head, she felt a knife penetrate her temples. The pain shot through her entire body, pooling at her wrists and ankles. Daggers, why daggers? Mary moaned aloud.

Someone was flashing a light. No, it stopped flashing. The room, now illuminated, was cruel. Mary moaned louder. A soft footfall must be rubber shoes, she thought. Why did everything hurt so much? She shut her eyes again. The voice came from somewhere close.

"The water is out of her reach. Not what I told him."

It was a woman's voice. There was exasperation in it, and an undercurrent of fear. Mary found herself being pulled into a sitting position. She kept her eyes shut.

"Drink."

The water trickled down her chin from the plastic bottle being held to her lips. Mary opened her mouth and sucked.

Almost at once the pain lessened. She drank and drank until the bottle was empty. Like a baby, she thought, disgusted.

"More," she gasped.

"I'll get you some," said the woman, clambering up from the floor. She was dressed in black: combat trousers, long sleeved t-shirt, and a black scarf over her head with eye holes cut by scissors. She'd been propping Mary up and now moved around to gaze at her prisoner.

"And food," croaked Mary. It was not a request. The woman's annoyance about the water showed they wanted her alive, at least for now. The woman nodded. With her long body and well wrapped head she looked like a giant insect. As the figure turned, Mary called out.

"You're not going to kill me?"

The figure in black hesitated for a millisecond before scooting out the door. Mary noted that suggestive pause. Bloody Celts. Then, feeling more of the pain drain from her head: *Bloody* Celts want my blood.

Propped up, her back was getting chilled. The stone walls: walls she could see now with the blazing bulb overhead. Windowless, and with one door, the room appeared resistant to rescue and to egress. It offered nothing besides dust, spiders, and a wooden rack on the opposite wall for wine bottles.

Mary was almost sure that her jailor had been Simmy. Perhaps she could get through to her? After all, she'd known Simmy back when the climate scientist visited the Archive.

There was a rattle behind the door and the woman came back in with the bucket. Mary flinched. The black figure paused, then knelt in front of her, taking out three small bottles of water and a wrapped loaf of black bread. Mary was very hungry. She held her arms out and the bread was put in them. The woman sat cross legged watching her. Was she supposed to remove the supermarket tie with her teeth?

"Please," said Mary, rather stiff, indicating the dried blood alongside the ties at her wrists. "I need hands to eat."

For a moment, the figure stared. Then peered at Mary's wrists. At last, she nodded and took a very small pair of pruning shears from her trouser pocket. Mary forced herself to keep still as the steel blades were worked under the plastic ties that felt like wire.

"Too tight," grunted the woman. She was gone. Something in her movement told Mary she would be back sooner this time. She reappeared with a jar of Vaseline. With the lubricant, she could get the shears to cut the ties.

Without a second of hesitation, Mary fell on the loaf and tore off the wrapper. It was hard black bread, already sliced. Stuffing a whole slice in at once, Mary noticed the woman was holding up a pack of bandages and a bottle of antiseptic. She nodded and held up a bruised hand. Let her wait while she got a bottle of water to take a swig first. Rye bread was so *dry.*

It was oddly intimate, Mary thought. She was chewing the salty bread while the woman wiped the dried blood from the torn skin at her wrists and ankles. There was an earthy taste in Mary's mouth, and an obscure sense of comfort in the damp cloth stroking her skin.

"Why are you doing this to me?" said Mary. This was her chance to see if she could make it more like a tea party than a hostage situation. The woman froze, then resumed cleaning Mary's right foot. She had not untied her ankles.

"Family," said the woman, not looking at her through the mask. Then added, "The earth is my family. The sacred waters can save us."

"Water, or blood?" Mary could not help saying. The woman ignored her remark and started to pack up the used swabs.

"Do you mean blood is the water of life?" Mary was desperate to stop the woman from leaving. She had to try to change her situation. "Simmy. It is Simmy, isn't it? I *knew* you. We chatted back when I was in the Archive? Back when you were a scientist?"

"I am a scientist!" The shout bounced off the damp stone.

Mary forced herself not to show fear. The woman continued. "Your bloody Archive had the clues to the lost river Eponia. I found them. As a *scientist* I've proved the Eponia is an artery of the Thames, the *sacred* Thames! The Eponia in London contributes vital minerals to the river gods as far as Oxford." Simmy was shaking now.

"That's wonderful, Simmy," Mary said. Just who is the vulnerable one here? She was cross. "If you let me go, I can help. . ."

"Noooo." There was a touch of anguish. Simmy scrambled for the door as if she'd discovered Mary had a contagious disease.

"Wait, wait! Please, please untie my ankles. They hurt. I can't get out of this room. . ."

Simmy stopped, then slowly turned back. The black insect-like woman was tense.

"Understand, Miss Wandwalker, the Reborn Celts care about the gods. We're going to wake this one. It will tear open the rotten heart of London. Blood for water."

There was a crash as she banged the door shut. The room was empty but for Mary. This talk of sacrifice and blood sent shivers up her spine. There was something else she should have noticed. Yes, that's it! After the door slammed there was no rattle. Could Simmy have. . .? Mary threw herself forward on the gritty floor. She began crawling on her elbows, then trying to use her knees. So difficult with the tied ankles. I'm a mermaid struggling on land, she thought.

Nevertheless, she got to the door and tugged at the handle. *Yes.* Simmy had forgotten to lock it. With creaking elbows, Mary pulled herself up to standing. She would have to jump with her feet but perhaps out there would be a sharp knife. She tried to ignore the cutting sensation around both ankles as she pulled open the door.

Simmy, was standing there without the mask, her eyes blazing above the black. In her hands was a golden torc.

"No," she said, too quiet. "You're not leaving. We have the torc now. Wait until the solstice." Then pushing Mary back, Simmy slammed the door and locked it before the prisoner had thumped back down onto the cellar's cold floor.

CHAPTER 34
CELTIC LONDON

"The solstice is the day after tomorrow," Caroline muttered while staring into the plate glass window on an obscure side street in London. Too soon, she left unsaid. On one side of her, Sarah's eyes flashed at her in empathy. Anna, on the other side, grinned at her reflection. Neither had a comment.

The three women faced a modern office building in Clerkenwell Lane. Behind them stretched a sleeping snake of parked cars with an occasional white van passng. This lane joined the ceaseless currents of the high street. That busy road was a mix of 1960's high rises and Victorian shop conversions. Caroline, Sarah, and Anna heard shrieks from its traffic before it intersected a major channel of the city. This afternoon heat was intense, bathing pedestrians in wave after wave of oily grit.

It was Anna who spoke first.

"Wife of Lir sees the well."

"Yes, we can all see the Clerk's Well, like the website says. Unfortunately, there doesn't seem to be any clue as to the river Eponia. You remember," continued Caroline, "we are looking for the river so we can rescue Mary. We hope."

"This well is just old stones and bricks," agreed Sarah.

"Apart from the hole." That was Anna; or was it still the wife of Lir? As they exited the Underground she had reared up, a nervous mare at the assault of full-throated London. This peculiar monument was a two-minute walk from the station.

The three women ignored the desks, screens, and the well-dressed citizens of the busy architectural practice that occupied most of the ground floor. Instead, they were concentrating on what was immediately on the other side of the glass. The space was a pie-shaped slice partitioned off to separate medieval London from the twenty-first century. The thickest part of the wedge contained the well, or at least its remains.

All they could see was an uncovered shaft, a dark hole dropping down to the dank world below. It was frustrating not being able to peer down it, thought Caroline. That well was an open mouth leading to Celtic London, said a couple of speculative web pages. One suggested that the Clerk's Well could connect to the Eponia River.

"At least it looks like the sacred well at Exmoor College," remarked Sarah.

"You mean if you forget the funny colored bricks instead of stones, and nothing on top."

"Wife of Lir eat now," said Anna.

"Now? We've just had lunch. . ." Caroline was still staring at the well. "This can't be a dead end; it just can't be. All we found for the river Eponia is that it linked the Celtic sacred wells of London. The site of two of these wells have been identified. . .Mary. . ." Caroline stopped and put her palm to the glass. If only she could push through it and stare down the well. Seeing its water might provide some clue, some trace of Mary.

Sarah put her hand on her arm. "I'm sorry I can't search like Anna. . ."

"Nonsense, Sarah! No one can search like Anna! She's a cyberwitch. No, really, I've seen her do what no one can. If she can't do it now, there's a reason. Janet said to respect that."

Caroline and Sarah turned to look at Anna. She was hopping from side to side. A grin split her face.

"Darling, do you need to go somewhere?"

"Wife of Lir eat horse."

"Anna. . .what?"

Anna pointed at the second plaque, black with white lettering. It was a list of historical finds from the well shaft: glass from beer bottles from fifteenth to twentieth centuries;

coins, including several with the profiles of Roman Emperors; broken knives, decorative iron from horse bridles, stirrup heels, small votive figurines of Christian saints; two Roman gods, and a bronze carved horse of the same era.

"Horse," said Anna, stamping her foot.

"Yes," said Caroline, with a rush of gratitude. "Well done, horse. Offerings that indicate horses. You're right, this must be a link to the Eponia." Now that she was facing two hopeful young women, Caroline had a moment of panic. She had no idea what to do next.

Earlier in the morning, all had seemed possible in the hunt for Mary. Yet, apart from an exhibition of five years ago on "The Lost Rivers of London," they had found only two Celtic wells: Clerkenwell and Bridgit's Well. Visited for centuries by women hoping to conceive, Bridgit was a goddess of fertility and christianized as St. Bride.

"The well is now under St. Bride's Church, Fleet Street," Sarah explained.

Now that the hollow mouth of the Clerk's Well revealed so little about the lost Eponia, Caroline found her mind dwelling on those items that came from actual horses. Through her sandals, she could almost feel the rhythm of hoofbeats on the hot cobbles.

An hour later, the hopeful trio arrived at St. Bride's Church forty minutes before closing. Its white round towers seemed oddly familiar, thought Caroline. Then she grinned. Sarah had mentioned that the church's multi-layered spire launched centuries of wedding cakes. Indeed, courtesy of Rhiannon, one such cake gathered dust in Oxford.

"The crypt is this way," whispered Sarah, overawed by the moody statuary and tall windows. Anna skipped as soon as she saw the stone steps leading down. She went ahead, stretching her palms against the raw bricks on each side. When the passage became vaults, Anna darted through several small rooms.

Bulky display cases meant visitors had to go in single file. Anna stopped at a rope that marked off the remains of a Roman floor. Kneeling on stone flags she held a hand over part of the mosaic. Her body trembled in response, as if a teaspoon of freshwater had entered her. Then Anna crouched to the side to let the other two see.

They bent over a design with faded, yet recognizable, colors. What could have been a snake in chalky violet and blue appeared to be chasing a four-legged creature. Above was a black strip with what looked like a flame or a star. A card under glass admitted that this unusual motif had never been identified. The purple was a royal dye, very rare back then.

Modern archaeologists speculated that the floor owes more to Celtic mythology than to the Romans, Caroline read. Dating evidence suggests the mosaic comes from the first decade of imperial Londinium. One theory is that the four-legged animal was the horse, Pegasus, his wings lost to time and theft.

"A horse," breathed Caroline. "Not Pegasus, the flying horse, please the goddess, not. Couldn't that long creature be a river, the Eponia? Royal colors might be about its importance, not. . .not how it looks in real life."

"The river is a god," said Anna. "The wife of Lir says, and I do too." She got up and looked straight into Caroline's eyes. Her smile was the most relaxed it had been for days.

"Anna, is that you?"

Anna nodded. Caroline wanted to kiss her, but it would mean crushing Sarah between them. There was no room to turn round if all three of them moved at once.

"Don't fuss, Caroline. We both need to be here." That was the harsh wife of Lir. Caroline was getting to know that metallic tang. Oh, she's staying, Caroline sighed.

"Can we get out of here?" said Sarah. "Those bricks in the ceiling are so. . .so *old*."

"Don't worry. They'll last a bit longer," said Caroline, leading the way back. Stop sounding like a kindergarten teacher, she told herself. Anyone would be claustrophobic under these flaking bricks. Sarah's history of trafficking probably included confined spaces. She quickened her pace out of the vault.

At the Church's exit they found the gift shop with a bald man in thick glasses busy counting cash. Suspecting the three women were not customers for scale models and postcards, he returned to checking the new ten-pound notes. While Caroline fumbled to put change in the donation box, Anna and Sarah slipped away. The man placed a bunch of keys next to the till then glared at Caroline. Nodding, she followed the others into the yard.

Sarah was concentrating on a plaque next to a huge horse chestnut tree. Its leaves were still green, unusual for this drought afflicted summer. Caroline realized that its roots must reach beneath the crypt they had just visited. Looking over Sarah's shoulder, Caroline saw that the tree had been linked to a lost water source: the Bride's Well.

"See this." Anna waved an expensive looking book from a bench beneath the tree. At that moment, a vigorous rattle marked the official closure of St. Bride's as the man locked the outer door. Instinctively, Caroline moved in front of Anna, as the man stomped out of the churchyard. As she feared, the book had been prominently displayed inside the church.

"Anna, no," she hissed.

"Give it here." Sarah seized the book and passed around a bottle of water.

"Anna, you stole it. Not again! We've talked about this. Mary said. . ." Caroline wanted to be cross. She could not stop smiling. The wife of Lir lacked the guile to purloin a book from a tiny kiosk with the assistant in place. But Anna didn't.

Anna's grin was broad. "See," she said, grabbing the book back and pointing to the title: *The Lost Rivers of London Exhibition, curated by Dr. S. I. Morrigan.*

"Dr. S. I. Morri. . .Oh, Simmy. Simmy did that exhibition."

"Does it have anything about the Eponia?" Sarah was ever practical.

"Yes, there's a section on each river. . ."

"A map?"

"Oh God, I hope there's a map!"

There was a map. To their frustration however, it only showed where the lost rivers of London were known and accessible. Sarah had found the very same image online. Bold red denoted deep drains that predated the Victorian sewers. They could follow the whole of the Fleet River, and there was the northern Lea, with its own valley leading out of the city.

Caroline held her breath on spotting the Eponia's exit into the Thames, exactly where Rhiannon's torso had lain. Unfortunately, that was all the map showed. Caroline sighed and Anna gripped her elbow.

Caroline fought her disappointment. Anna took hold of the book. Shutting it with a snap, she held it like a shield. "Wife of Lir not like. Dragon here."

"Dragon?"

"The great serpent. I see him from the house that moves." Anna was taut. She turned the book around as if it could protect her.

"Anna, come back, please." Caroline was wringing her hands. Sarah was more forthright.

"She means the Thames. We came over the Thames in the train. It does look like a massive snake, the way it bends around. On a map, it's a snake-dragon running through London."

"Just like that purple and blue wave on the mosaic," Caroline was thoughtful.

"You were saying how you saw the Eponia join the Thames."

"I was remembering the blood." Caroline turned to Anna. "Did that bring back the wife of Lir?"

Anna wriggled. She announced: "Thames. Great serpent. Big power, big god."

"Yes, oh yes! You're so clever Sarah, for making the connection." Sarah glowed for a second. Caroline sighed. "Anna, wife of Lir. . ."

"*Wandwalker,* I see her." Anna trembled. Caroline put her hand to her mouth.

"Miss Wandwalker? Where?"

"Her. . .mark. Signs. Here."

Anna put the book face down. Her body relaxed, became intelligent. Caroline saw her expression take on the ferocious spark she knew to be Anna.

"Look Caroline," Anna said. "It's Mary. Her name."

And there she was, in tiny letters on the back of the expensive catalogue: "Thanks to Mary Wandwalker of the National Archives for her assistance in researching this exhibition."

"It's Mary," whispered Caroline.

"She helped Simmy?" said Sarah, wondering.

"That's right," remembered Caroline. "Because they did not find the Eponia Simmy was cross."

"Anna will find the Eponia in the Archives."

"Oh, bless the goddess," gasped Caroline. "Since Mary the Archives have been digitized."

In the silence none of them dared to breathe.

"Then why. . ." Sarah began.

"It's not connected to the internet," explained Caroline. "That's why we couldn't find anything online. The Archives are too sensitive. They vet scholars and then invite them on the premises near St. Paul's Cathedral." Caroline's huge green eyes found Anna frowning at her bag where she carried her laptop.

"The Archives are shut until tomorrow," Sarah said, looking at her phone. "You, I mean *we*, can't search the catalogue. It's not accessible to the public. Anna. . .?"

"No," said Anna. "Not with Caroline's machine. Unfortunately, the wife of Lir interferes."

"There is a public terminal for a limited search in the Lobby," said Caroline, remembering.

Anna showed her teeth in a wicked grin. "Anna and wife of Lir will quench that fire."

"Firewall. Good. Tomorrow then," said Caroline. "We'll be there bright and early."

"The day before the solstice," whispered Sarah. As she met the eyes of her companions, she could see the same fear.

The solstice was an unstoppable river of blood on the horizon. Caroline caught a new note in the roar of the city. Somewhere, far away, the sky was splintered by thunder.

CHAPTER 35
TOWER OF RAIN

Mary lost track of the days. The summer solstice must be close. Perching in front of her, Simmy refused to confirm or deny whether it was the 20th of June. Rather, she lectured Mary about this part of Celtic London.

"Oxleas Wood is eight thousand years old. Even to the Celts it was ancient. To them it was holy ground."

Talk of the Celts increased Mary's sense of threat. Simmy in black ignored Mary's attempts at reasoned argument. They were a meter apart on battered wooden chairs. Over the last couple of days, Simmy had dropped the ski mask and cut the punishing ties on Mary's ankles. Free hands and feet helped with eating and bodily necessities. She was dissuaded from rushing Simmy by the rope tying her waist to the iron ring in the stone walls. At least its length now allowed her to reach the light switch.

Mary was both glad and pained by the artificial light. Every time the bulb flickered, only to flood the room— every time, she knew herself more cut off from the natural light of day. She missed waking in the summer dawn. And she longed for real night. She ached for Caroline's earnest fascination with the moon as cycles of death and rebirth. She even regretted Anna's scorn for her skepticism.

What Simmy did not know was that Mary had a plan. She had found shards of bottle glass down a crack in the floor. Every time she was alone, she sawed at the thick rope that held her. Now she fished for more clues about what was outside the cellar door: her strategy for escape was almost complete.

Mary sniffed. "I don't need more history, Simmy. We're not in class now."

Too tart?

Mary tried again. "Simmy, why are you trying to confuse me? You said, we're in London. Now it's some mythical forest. How can I rely on anything you Celts say?" Mary took another swig from the water bottle. She was lean and hungry from the diet of rye bread and water. At least her caffeine headache was starting to wear off.

"Coffee would be. . ." she began.

"This was once a castle." Simmy was staring through Mary's head to another world. "In Oxleas Wood, now part of Southeast London. During the eighteenth-century highwaymen would attack the rich travelers on Shooters Hill down the road. The robbers were rounded up and kept here until they could be taken to the Clink. You know," she glanced at Mary. "That old prison by the Thames. It's a museum today."

"With gruesome banners and bloody chains to attract the tourists," Mary added. She remembered the Clink. After all, she used to live in London. Weekdays working into the night, she'd slip through the streets to her second-floor apartment in a Victorian house. Weekends she ignored her loneliness by walking.

For an instant Mary wished she was back striding through cobbled alleyways and along the Thames towpaths. No time for daydreams, Mary scolded herself. She resumed her casual manner.

"Umm, so this, er, castle was a prison too," said Mary. "That would account for these iron rings. How. . .how convenient. Is it close to a main road?"

"Convenient, yes." Simmy refused to react to sarcasm. "Let me explain why we are here, Miss Wandwalker." Simmy the teacher was the mask she had not taken off.

"All that remains of the castle is a watchtower surrounded by trees. My father used to bring his students here during our festivals. Winter solstice was my favorite when the trees are naked." She took a breath. "We'd climb to the top and see what was once— and WILL be— a Celtic city."

She leaned forward. "From the top of this tower you can see the three sacred hills of London." Mary tensed. "From one of these, we. . .that is, the Reborn Celts, will open the door to the Otherworld at summer solstice. We will release the lost river, the goddess Eponia."

She turned her remote expression on Mary. "It's the culmination of our work: the Blood Rising. The rite means everything to Colin."

Simmy flushed. She got up to leave.

"What about me?"

The words flowed unbidden from Mary's fear. Simmy paused for a second.

Mary leapt to her feet. "Why did your father kill himself?"

Simmy turned around. With no warning she threw up her head and cawed like a crow. The cry tore through Mary, a lightning bolt of hot pain. Then silence. Mary had diverted the polluted river between them.

Simmy's jet black jacket flapped. Jamming her hands into pockets, her head tipped as if she had a beak and talons. Mary raised her chin. Her life was at stake.

"Why the Thames?" she whispered into Simmy's inhuman eyes. "Why did he jump into the Thames just there, at Waterloo Bridge?"

"My father," the words rasped. "My father sacrificed his life-blood to the river to save. . ." She choked. The human Simmy was back, enraged. "He ruined our family! This Blood Uprising is the true sacrifice, Colin says."

She strode out, banging the cellar door. Mary winced at the scrape of the key in the lock. She'd wanted to ask about Rhiannon and Joe Griffith. She'd hadn't dared. There was something vulnerable as well as dark in Simmy. Mary was left wondering about Simmy's place in the Morrigan family, as well as her role in The Reborn Celts.

Today, Simmy reminded Mary of Anna. She had once said: "Trust the body of your enemy. The body does not lie. Most people," she'd looked directly at Mary, "most people do not know how to make the body lie."

Mary remembered how she'd seen how Colin mirrored Joe. He was desperate to be like Joe, the warrior, she realized. Would that impel Colin to kill? She remembered Caroline's account of the storm that frustrated the sexual rite, and Colin's rage. That too was part of the story of Simmy and Colin.

It went without saying that Anna, the trafficked woman, could make her body a skilled participant in deception. Mary, alone in the cellar, tried not to think about beheading; tried instead to understand Simmy's body. What roused the crow in her? What was behind that talk of blood?

"You have to live it yourself, in your body," Anna had said. "It's not a thinking. It is being in the bones that soaks the flesh. It is re-creation."

Mary sat gingerly in Simmy's chair and tried the stiff posture of her captor. Then she retraced the moves to the door. Yes, even the twisting of mouth and eyes that suggested a beak with blood on it. When she imitated that sound (more quietly), that tearing crow noise, it had come from the predatory curve in her spine. Was that why Simmy dodged the question that every prisoner asks: What about me? Will you set me free? Will you let me live? Simmy had indeed disconnected from the human world.

This glimpse of Simmy's wild nature was not reassuring. There was also that story about Simmy's lover taking away their child. Mary shivered. Then she glared at the locked door and took out the biggest piece of glass from her pocket.

There were a couple of other jailers besides Simmy. Mary assumed these hooded figures were like Colin's dead parents, believers whose obedience took them across the line into crime. Now, given that Simmy had brought more bread and emptied the damn bucket, Mary judged that she had time to finish sawing

252

the rope. The next stage would be to dispose of the maddening lightbulb.

Approximately two hours later, the door opened again. Mary held her breath while gloved fingers felt around for the light switch. A click. Nothing. A surprised grunt. The person dropped his package of water bottles and stepped further into the room. Before he could pull out a torch, Mary slipped out from behind out the door. She took immense pleasure in locking it with the captor inside. At once, there was a yell and a hammering.

"Gav is that you 'aving a larf! Open the door. Gimme the torch!"

No torch. Serves him right. He can't be sure she was gone. Not in the dark, not at once. Thank goodness the door is solid oak, thought Mary.

She darted up the stairs, her breath sobbing. Please let there be a way outside. The steep winding staircase smelled different than the cellar, an earthy fragrance. Gasping, Mary's chest hurt by the time she reached the top. Daylight, the blessed outside was calling. The tower's door was ajar. Mary filled her lungs with the breath of trees, and the fainter diesel. London traffic, what joy.

She was about to run out when she caught voices, voices very close. She was frozen behind the open door. Noooo. Noooo, she wailed silently.

"He's down checking on her now. I wonder what's taking so long?" A man's voice. Mary dared not breathe. Quickly, she removed her shoes and held them in each hand.

"You back yet, Steve?" He was suspicious. And closer. Mary flattened herself to the wall. "OK, Steve, another five minutes and I'll be down!"

The male voice was moving away, and Mary heard a match strike. The smoky odor took on a hint of tobacco. He was having a cigarette! A sliver of possibility remained. If the men outside would wander, she might just be able to. . .

Mary jumped back. He was coming. He would go to the cellar for Steve and find her gone. All Mary could do was hide further up the stone staircase that continued to wind above her. Mary half ran, half climbed, holding her shoes with one hand, and using the other to balance on the cool walls.

Her body felt like a sack of stones; blood drained into her feet, then trickled out. Yes, her feet were bleeding, leaving telltale smears. On and on she climbed, until she saw a flicker that grew into square. The trap door to the watch tower platform had been propped open.

Mary pushed through her head. Water cooled her hot cheeks in a fine wet drizzle. It was raining. How could it be raining? It had not rained in England for five months.

She scrambled out onto the wooden floorboards and made for the battlements. Spreading beech trees dwarfed the tower, even though it was built on a low rise. An overgrown rose garden lapped the stone walls. To the right, she glimpsed the road to Shooter's Hill between branches. And it was certainly raining.

Mary lifted her head to the first rainclouds for six months and her first daylight in many days. She wanted to lie flat and let the water soak into her aching limbs. It was starting to wash the blood off her feet. From a tiny porthole in the entwined beech and oak of Oxleas Wood, London loomed. As the leaves flickered with drops of water, Mary spotted domes, spires, pyramids, and glass of the historic and fantastic city. Time contracted like her vision. The porthole vanished as fog rolled in from the Thames. Mary was left in a world of air and water.

Mary kept staring into the fog. She tried to remember Simmy's three Celtic hills of London. Was that a darker mound beyond the skyscrapers? Oh, it was too hard. Mary sank back onto the slimy wet boards.

The rain beat down harder. It did not muffle the sound of boots on stone. She had nowhere to hide. Oh, the irony of rain, rain at last, what she, Caroline and Anna had hoped for. Despite her imminent recapture, Mary felt something stir.

Rain after drought brought her closer to Caroline who had been learning rain rituals at Holywell. Caroline wrapped herself in rain that night on the field trip when Joe Griffith died. Rain had no effect on Anna. Where were Caroline and Anna? Mary's jaw tightened. They would never give up. She knew that in *her* wild bones.

Mary watched a man climb out of the trapdoor. She would not yell or throw herself off the tower. She showed no fear. He leered through his mask.

"Thought you could get away, did you? No way. You are for the Blood Rising. The Celts promised it will make this country white again."

All Mary could see of him was olive hands waving a baseball bat. Mary did not think that this was a moment to bring up irony and skin color.

"It's alright. I'll come down," she heard herself say, even though the sky was falling. The ski mask nodded. Mary collected her shoes. Although they hurt her grazed feet, she'd wear them anyway. She was just starting to climb down when the man spoke again.

"Simmy says to make you coffee."

Mary bowed her head, then carried on down the steps. Coffee was her fuel of choice. Just what were the Reborn Celts fueling her for?

CHAPTER 36
MR. JEFFREYS AT THE ARCHIVES

At the time Mary was slipping out of the cellar, Anna was entering the lobby of a classical style building close to St. Paul's Cathedral. She homed in on the old-fashioned computer terminal and, after a slow start, her fingers rained down on the keys. Soon the firewall into the restricted databases was mere flotsam on the tide. Anna grinned.

The temple-like headquarters of the National Archive had once been Sir Christopher Wren's Library. Employees joked that the magisterial Mr. Jeffreys had been there at its inauguration. They used to say that he found the Chief Archivist, the formidable Miss Wandwalker, already at work in its vaults, where its documents, letters, telegrams, files, reports, tapes, treaties, and of course maps, were stored underground. Over the centuries, the original cellars and vaults sprouted extension tunnels that crisscrossed the Square Mile of the original City of London. An indiscreet civil servant once complained that the Archives took up more space under the city than Roman London had above. Most of the collection required high security clearance.

Caroline hugged her chest in gratitude at the return of Anna, her very own computer goddess. At last Anna was herself enough to use her extraordinary prowess. Caroline and Mary both believed that Anna had mysterious cyber-powers. If anyone could dive down to ancient London's maps it would be Anna.

After a few minutes, Anna's black eyes were enormous. She could climb into this old box and disappear into the veins of

257

code, thought Caroline. Just as London's rivers sunk themselves into the bedrock to be forgotten.

Across the street Sarah and Caroline were pretending to browse in St. Paul's Cathedral Bookshop while keeping watch for the Reborn Celts. In fact, they were too anxious to concentrate. Caroline insisted it was their last chance to save Mary. If Anna could not find the Eponia they would have to involve the police. They had twenty-four hours until the solstice.

To herself, Caroline had set a deadline of six p.m. She and Sarah tried not to glance at Anna. Visible from the side, her hands flickered over the computer. Her anxiety rising, Caroline's squishy insides were electrifyingly in tune with Anna's frenzied fingers.

Sarah was glued to a book on menstrual magic when Caroline stiffened.

"Look, Sarah."

A hissing sound came from the open door. Big drops hit the hot pavement and instantly evaporated, followed by more and more. From the sour sky came the wrecking sound that reminded Caroline of the hillside falling.

"What's that noise?" said Sarah wondering. "Can it be rain?"

"No, not rain. I mean, yes, rain, a storm. That was thunder." Caroline took hold of Sarah's arm, "Look who's found Anna."

No longer at the terminal, Anna tossed her head at an imposing-looking man. His suit gleamed even more than the wet streets. It was Mr. Jeffreys. Caroline groaned. She was kicking herself for not realizing that Anna could be spotted from *inside* the building. There must be cameras in the lobby.

"Isn't that Mr. Jeffreys?"

"I'm afraid so," said Caroline.

"Anna's waving us over. Shall we make a run for it.?"

"Certainly not," said Caroline, feeling like Mary. "We have to support Anna. She'll have told him about Mary by now. He'll be incandescent. Come on Sarah. Put that book down. Janet doesn't want you reading that stuff."

Three minutes later Caroline and Sarah caught up with Mr. Jeffreys and Anna. Under raised eyebrows, Mr. Jeffreys held the door open to the elevator. His expression suggested a complex set of emotions. Caroline decided to save explanations for Mr. Jeffreys office. After he unlocked the door, the women fell into the room, and into speech.

"Mr. Jeffreys, we can explain. There's an important development. . ."

"Mary, it's Mary. I see her now."

"Whaaaat?"

Caroline and Mr. Jeffreys rounded on Anna. She had taken command of the room from dead center. Caroline put her hand to her mouth. Mr. Jeffreys was less impressed.

"What did you say, Vronsky? If you are involved in Mary's disappearance. . ." Mr. Jeffreys swiveled to pounce on Caroline. "As for you not informing me that she. . ." He choked, thunderous.

Anna paid him no attention. She was concentrating on something the others could not see.

"Mary, I see you. Tell me where you are?"

"Stop this nonsense at once." Mr. Jeffreys was threatening. Sarah shrank back, Caroline stepped towards Anna.

"Anna. . .?"

Anna turned to her with blazing eyes.

"I am wife of Lir. She, Wandwalker the crone, she is with me."

Mr. Jeffreys crashed his fist on his beautiful desk. Sarah jumped. Mr. Jeffreys stomped around to take his chair, his bulk blocking the window. He glared at all three women.

"I will not. . .I will not have. . ." He was at a loss for words. Caroline was astonished.

At last Anna noticed him. "You made me lose wife of Lir, Mary was about to speak." She folded her arms again, like Mary.

"Sit down, all of you," ordered Mr. Jeffreys through gritted teeth.

Caroline's knees shook as she sat, whereas Anna stared through Jeffreys at the increasing rain out of the window behind him. Sarah retreated to the door while Mr. Jeffreys struggled to regain his composure.

"Now Mrs. Jones, let me start with you. You're the sensible one, or so I used to think. Just what have you done with Wandwalker? No, shut up, Vronsky, or I'll have Inspector Walbrook take you to the cells."

Caroline searched for the right words. For days she had agonized over where Mary could be. She looked at Anna, whose scorn was palpable. Caroline was comforted. She had not seen Anna so much like her old self for weeks.

"Mrs. Jones? I'm losing patience."

"Kidnapped, Mary's been kidnapped." Caroline was weary. Emotion did that to her.

"There's not much time. We are almost at the solstice," said Anna.

"Kidnapped? That's what Vronsky said in the Lobby. What's the solstice got to do with it?"

Mr. Jeffreys leaned forward; his expression unreadable. "You had better tell me everything from the beginning, Mrs. Jones. Leave nothing out. I called that Holywell witch of yours when I couldn't get hold of Wandwalker. She says Vronsky needs another dose of the antidote she's cooked up. I've had people looking for you."

He banged the desk again. "God in heaven, If Mary was taken, why oh why didn't you call me? Or the police?"

"They said they'd kill her," said Caroline. "We didn't want to risk contacting you. She's going to be a sacrifice at the solstice the day after tomorrow. They're making her the next victim after Rhiannon and Joe Griffith."

Jeffreys opened his mouth to shout again. Caroline held up her hand. "No, no more shouting, please. We'll tell you everything. Listen. Please listen. Don't get angry until I've finished."

Mr. Jeffreys grunted, his dark palms flat on the desk, body taut. After Caroline began, he leaned back and took out his phone. Motioning Caroline to continue, he started tapping at the screen. Even the tapping sounded like orders. Anna interjected a few words and was told to be quiet. When Caroline finished describing their hunt for the Eponia, Sarah crept from the door and pulled up a chair.

"So, you see, Anna was trying to get into the restricted maps in the Archives to find out where they might be taking Mary."

A scowl passed over Anna at "trying." Caroline did not notice. "We know it's all about tomorrow, June 21st, the summer solstice. The Reborn Celts have been talking about this Uprising or Blood Rising ceremony for weeks, it's their third rite. We know it involves. . .um, what they call waking or setting free water from under the ground. This time it's not a well, like in Exmoor College. They're going to bring a river back to life here in London. The river Eponia was once sacred to the Celts. The problem. . ." Caroline faltered.

"Go on." Mr. Jeffreys was no longer on his phone. His eyes drilled into Caroline. She almost expected high pressure water to follow.

Caroline swallowed. "They think they need blood. Sacrifices. First a virgin. . ."

Anna snorted.

"Then a warrior; that was Joe Griffith on the field trip. Then a crone. So, they plan to sacrifice Mary. Her lifeblood will feed the lost river, the Eponia.

"What?" Mr. Jeffreys snapped.

"Well, it all fits, you see. We did a dream divination and Janet said. . ."

"Harrumph." Mr. Jeffreys snort resembled Anna's. His sentiment did not. "Dreams. Give me strength. *Where is Wandwalker?*"

"High," said Anna.

"Erm, we don't know. She'll be at the source of the Eponia on the solstice. . .we believe." Caroline's voice wobbled. Then she realized that Anna had spoken. "Did you say high, Anna?"

"High."

"You mean they've drugged her?" Mr. Jeffreys was furious again. "Mary Wandwalker drugged."

"Ha," said Anna, as if she had caught him out. "No drugs yet. She is somewhere high up. I see sky, tops of trees, rain on her face."

"I suppose that's another of your dream visions," growled Mr. Jeffreys. He continued. "Thankfully we have, no scrub that, *I* have better resources than drug-fueled ramblings and mythical rivers." Then he went back to tapping on his phone.

"Not a mythical river," came a quiet voice. Three heads turned to Sarah. "Miss Wandwalker knows the Eponia. It goes into the Thames just where Rhiannon's body was found. She saw the river washing the body. Well, that is, without the head. Miss Wandwalker was. . . Miss Wandwalker *is*. . .haunted by Rhiannon."

Sarah spoke with a little of Mary's dignity. Mr. Jeffreys looked hard at her. He waited until she'd finished before scrolling again.

"I found it." Anna put her hand on Caroline's arm. At that moment the window blazed behind Mr. Jeffreys. A molten fork shot wild electricity into London. Caroline held Anna's arm very tightly.

"You found the Eponia?" Caroline whispered. Thunder rolled over the city and Caroline's exclamation. Mr. Jeffreys was not spooked. He scrutinized Caroline.

"The source of the Eponia," corrected Anna when the sky had drained of noise. "I found the spring on the oldest map in the Archives. It took extra decoding to read the symbols."

Sarah edged closer. Caroline almost stumbled over her words. She knew that Anna was baiting Mr. Jeffreys, but it was Mary who mattered now.

"Anna, where is it? Where are the Reborn Celts taking Mary?"

Anna was tracking Mr. Jeffreys with her large black eyes.

"I will not tell unless you listen," she shot at him.

"And why should I pay attention to a murder suspect?"

"Because Mary would."

That made Jeffreys put his phone down. Sighing, he nodded at Anna.

"Proceed."

"Eponia's spring is buried on Parliament Hill; one of the three Celtic Hills of London. The hill is part of Hampstead Heath."

"I know it," said Jeffreys impatiently. "You're certain Parliament Hill is the right one?"

"Tower Hill is almost gone. Celts built the first towers by the great river to protect the city. The head of King Bran is buried underneath. He is why there must be ravens. If they ever leave, then the city will fall." Anna enjoyed an audience. "There is another Celtic mound. You call it Primrose Hill. It is not where the Eponia goes, because a Roman map records a different direction. Then I found the map with the most magic. Earlier than Roman. It has the whole course of the river. And. . ."

Anna paused for effect. Caroline wanted to shake her. "It begins in a Celtic shrine with a horse symbol, on Parliament Hill. This Eponia's spring is another sacred well." Anna folded her hands and waited. Caroline spoke first.

"The Reborn Celts are going to make it like Tower Hill," she said in horror. They are going to dig up the river source and behead Mary."

"Her head will be thrown into the new well," agreed Anna.

"Why Mary?" Mr. Jeffreys was talking to himself. Caroline answered.

"They called her a crone. After Rhiannon, a maiden. . ."

Anna snorted again.

"A maiden," repeated Caroline, "and Joe Griffith, a warrior.
. .He was in the army. In fact, he saved Dr. Wiseman's life in
Afghanistan. You know him, don't you, Mr. Jeffreys."

"Mary's a crone? She won't like that." Mr. Jeffreys wasn't
buying it.

"It's not just that she's so old." This was Sarah. She, a
mere twenty, could call Mary old to her face. "They see her as a
queen. Like that other head, Anna. The one at Tower Hill."

"Bran, the Celtic king and his ravens? Perhaps." Mr.
Jeffreys stared at Sarah.

Anna turned to practicalities. "We rescue Mary. At night,
at the solstice."

"You will do no such thing," thundered Mr. Jeffreys.
"Amateurs. Give me strength." He strode across his enormous
office until he could mutter into his phone out of the women's
hearing.

"Yes, weapons, trained officers," they heard. "Get
everything ready to move in tomorrow. I want the entirety of
Hampstead Heath locked down six hours before sunset."

Mr. Jeffreys returned to his chair facing the women. The
desk between them was bare, even free of dust. Caroline did
not need to look beyond Mr. Jeffreys for the rain. The streaming
windows were reflected on the pristine oak.

"You're trusting us about Parliament Hill?" Caroline found
that hard to believe.

"Of course not," said Mr. Jeffreys. "Well, not just you," he
conceded. You'll remember Frederic North, Rhiannon's father?
His lawyers have been in constant contact." Mr. Jeffreys' lips
gave a wry twist that Mary would have recognized. "First thing
they did was to hire operatives in London. From a *very* different
outfit than your Enquiry Agency."

Caroline nodded. She did not want him to stop. He didn't.

"Due to certain. . .shall we say. . .friends in common, these
men, and they are all men, Miss Vronsky. . ." Anna tossed her
head. "These men with certain *unusual* skills were persuaded
to work with me. They've been tailing the lunatic fringe of the

Reborn Celts since the death of Griffiths. It so happens that they have mentioned unauthorized digging on Hampstead Heath. I will admit that your information, Miss Vronsky, has clarified the situation."

Anna radiated satisfaction.

"Now, as to the solstice itself. Yes, we have word of something big. All the Reborn Celts have been told to prepare fire and water rituals. The chatter is the solstice will be "fertilized by blood." Mr. Jeffreys quoted with revulsion. "If these men cannot locate Mary before noon tomorrow, I will supplement their resources from Special Branch, and lead the raid myself."

Caroline was astounded. "Not you, Mr. Jeffreys."

Anna remained enigmatic; Sarah lost.

Mr. Jeffreys ignored Caroline. "As for you three, you will make your way back to Oxford tonight. There you will wait." He held up a hand. "Wait for me to return Miss Wandwalker to you. This is not a negotiation. Do you understand?"

Caroline got to her feet and the others followed. Rain had washed away much of the daylight. Another flash of lightning could have showed Mr. Jeffreys something pertinent, had he cared to watch the women. Caroline paused at the door.

"Very well, Mr. Jeffreys," she said. "At a time like this, it is up to us to do what Mary would do."

It said a lot for Mr. Jeffreys' anxieties that he did not ponder this remark. Instead, he leaned back in his massive chair and waved the women away. He was speaking into his phone before the closed the door behind them.

"We're not going to Oxford," said Anna in the elevator. It was a statement of fact.

"No, we're not," agreed Caroline. She was resolved. "We're going to do what Mary would do – pay no attention to Mr. Jeffreys when one of us is in danger. I can't bear thinking about it," she added. "A bunch of men with guns who don't even know what Mary looks like. Far, far too dangerous! She needs *us.*"

Anna worked her phone. "I booked us into a hotel in Hampstead. Very expensive. Overlooks Parliament Hill. See." After thrusting the photo at Caroline, she led the way out of the Archives building. For a moment, the three stood with their faces up to the rain. It was a silent tribute to Anna's image of Mary somewhere high up. No words were exchanged.

They followed signs to the nearest Tube Station. The violence of the storm had passed over, leaving a steady downpour to soak into the parched trees and the city parks. Several miles to the north, late dog walkers were venturing onto Parliament Hill.

"If the hotel is expensive. . ." began Sarah, as their train dived back into a tunnel.

"Oh, we're not *paying*," said Caroline. She was far more blasé than Mary about Anna's disregard of the law. "Found details of our suite. Great choice, Anna. We'll pop into one of those organic delis for food so we can keep a low profile in Hampstead. As for tomorrow night, Anna, you can get us past any kind of barrier, can't you?"

"Wife of Lir can."

"Ah," said Caroline, less confident.

They exited West Hampstead Tube Station onto wet evening streets. None of them had coats or umbrellas. Sarah shivered, her soaked jeans rubbing her thighs. Caroline was too preoccupied to worry about water frizzing her faded copper curls, while Anna was reveling in the kiss of water on her skin. Or was that the wife of Lir smelling the rain on her own hair? Caroline decided not to ask. Crawling traffic and mist marked their approach to the three Victorian Houses that made up Hampstead Heights Hotel. None of the women noticed they were being followed.

CHAPTER 37
DEATH BY WATER

Once again Mary was tied up in the dark. No light, and the rope looped through ankles, waist and hands restricted her movement. It bound her— tighter this time— to the ring on the wall. They weren't taking any chances.

Fear is exhausting, thought Mary. Too worn out to try shifting her position, the cold of the stone floor seeped into her cheek. Don't sniff, she reminded herself. The last time she's tried to clear her nose she'd inhaled sticky dust. Most unpleasant was coughing with hands tied behind.

"It won't be long, now," Simmy had said hours ago. "They'll bring you food in the morning, and again before the sacrifice." Her voice had been gentle in the pitch-dark room. She'd made a point of telling the masked man, Gav, or was it, Steve? not to pull too tight. He did anyway. Mary gritted her teeth instead of whining.

"She'll be OK until tomorrow night," he'd said.

They left her, having made sure she could use that stinking bucket. Mary heard one set of steps pause at the door. At least her mouth was free.

"Simmy please. . .let's talk. . .These men are racists. That's not you!"

"Colin has some unfortunate friends," she dismissed. "Reborn Celts are not racist. No one pays attention to the white supremacists."

Mary wanted to argue. A wave of exhaustion stalled her.

"It won't be long," Simmy said again. "Just wait, Miss Wandwalker. Death by water is a privilege. Only for a few. You are a gift to sanctify our Blood Rising. I almost envy you."

The door banged. She was gone before Mary could say that she was willing to forego the honor.

Yuck. It was that voice. Mary ignored it.

Tired of the cold, Mary tried maneuvering into a sitting position. Grunting, she managed to wrench upright and find the wall to rest her head. If only the voice would drown.

Mary, Mary, always contrary.

Mary shut her eyes. Big mistake: now the voice had a head, a gapping mouth surrounded by rotting flesh. Bathed in eerie radiance, the hair was greenish, framing black and purple discolored flesh.

"Go away, Rhiannon," said Mary aloud. "I want to be alone."

No, you don't. You hate being alone; you're terrified of it.

"I lived alone for forty years," said Mary, furious.

The decaying mouth showed yellow teeth. Yeah, because you gave away your baby.

Mary's wail had a baby's cry in it. She bit her lips and longed to stuff her fingers into her mouth. The rope dug into her wrists behind her back. She squeezed her eyes to dissolve them. Anything to block that hateful face and voice.

You've punished yourself for forty years. You're terrified of dying alone. Even worse is the pain of what you did. So, no one gets too close. Even Caroline and Anna.

"*Shut up,*" yelled Mary. "Stop. You fucking demon. You're not real. Get out of my head. Now *fuck off.*"

Mary rocked herself, straining against the rope. A cold ache enveloped her shoulders. All that pulling and wriggling simply added more strained muscles. At least the physical pain distracted her from the that damn voice.

While I'm here, you are not alone.

"Go away."

Mary made one last attempt to force her wrists apart. No good. That slipperiness must be blood. The scabs have opened. She flopped back down, careful to put her other cheek on the floor. I'll just go mad, she thought. Perhaps I can't get rid of her. They'll cut my head off with this fiend laughing inside it.

You're not crazy, said the malicious voice. I'm here because it's your fault I'm dead. Now you are going to die like me. They're gonna make a new well for you.

Mary's words flowed where they wanted to. "You can't be Rhiannon. She was an American teenager with too much make up. Her body is locked in a steel drawer." Mary took a breath as a new thought surfaced.

"Are you, whoever you are, behind Simmy, Barin and the Reborn Celts? Was it you all along?"

Of course, I'm Rhiannon, said the voice with the energy and life that was ebbing from Mary. I'm what Rhiannon has become.

The head closed its eyes and sank back into the dark waters. Bile in Mary's throat was diluted by salty liquid. She swallowed. Water rose, sweeter this time. Then came Rhiannon, not the putrefying head, but the girl, restored. She was dressed in the same clothes as their first meeting.

"I'm sorry," Mary found herself saying. "I am sorry I did not keep you safe. I didn't like you. I've said it before. When I was safe in bed. Because I felt guilty. Because it was what I was supposed to say. I thought I meant it."

Blood from Mary's wrists dribbled onto her dusty suit. She was going to die. She was going to die *in dirty clothes*.

"Rhiannon, I'm scared. I'm sorry about what happened to you. I did not— care— for you—as I ought to have."

Poor Mary Wandwalker. It was mockery. And not.

Rhiannon's inscrutable face glimmered.

"I still don't like you," said Mary, surprised at her words.

I don't like you either, came the reply.

The water in Mary's throat flowed onto her parched tongue.

"But you'll stay with me?"

Until the end.

CHAPTER 38
THE RESCUERS

On the morning of the summer solstice, Caroline woke up with her arm around Anna. The young woman slept like the dead. That was normal for Anna. Caroline told herself to stop worrying about Anna's recovery, retrieve her arm, and put the kettle on for tea in the next room.

Strewn with their bags and soiled clothes, the room included Sarah asleep on the sofa. The girl's eyelashes began flickering as soon as Caroline turned on the tap. Although assigned a pleasant room on the next floor, Sarah asked if she could sleep closer. Anna sniffed; Caroline agreed at once.

"I don't like London," was all Sarah offered in explanation. Nothing more was required to jog Caroline's recollection. As one of seven trafficked teenagers rescued from a brothel in East London, then Sarah suffered arrest as an illegal immigrant. She and the other young women were confined near Woolwich during the subsequent trial. Afterwards, Holywell provided their refuge.

Caroline spoke as Sarah stretched herself awake.

"We'll head back to Oxford as soon as we get Mary," she said, shoving the plug into the kettle. "Take the first shower, Sarah. I'm hoping Anna will sleep for a few more hours. Janet says rest is the best thing for her, if she won't take that last dose of the antidote. I've got it in my handbag, just in case. Janet texted instructions to my phone."

Sarah nodded. "She sent them to me too."

Throwing off the big t-shirt she'd slept in, Sarah draped a huge white towel around her like a sari. She grinned at sight of herself in the floor length mirror opposite the door. For a second Caroline saw a model on a photoshoot: graceful ebony curves, a tilt of her queenly head above a strapless gown.

Sarah turned and did a curtsey for Caroline. Touched, Caroline was about to speak when she glimpsed the track marks and knife scars. Following Caroline's eyes, Sarah dodged into the bathroom. Caroline hated that her face betrayed her. She sighed and went back to making tea for the two of them.

It all blew up a few hours later with the news from Mr. Jeffreys. His American agents discovered where Mary was imprisoned: an old watchtower in a Southeast London wood. So far, she was unharmed, Mr. Jeffreys assured Caroline on the phone. The Americans had agreed to join forces with Special Branch under his direction. That had been the good news.

The bad came with the information that Mr. Jeffreys judged it too dangerous to rescue Mary from the tower. The Reborn Celts had scattered lookouts throughout Oxleas Wood. They had turned it into a fortress.

His information was that Mary was confined in the cellar. Her location made her too vulnerable to reprisals in the event of a raid. Instead, the plan was to intercept the Celts transporting her to Parliament Hill. In the event of failure, a backup would be provided by a second wave of rescuers stationed on Parliament Hill itself. These men and women were lurking incognito by swimming in the park's outdoor bathing ponds. (Caroline smiled at a vision of a SWAT team in bathing suits).

Perhaps sensing her doubts, Mr. Jeffreys said that the surrounding trees provided cover to store their flak jackets and other equipment. Anna muttered that trees worked for militant Celts too. She was all for setting off to the Watchtower before the Celts moved Mary. Never mind it was late morning in brilliant sunshine. Waiting was not in her nature.

Horrified at Anna going alone in broad daylight, Caroline threw herself in front of the door. There was a fierce exchange, culminating in Anna yelling, Caroline white and pinched. Afterwards, Anna slammed the bedroom door, leaving Caroline drained.

Sarah, who had retreated to the bathroom, emerged with tentative steps. She passed Caroline facial tissues, then, to Caroline's surprise, went after Anna with a mug. After five minutes, Caroline decided that she was too agitated to wait any longer. Yet, before she could get to the door, Sarah came out. She was smiling.

"She's asleep," she whispered.

"What do you mean?" exclaimed Caroline. "Anna's unstoppable in that mood. I was terrified she would push past me."

"Not you," said Sarah. "She would never push past you. Listen, I gave her the last dose of the antidote from your handbag. She got sleepy right away."

"You did what? Sarah, that's dangerous."

"No, Caroline. It's not dangerous at all. I've been texting Janet. She said to put it into ginger ale so Anna wouldn't taste it. I did." Sarah remained composed. "Janet says it won't have so much of an effect as last time. Anna will wake up in a couple of hours."

"She's going to be furious." Caroline was uneasy. Still, if Janet said it was the right thing to do. . . "Thank you, Sarah. I suppose."

At 2 p.m. they roused Anna to eat. Sarah stood at her door with a tea plate piled high with sandwiches from a shop around the corner. Caroline was sitting on the bed jiggling Anna's arm. One dark eye opened, then another.

"Anna, darling. You're, OK? Please say you're OK."

Anna yawned and put on her inscrutable face. She squinted first at Caroline, then Sarah. Caroline heard the bedside clock ticking.

"Ha."

Caroline and Sarah jumped. Anna let loose her wicked laugh. "Wife of Lir say OK." she said.

"Um?" began Caroline.

Anna pulled her in and kissed her quickly on her lips. "Anna is here too," she conceded. "I'm hungry. Give me a sandwich, please."

Just before 6 p.m. came the news they were expecting. For hours no activity had been observed at the watchtower where Mary was confined. At last, Mr. Jeffreys made the call. A couple of agents broke in to discover— nothing at all. The whole building was empty, although Mary Wandwalker's handbag and phone had been tossed and trampled in the cellar.

Mr. Jeffreys admitted to a patch of dried blood on the bag. He emphasized that wound to Mary was probably not severe. He made no comment on his teams missing the Celts moving Mary to Hampstead. Rather, he stated that everything was prepared for an evening raid on Parliament Hill, *well before any funny business*, ended the message.

"Jeffreys's agents are no good," said Anna, with satisfaction. Caroline and Sarah picked up her implied, "I told you so," about her plan to go that morning.

"We have to be there for Mary," accepted Caroline. "At the well site where they... plan to do it."

Sarah held out the paper bags of clothes she'd bought from charity shops that afternoon. Anna grabbed the best quality garments. Black jeans and green silk shirt that fitted her perfectly. Sarah felt comfortable in small size army surplus. She watched with anxiety as Caroline struggled to zip up the trousers she'd picked out.

"No problem, Sarah," puffed Caroline. "No really, you did a great job. These are not too tight at all."

"If you do not drink anything," said a heartless Anna.

"Who needs to drink?" returned Caroline. She had her man's shirt to hide the bulges.

Now they watched for the solstice sun to set. Soon it would soak the sky red before the shortest night of the year.

It was a matter of waiting; the hardest part.

Anna was itching to practice with the wicked six-inch blade she'd carried for years (despite Mary's stern views). In the bathroom, Anna strapped the dagger beneath her jeans. She knew that Caroline was not fooled. Mary would have been.

Caroline and Sarah's defensive devices were pen knives bought for pennies along with the secondhand clothes. They had tried to sharpen them without much success. After all, Mary would be tied up, so the ability to cut her free was imperative. At least this was their plan. Caroline envisaged creeping through the bushes before Mary came to harm. Sarah trusted Caroline. Anna said nothing.

Caroline wouldn't admit it, but she was relying upon her intuition. The witches of Holywell taught ways to extend the mysterious knowing that ended in darkness. More practically, it helped with the tide of fear in her stomach. It must be time to go; soon, very soon.

Sarah gazed at the picture on her phone's screen with longing. It showed the watchtower they now knew had been Mary's prison.

"Don't worry," Caroline whispered, squeezing Sarah's shoulder. "We'll get her back. Safe and bossing us around. You'll see."

Sarah returned a half smile.

The appointed time drew close. Before anyone could say so, they heard heavy footsteps approaching. Worse, the steps were hesitant, as if searching for a particular door. Anna frowned and patted her leg with the knife. Caroline rose to her feet, heart sinking.

Bang, bang. Heavy breathing accompanied the hammering on their door. Sarah was nearest. She shot Caroline a desperate glance as she undid the chain and drew back the bolts.

Mr. Jeffreys stormed in, neck to toe in aquamarine Lycra. Caroline stepped back and covered her mouth at the giant bluebottle. Anna looked him up and down, grinned, and folded her arms. Sarah tried not to giggle.

"I know what you're up to," said Mr. Jeffreys, glaring at Caroline. "I had you followed. Although I could have you arrested, I've decided you could be useful when we get Wandwalker."

He scowled at Sarah and Anna. "I'm coming with you. You will all. . ." he paused, "do what I say. No arguments, no questions."

His blue-clad barrel chest dazzled in the sunlight dying over London. Caroline drew herself up. Just what *would* Mary do? She folded her arms alongside Anna. Sarah followed suit.

"No," said Caroline. She swallowed, then spoke with more firmness. "No, we won't do as you say, Mr. Jeffreys. Mary's too precious for that."

Mr. Jeffreys' eyes widened. He threw out an arm, grabbed a chair and sat, despite the moaning from the wooden legs. Just after his full weight hit the upholstery, he started up again, "Aaaaaaaaargh," he roared.

Caroline recognized the tone.

"Oh, you've hurt your back! Come on, Mr. Jeffreys. Try the other armchair, over here. It's firmer. Sarah, pass those cushions. They give better support. "Poor Mr. Jeffreys. I guess you went to the gym, and it's been a while."

Mr. Jeffreys gritted his teeth as he heaved himself up and onto the other chair. Easing down, his stomach bulged over shiny blue legs. Frowning at the women, he seemed to be at a loss.

"Is that why Special Branch wouldn't let you go with them?" Anna asked without sympathy. "Because you hurt your back? Or is it that you are too old?"

Mr. Jeffreys mumbled something that could have been swear words. After he'd eased his back against the cushions he breathed more easily and nodded to Caroline. She took the chair facing him, while Anna and Sarah leaned against the wall, Sarah mirroring Anna's superior look. Faced with a giant insect unable to move Caroline tried to keep a straight face.

"We've got a few minutes," she said. "Before we set out, that is. So, Mr. Jeffreys," she inquired of the human bluebottle, "you went to the gym?"

"Yes," said Mr. Jeffreys, rubbing the small of his back. "First I discovered how long it had been. And then my back did."

He sighed. Then he glanced at Anna. "You're right, Miss Vronsky. Special Branch told me I was too old to go on the raid. *That's* when I went to the gym."

"Ah," said Caroline, understanding. "Well, if you can walk, you can come with us. . ."

"Wife of Lir say no," Anna hissed. "He not one of us."

"None of you should be on the Heath." Mr. Jeffreys heaved another sigh. "Leave it to the professionals. You're. . .you're. . ."

Caroline felt Mary watching her. "Yes, Mr. Jeffreys? We are what?" There was a pause.

"Untrained."

"Do you mean women? We're just women?"

"I mean untrained," he snapped. "Kidnapping is a serious business."

"Yes, but this isn't," said Sarah unexpectedly. "Business, I mean. For these people."

They all looked at her in surprise.

"I was kidnapped. They took me from my family and my village. To them it was just business," she said. "Your men," Jeffreys frowned. "These professionals could have stopped them. . ." she looked at Caroline for the right word. The older woman smiled, encouraging.

"Effectively," Caroline said.

"That's right. Effectively. You see, I've thought about this a lot." Sarah stopped, noticing three pairs of eyes waiting. Emboldened, she continued. "Businesspeople, even criminals in business, they know the rules. Know how kidnappers behave and what the police do. They know how to work so that people don't die. But now, tonight, the Celts who have Mary are. . ."

"Amateurs," said Caroline.

"Terrorists," said Mr. Jeffreys.

"Dangerous," said Anna.

"Yes, that's it," Sarah continued. "They're dangerous because it's not a business. It's everything to them. Their whole world is on Parliament Hill tonight." We *know* them." She shuffled her chair back behind Caroline's chair, watching for Mr. Jeffreys' reaction.

"I am them," said Anna.

Mr. Jeffreys put his head in his hands. "Oh Mary Wandwalker!" came from between his fingers.

Caroline had a sense of Mary smiling. "You said we're untrained," she said. "That's the exact point. That's why we must be there. We're *un-trained*."

"If you mean," said Mr. Jeffreys, "that you are untrammeled by experience in unarmed combat and hostage negotiation. That you are without toned muscles, tasers, razor sharp *trained* instincts. . ."

"Stop it," Caroline interrupted. "You listen. You with the bad back."

Mr. Jeffreys bit back his retort. Caroline nodded. Always wary of Mr. Jeffreys, now she was acting for Mary, she had to *be* Mary.

"Your men haven't done too well so far, have they? They missed the Reborn Celts taking Mary through London and onto Parliament Hill. No, we haven't time for excuses." Caroline raised her hand, imitating Mary. Mr. Jeffreys closed his mouth. Caroline continued.

"Your team expected the kidnappers to follow usual patterns. They won't. The Reborn Celts are not regular criminals." She slapped a hand on the desk. "They're not even regular people. All the stuff *we* do that you reject: the spells, Janet's herbs, dream divination, even Anna becoming the wife of Lir, it is part of this . . .part of what's happening tonight."

Now it was Mr. Jeffreys who folded his arms. Caroline tried again.

"Look, we're very glad your men plan to rescue Mary. We really are. Perhaps they will succeed. But you need to understand us. We can't leave it to the professionals because it is not about money. It's about craziness." Caroline stood up; her cheeks flushed.

"By the goddess, Mr. Jeffreys, they are going to murder Mary to bring back a river. It's all part of some fantasy that the Celts will save us from the rising seas. They're confused."

Mr. Jeffreys raised his eyebrows. "Confused," he muttered. He stared at each of them in turn. They were serious. Caroline felt her pockets for the penknife and unlocked the door.

"If you can walk, Mr. Jeffreys, you can come with us. Not lead us; rather you will accompany us, because you care about Mary too."

CHAPTER 39
THIRD RITE: THE CRONE
IN THE WOOD

On Parliament Hill, where beech and oak grow thick, Mary Wandwalker strained at the ropes that bound her to a tree. They had taken her shoes. So dense was the undergrowth that everything was still damp from yesterday's storm despite the return to blazing hot weather. Mary wedged her head on the tree trunk and looked up.

Pools of sky were visible through scorched leaves. Blue fading into white would soon turn pink, followed by the dark blue of twilight. Then everything: city, sky and speckled stars would fall into the deep well of the shortest night of the year. To consecrate it, they were going to pour her life into the rediscovered source of the Eponia, a few meters away.

Mary listened while the Celts dug. Their spring so far resembled a muddy pit. Rhiannon said that she'd seen it. She was not impressed.

Perhaps they'll wait until it fills with water, she'd said hopefully. Could be a few days.

"I'll suggest it," Mary croaked. Both knew that the Celts would not forego the solstice as the propitious time for their rite of blood.

Someone's coming, whispered Rhiannon, and dived back down. Mary groaned. She should be working on some last appeal for her life. Unfortunately, her mind was blank as pond water.

The sound of squelching leaves came from behind her. Someone was trying to be quiet. Mary almost choked on the flood of adrenalin. Rescue, it had to be. About time too. Even now the Reborn Celts were building the bonfire next to the pit. Lighting it would begin the ceremonies. The footsteps were very close. She could hear puffing and smell human sweat, male human sweat. She was about to speak when she heard the rasping she longed for. Someone was sawing through the rope.

"Who are you?" whispered Mary. "Try not to pull so much. My wrists hurt already. Did Mr. Jeffreys send you?"

Since it was a man, it could not be Anna or Caroline. Muttered curses reached her. Now Mary knew the voice. One of the last she'd expected. The man crawled on his knees in front of Mary to work on the rope binding her feet.

"Dr. Barin! Why are you doing this? I thought you killed Rhiannon."

That stopped him. He stared at up her, then resumed sawing. Although the clothesline was even tougher than the rope in the cellar, Mary found her arms were almost free. Now if Barin would get a move on. . .

"I'm not a killer," Barin said at last. "They're after me because I took the Sacred Well Torc from the tower." There were more sounds in the woods, human sounds. "I'm not a racist like that Colin. He's evil. He stole my sister; her soul, I mean."

"Well, then, who did kill Rhiannon?" said Mary forcing herself to stay calm. The thumping of booted Celts got louder.

I know. . .! said, Rhiannon, popping up again.

Yes, but you won't tell me, so keep quiet, Mary said soundlessly

"Joe Griffith killed the girl," said Barin, working on the last strand. "Suffocated her first, then lopped off her head for the well. I'd left by then. A couple of his minions took the rest of the body and put it by the Thames the next night."

Mary told herself to keep rubbing her knees and wrists. "On the field trip, Colin went mad and fell on Griffith. I always said that brat was the devil. He was raving after the storm interrupted the er. . .ceremony in the forest. Couldn't bear for Simmy to be touched like that. Afterwards he said killing Joe meant the Celts sacrificing a warrior after the virgin. He insisted on a crone to complete the three. It takes three sacrifices to release a river, you see. Simmy chose you for the crone. She's so under his spell she thinks it's an honor."

"And what about you?"

Mary was free, she staggered forward. Uh-oh, no sensation in her scarred feet. She could not walk. Angry calls came from two directions. With one hand on a branch to hold herself steady, Mary started banging her ankles. She had nothing to put on her bleeding feet. But if the Celts thought that would stop her running away, they were dead wrong.

"Just go!" said Barin, almost as frantic as Mary. "I've got the Torc in my backpack. That's all I've ever wanted. Gold doesn't let you down. It doesn't abandon you or die."

Mary grabbed his arm. "Why didn't you stop the killing? Stop Colin dragging Simmy further and further?" Wobbling, she took a step and bit down on the pain.

"Ever held a tiger by its tail, Miss Wandwalker? Thought not. It's too late to save Simmy. Go right for the nearest park gate." He pulled his arm away and slipped off in the other direction.

Mary managed a few strides before her heel was pierced by an invisible thorn, threading pain across her entire foot. Blood seeped out. She limped on.

She was dizzy by the time the shouting caught up with her. Along with yells and bangs, others were trying to reduce the commotion.

"There he goes! The slimy traitor. Get hold of him, Steve. Colin—"

"Not too loud. We've got him now! Here, hold him still."

Mary dived for a bush. Any snap of a twig would betray her.

It was as if running water went still.

"Simmy, I beg you, just stop. This is madness. Give yourselves up before you're in too deep. You're my sister." The professor's voice quavered.

"Colin's my son. He'll rise as Mabon, God of Light, before tonight is over." Simmy's human part was edging on hysteria; the rest was all Morrigan.

Mary thought she saw the image of a man whose white beard matched the white stone of Waterloo Bridge at dawn. He jumped into the light and down into the underworld.

Mary huddled in a ball. Dreadful, inevitable footsteps converged on her location. Meanwhile, Simmy had not finished with Barin.

"—you're no brother of mine. Not after taking the torc that we need for the sacrifice. It's just money with you. Always money. Our father would disown you."

"He did disown me." Barin was almost in tears. "I would have done anything. I told him we could make fortunes from the stuff he was digging up, like the Sacred Well Torc. He could endow his bloody Celtic Studies forever. No, he had to save the world. . .and recruit crazies and drug addicts like those that spawned this psychopath. . .Ahhh! Stop it, stop it!"

Mary blocked her ears against the cries and grunts of Barin being beaten. His louder screams were cut off. They must have gagged him.

"Enough. Get the backpack. I want to see the Torc." That was Colin.

Mary guessed that was the backpack being stripped off his bruised body.

"Got it, Simmy."

"It's worth millions, Simmy. Don't let him do this to you."

"Shut up, Barin. Traitor to Albert Edward. He's *my* grandfather. Simmy belongs to me. I'm the Morrigan heir. I'm going to be reborn as a god." Colin's voice was shrill. "Dave, let the fat slob have it. The Torc— and the crone— go to the underworld via the sacred well and the river."

"Sure, sure, Colin. No worries."

"Take him to the van," ordered Colin.

"He might need a doctor." That was Simmy. She was cold, yet practical, thinking of the future.

"Later, mother dear," said Colin. "We need to prepare the crone. Her white blood will sanctify a white land."

The Reborn Celts really have gone over to the white supremacists, Mary thought, no matter what Simmy said. If I could just tell Mr. Jeffreys. Colin continued:

"Give me the torc. The sun is almost leaving us. He needs blood to return; her blood and the sacred river."

"The crone's over here," came a voice that sounded inches from Mary's ear. She shut her eyes, hoping that it made her invisible. (You've sure lost it, commented Rhiannon.) The voice close to Mary was a woman's. Mary did not recognize it. With eyes closed, Mary could hear her own ragged breathing.

They were coming. Not as she imagined the ancient Celts, creeping through the trees they revered. These so-called Celts tore through the undergrowth smashing the tiny bones of tree seedlings. Hope the stinging nettles get them, thought Mary, biting back tears. She never cried.

"She's in that bush."

"Got her. Come out of there or we'll drag you by your hair." Colin's satisfaction was hateful. Mary forced herself to open her eyes. On her fists and scabbed knees, she crawled out of the tangle of branches and struggled to her feet. A masked woman stood over her with a pickaxe. Alongside were a couple of men along with Simmy and Colin.

"Mary Wandwalker," began Colin, his mad eyes a darker blue. "Uncle Barin the thief tried to free you. Too late. You have to change history."

"I'll pass," croaked Mary. She would not beg for her life from him.

Colin held the golden torc to his lips then placed it around Mary's neck. She tried not to flinch at his sour breath. Too sticky for beer; mead perhaps.

"With this torc you are ready for the gods. With your blood, I will be reborn as Mabon, Son of Light."

Mary wanted to spit at him, but her throat was too dry.

"The waters do not rise for you," she heard from her own mouth. Rhiannon was speaking now.

CHAPTER 40
IN ANOTHER PART OF THE FOREST

They were walking single file towards the oldest part of the forest. Anna led because she had found the trail. Bringing up the rear was Sarah, who tapped Caroline's arm and pointed at Mr. Jeffreys. "Those blue legs," she whispered. Her eyes were alight. Caroline patted her hand. Before they'd set out Mr. Jeffreys had peeled off his blue Lycra top, replacing it with a chocolate shirt of Caroline's. It was the one item that had a hope of making him less visible.

Mary called it Caroline's "comfort shirt," worn when she felt too large to wear anything else. Even this garment had begun to split across Mr. Jeffreys shoulders. It was ridiculous, Caroline knew, but she wanted to rip it off him. Instead of wearing it, she would hold it to her breast as if it were alive.

Nerves, she said to herself. At Sarah's giggling Anna stopped, waiting for the party to regroup. She stabbed a fallen log with her knife. Spurred by familiar jolt of anxiety, Caroline pushed past Mr. Jeffreys.

"Anna," Caroline hissed. "What are you doing? Be careful with that knife."

"Testing." Anna stopped stabbing the log. She pulled Caroline into deep shadow and kissed her on the lips.

"P. . .put the knife away," gasped Caroline. Anna laughed soundlessly. She could do that.

"Be quiet." That was Mr. Jeffreys, off his phone at last. He did not know how *not* to give orders, thought Caroline.

"Tracks to the left. We move closer to the well," said Anna. "It's time. Wife of Lir say." Without waiting for a response, she slipped into the dimness between the trees.

"She's invisible." That was Sarah.

Caroline grabbed her arm. "When she wants to be. Come on, we're going to follow."

Mr. Jeffreys coughed, making Caroline pause. Not another confrontation. His brown eyes met hers. He shrugged. On tiptoe, trying to avoid cracking sticks, they entered the forest into which Anna had disappeared. Caroline noticed that Mr. Jeffreys began to relax. Plus, he was checking for footprints. Mud churned in yesterday's storm turned to pliable clay. Today, in between stones, moss, and leaves, the occasional boot print betrayed a human presence.

It must be the Celts, Caroline hoped. The prints were sunken, so perhaps the owners were carrying something heavy. Like digging equipment, or a woman. Mr. Jeffreys nodded at the fresh indentations.

He did have military training, Caroline remembered Mary telling her. That's how he knew Jez Wiseman. Although hardly contemporaries, Mr. Jeffreys' work in intelligence had connected with Wiseman in Afghanistan. He's a panther, rather than a beetle, she decided, comforted. Mary's smile pulled her forward to where the trees grew closer together and the darkness flowed into them.

CHAPTER 41
SOLSTICE LATE

Night descended on Mary, alone and surrounded by crazed people. I've had enough of being tied to walls and trees, she thought. Here she was against yet another tree. All she could tell was that it wasn't an oak. This new trunk had smooth bark and was slender enough that they could tie her wrists together behind it.

It's an ash tree, came the voice from below.

"Where've you been?" said Mary, sick of her fear. "It's been hours. I've not got much time, you know."

Hey, even a ghost needs a break said Rhiannon. And you can't be using me to avoid what's happening. It doesn't work like that. Watch.

Mary watched.

Despite the twilight, they were close enough to the bonfire to make out the preparations. About fifteen Celts had gathered, some with masks, some with charcoal smeared on their faces. A few meters away, the clearing was marked by piles of dug up earth. They'd lit torches from the embers of a small fire next to the well, or rather, the big muddy hole.

Some earth had been shaped into a rim that gave Mary the unpleasant suggestion of a gaping mouth. Together with the torches, the rim was meant to stop them tripping into it in the dark. Whatever wood they were using, it burned slow and red, with pulses of smoke. Several figures held the torches over Simmy and Colin as they fastened their robes. Other Celts were using twig brooms on the ground between Mary's tree and the well.

The well's wet rim shone in the red flames like a slimy animal's skin. Yes, it was the head of a snake that would swallow her into the underworld. Mary wanted to scream; instead, she choked. The well resembled the one at Exmoor, and she felt Rhiannon shift in response; Mary was not alone. She shut her eyes and thrust herself back to that night in the Well Garden. There she saw the intoxicated face of Joe Griffith's intoxicated face holding out a cup. She had known, without being told, it was made of deer horn.

Flames had licked Joe's curls in the darkness. She could see little snakes all over his neck and remembered thinking, those veins would have gushed a red river of blood when Colin hacked at them. No, I won't think about that.

"Come into the circle, Mary Wandwalker," Joe boomed. The cup hovered in front of her, growing larger, blotting out everything else. "Drink a libation to the Waking of the Well!"

Despite the soreness of her tied wrists, Mary dreamed her right hand reached for the cup with its glittering contents.

Noooo! shrieked Rhiannon. Not that night. It's mine. Open your eyes, Mary Wandwalker. This is *your* night.

Mary obeyed. She had no energy of her own now. It was all up to Rhiannon.

"Drink this. It'll help." Simmy loomed in front of her holding a small silver bowl. A set of horse heads chased each other around its sides.

Mary opened her lips. It was automatic. She was thirsty. It was hard work, watching her death being prepared.

"Yuck." She spat out the brown liquid onto the chest of Simmy's yellow robe. The priestess took a step back, and locked eyes with Mary. Simmy raised the bowl to her own mouth.

"I thought you were giving me water," Mary said. "I suppose it's more of that drug. Horrible, bitter stuff. I won't drink anymore."

"Suit yourself, Mary Wandwalker," said Simmy, taking a second gulp. "Danu's Root is for the chosen. For those about to be gods."

"No Simmy. I won't be a god. This isn't what you think it is," said Mary. The harshness of the liquid stimulated a flicker of defiance. Simmy vanished and Mary was left with the rising waters of this terrible night – and Rhiannon.

They gave me that stuff as well, said the girl. Nasty, true. Then wow, like swallowing lightning. The high!

You didn't end up high, Mary silently muttered. You ended up at the bottom of a well.

Not just at Exmoor. Don't forget the rest of me, where the Eponia meets the Thames, said Rhiannon in an annoying know-it-all tone.

Given her situation, Mary didn't need a reminder of that morning. "At least," she said between her teeth. "At least what they are about to do to me will wash that image away."

You're so ungrateful, Rhiannon replied. It would not last.

Afterwards, Mary concluded that some of Danu's Root had soaked through the membranes in her mouth. She noticed changes. The night got darker, as if the million lamps of the city were snuffed out. A duo of homemade flutes began a somber melody. They were joined by the insistent beats of a drum.

She saw red dots circling the well and the fire; those must be the torches. They were dancing faster and faster. All at once, the torches made a circle then were still. There was a bit of banging as they were stabbed into the wet earth around the well's mouth. Now she could hear a rustling, like leaves, but much more intense. Robed figures with painted faces came up to Mary in solemn procession. Each whispered words she didn't understand. They wanted to touch her face and bare forearms.

Mary's body was melting. It didn't hurt at all, this liquefying flesh. First her clothes became so wet they streamed down her torso and pooled at her feet. Then her skin began to loosen as if she were an ice sculpture left in the sun too long. Great gobs fell off and into the dark.

It was not just her body that was taking a new form. Pressed against the tree, she started to feel faint pulses. She was a drum, and the tree became hundreds of tiny drummers. I ought to be afraid, thought Mary. This must be what dying is like. She tried wiggling a bony finger to attract Rhiannon. She wanted to ask her: is this what it was like?

Instead of the dead girl, a hot vein poked out of her disintegrating hand. Fascinated, Mary watched it wriggle like a tiny snake then dart into the tree. She could feel the cool tree sap comforting the boiling blood that had been hers. Like a swimmer escaping a deep well, the vein flowed up the tree to a tall branch. Mary's finger was now inside a twig. No, not just her finger! She was oozing backwards into the tree. Her bones were going to mate with the grain of the wood. I am becoming part of the forest.

Without thinking Mary shot both arms above her head. Her world spun, and the tree was a giant net. She arrived, suspended on the topmost branch. She almost sang with relief from the pain and fear. Above her the milky way ran as broad river. The stars were bigger, their constellations more pronounced, almost insistent that she worship them.

The full moon rose fast, a glowing ball tossed into the celestial river. Moonlight bathed her. She saw that the whole forest stretched as far as the eye could see. There was no city, no London, just beacon fires on all three sacred mounds.

"*EEK.*" Mary's forearm was on fire.

"Sorry. My cutters slipped. Be quiet, Miss Wandwalker, Ma'am, while I get you free."

The unknown male voice had an American drawl.

"Are you police?" she whispered. Pain forced her back into her skin. The Celts, or at any rate, the red dots were gathered around the fire a few meters away. She could smell barbequed meat.

"Working with Special Branch. Hold still. Just a few moments."

A gunshot rang out from the forest, followed by incoherent shouts. The red dots were tossed into the fire. Oh no, the Celts are prepared for an attack, Mary realized. Why am I still tied to this sodding tree? The rasping stopped. Mary heard her rescuer call out.

"Get away from Miss Wandwalker! I'm armed." Incoherent sounds rose from the darkness. Yelling, blows, defiance and no one helping her.

"Fucking Hell."

"Y. . .under arrest."

"Drop that knife."

The man behind her was fighting a Celt, maybe two of them, Mary concluded. That shot had alerted everyone. What had she always said to Mr. Jeffreys about the uselessness of guns? Mary tugged at her bonds. After a few dangerous moments, the sound of fighting diminished, replaced by panting and stumbling. She could see groups of figures in robes wrestling with others in dark clothes. Electric torches were being wildly waved about, yet no one was coming for her.

"Help!" she cried. "Over here! Help! Help!"

"Kill the crone." Colin cried through the dark. More than one set of fighters paused for a second.

"I'm not a crone you little. . .fool. Release me at once."

At last, Mary felt something that was not a threat. Two faces swam from the dark. After a bit of sawing, she felt the wrist ropes peel away. A wet towel dabbed at the blood and bruising left by the tight knots.

"Mary, thank God."

"Don't you mean goddess, Caroline?" said Mary, weak with relief.

"She does," agreed Sarah, holding her by the other arm.

"We're getting you out of here," gasped Caroline. "There's an ambulance waiting to take you to hospital. Mr. Jeffreys is just checking with Special Branch. He'll meet us at the park gates."

"Mr. Jeffreys?" muttered Mary. "Here? Are you sure?"

I'm here too, said Rhiannon; she was cold. It seems you won't be joining me after all.

Mary was too busy to respond. Sarah produced soft shoes from her knapsack. Mary put them on, oh so tenderly over her bleeding toes.

"Your poor feet!" exclaimed Caroline, noticing the scabs and bruises. "Perhaps we can get a man to carry you to the ambulance."

"Definitely not," said Mary. "I'm walking out of here with you two. Come on. Wait!"

"What is it?" said Caroline.

"Where's Anna?"

CHAPTER 42
SOLSTICE NIGHT

At the park gates, they found Mr. Jeffreys glowering at Simmy, who was in handcuffs. Agents in black protective clothing surrounded them. Mary told herself: black bulletproof vests and bulging belts did not suggest the black clothed Celts who had held her in the tower. More Special Branch officers arrived dragging arrested Celts. But there was no Anna, and no Colin. No one had told Mr. Jeffreys because he was already furious.

"Who fired that weapon?" he thundered. "Firearms are last resort only! I was at the briefing. Nothing in our intelligence indicated guns."

The figures in black shifted from foot to foot, and several dodged out of Mr. Jeffreys' line of sight. A young woman coughed.

"Um, an accident, sir. I was assigned to capture that young man, Colin Morrigan. The profiler said he was the most dangerous. When I saw him waving an axe, I took out my gun. Someone jumped me from behind and it went off. I was trying to protect the crone."

"I am not a *crone*," Mary spluttered, her iron will rusting. Caroline put both arms round her. She was too worried to wait.

"Mr. Jeffreys, where is Anna? She wasn't with us when we rescued Mary."

Mr. Jeffreys face was in shadow. He stared at Mary with the streetlamp behind him.

"Miss Wandwalker, I am relieved you are safe. Your friends should be able to see the ambulance from the park gate."

He put up his hands. "No arguing. Now, as for Miss Vronsky. . ." He turned to his operatives, who shook their heads.

"She went after Colin." It was Simmy, shrouded in a blanket over her robe and handcuffs. "I know my son. He won't surrender. Colin's gone to the river, the Thames. The sacrifice must be completed. He'll become a god; you'll see."

She hissed at Mary. "It was supposed to be *you*. . .you useless old woman; not a boy brimming with the gods!"

Silence descended like stone. No one looked at Mary. Swallowing, Mr. Jeffreys clicked his fingers at his agents. Two of them started to talk into radios, while those with prisoners strode out of the park.

Too tired to move her throbbing feet, Mary slumped. Caroline and Sarah held her by her shoulders. Yet even now, Mary was a woman of words.

"Do you really believe that people like me are useless?" she croaked at Simmy.

"We must have fresh water," said Simmy. "Blood purifies water. You have no child, no lover, no future." She carried on muttering into the dark.

There was a snort from the direction of Mr. Jeffreys. "Take her away." He was frightening in his control. Agents either side of Simmy marched her to the police vans parked beyond the gates. Other operatives made haste to follow.

"Don't forget Barin," Mary called. "They hurt him and put him in some vehicle, left him unconscious. He did try to help."

A slim man acknowledged Mary. He beckoned to the last two agents to accompany him.

"My men will find Professor Morrigan," said Mr. Jeffreys. "Look, the ambulance has just parked next to the police vans. Do you think you can make it, Miss Wandwalker?"

"We'll take her." Caroline kissed Mary on the cheek and spoke directly into Mary's ear. "What that woman said. . ."

"Was true."

Mary grimaced at Caroline's shock. "Don't worry Caroline. I know it's her own emptiness that spoke." Sarah and Caroline helped Mary over the damp grass and onto the Edwardian streets.

They met towering houses and even taller trees. These living giants prized up pavements and made roads slippery after rain. Strong hands pulled all three into the back of an ambulance. Every second the absence of Anna weighed heavier on them. It wasn't over yet. Anna's disappearance drew them down into a whirlpool.

CHAPTER 43
A TRIP TO THE THAMES

"Get this thing off me." Mary tugged at the torc round her neck. Ignoring the shining artefact, the quiet paramedic carried on checking the sores and scabs around her wrists and ankles.

Sitting next to Mary, Caroline eased off the torc. Twisted for thicker male necks, the gold collar opened to let Mary go. Tiny dragon teeth glittered between Caroline's fingers. She handed the torc to Sarah who put it in her backpack. Caroline examined the other paramedic, a woman in a hijab fixing Mary's saline drip. She then produced wipes and a plastic bag with Medical Waste printed in it. Mary gave her a tired smile.

"Mary," said Caroline. Her name, also an appeal.

"Yes, I know. You're not going anywhere alone. We are sticking together to get Anna."

"Did they give you any drugs, Miss Wandwalker?" That was the male paramedic, a grizzled Scot bandaging her left forearm where the agent had let his cutters slip.

"They tried. Fortunately, your drip is clearing my head."

"You are severely dehydrated."

"Do you have anything to eat? Then we need to talk about where you are taking us."

"I think I should. . ."

"No, Caroline. It's all of us or none of us."

Caroline subsided, keeping a grip on Mary's arm. The older woman absently patted her hand. There's a wolf in my stomach, Mary thought. The woman paramedic handed out energy bars.

Mary ripped into hers and chewed. Sugar and heat coursed through her, driving the wolves back.

Mary studied Caroline and Sarah for the first time that night. Sarah's stillness was pleasure whereas Caroline's love was tinged with despair.

"Thank you for rescuing me. It was. . .close."

"Anna." A whisper followed by a moan.

"I know." Mary summoned the Archive Supervisor from a past that was another world now. She addressed the paramedics.

"Please listen carefully. We must go to the hospital via Waterloo Bridge. A man is about to jump into the river. Anna, our friend, will try to stop him. She's in danger."

"We have to get to them. Right now!" Caroline hugged her chest and rocked. Sarah stroked her arm.

"Our orders were. . ."

"Countermanded." Mary's unflinching eyes met the man's professionalism.

"The police."

"Are on the scene, no doubt. But we. . ." Mary glanced at Caroline and Sarah, then took another gulp of the water being held out to her. "We have information. . ."

"We can save them." That was Sarah in a whisper. Caroline was too tense to speak.

The woman pursed her lips. Then she peered at the instruments connected to Mary.

"Well, your vitals are improving, Miss Wandwalker." She checked her iPad. "I see that Charing Cross Hospital has available beds tonight. Tell the driver, Clive."

The man turned, picking up a phone. Meanwhile the woman was tapping into her own device. "I'm alerting the river police about your friend. We should be in the vicinity in thirty-seven minutes."

Anna's journey across London was simpler. She pursued Colin into the Underground, where he had vaulted over the ticket barriers and onto a train two seconds before it moved off. She reached the platform just to see him make a rude gesture through the glass door. Anna used her fury to sail back over the ticket barriers.

Racing up to the street, she spotted a parked Mercedes, hotwired it, and was speeding down an empty side road before Colin's train reached the next station. In three minutes, she persuaded the onboard computer to find the most traffic free route to Waterloo bridge. It wasn't necessary. If any night drivers ventured close, they skidded to the side as Anna shot the Mercedes forward. She was an unstoppable tide, like the unblocking of an ancient river on Parliament Hill.

CHAPTER 44
THE SACRED RIVER

Waterloo Bridge is never entirely free of traffic, either the two-footed or the rubber-wheeled kind. Yet, when Anna arrived on the shortest night of the year, the silence was eerie. Anna never paid any attention to clocks. If she had checked at Waterloo Station, she would have known that dawn hovered over the North Sea. Instead, she sprinted towards the river.

At that moment, in jeans and a short, cream robe, Colin was moving along the bridge, keeping one hand on the railings as he waited for the sun. Smelling the river as if she'd been born in it, Anna sprung up the steps onto bridge.

The boy's solitary figure turned around to face the young woman with a knife. Colin's robe was loose enough to sway in the river's breeze. Gold from an embroidered sun motif sparkled in the lamplight. On the opposite side of the bridge, a police car drew close to Somerset House. Shuttered windows indicated that the edifice was blind to the human dramas being enacted below. Police on foot arrived and began preventing cars from accessing the bridge.

Anna concentrated on Colin standing rigid before her. Light from dark from the churning water below reflected the blue glitter in eyes like two poisoned wells. Deciding to ignore Anna, Colin swiveled back to the river. He pressed against the barrier; his future was as avatar of the reborn sun for the great god Thames.

"Colin don't!" Anna shouted.

It was what Caroline would have said. Or Mary. For the first time it occurred to Anna that she didn't know what to do next. She wasn't Mary, with her well-wrought plans and reckless courage. Neither was she Caroline, with her fount of compassion. Joe Griffith swam into Anna's memory. Their love affair had been a mutual drowning until his drugs pushed her into possession by the wife of Lir.

The wife of Lir would kill Colin. Anna began to move towards him. Her strong left hand held a knife thirsty for his heart. Sensing her approach, Colin climbed over the steel railings designed to stop people doing what he planned to do. Once he got as far as he could without falling, he hesitated. Mesmerized by his face reflected in the waves, Colin communed with the river that linked the heart of England with the endless sea.

With the sure footing of her wild being, Anna's focus on Colin never wavered. She was unaware of two persons gesturing at the inhabitants of a second police car on the north bank. The thin one was trying to attract an oblivious Colin while grasping the other, rounder woman. She was signaling, in vain, to Anna. A third figure, diminutive in army fatigues began to sidle onto the bridge. After a few steps, two uniformed men grabbed her. They lifted Sarah between them and carried her to the first police car.

Anna willed herself into a shadow. Meanwhile, across the bridge a van poured out more plain clothes officers. Had Anna looked carefully, she would have seen a big man in a muddy shirt and blue legs shiny enough to cut through the dimness. One of the arguing women stamped her foot at him. Apparently, the blue-legged man was trying to calm her down. No, he must have conceded something, because she and her shorter companion were making their way across the bridge to Colin. Too late, decided the wife of Lir.

Colin could no longer ignore Anna's proximity. Without acknowledging her, he tried to stand up on the railings, wobbled, and came down again.

"Stop!" Anna commanded. She was so close she could smell his rancid sweat.

Colin shifted to spit at Anna. "Why? Why should I stop? Not for you."

Why indeed. He would die in the river. The wife of Lir wanted that, didn't she?

"Anna, wait." That was Mary limping into earshot. How her feet hurt. Caroline held onto her waist.

Ignoring Mary, Anna crept closer to Colin. He scrambled up again, this time jamming one foot between the bars, finding a balance that was half secure.

"Stop, Colin."

Less imperious, there was some of Anna in the wife of Lir, Mary judged.

"I can't stop!" said Colin, a defiant child. "*I eat the dark.*"

Anna shrank back, joining Mary and Caroline. The three women took equidistant positions around Colin, not needing to confer. He glared at them. Short of wrestling all three, his only escape was down.

"Move back," said Mary. "Give him space." They shuffled back a few steps.

Colin eased his position so that his vision encompassed the entire Depth Enquiry Agency. None of them could reach in quick enough to drag him off the railings. His back was to the water. Mary hoped that was a good sign. She wanted him to come down and be arrested. It is time to restore normality to the world. Enough of raving drug addicts pretending to be gods.

Caroline, she knew, feared for Anna. The young woman's fierceness would not falter tonight. Unfortunately, Anna appeared to still be possessed by a mythical figure. Would the wife of Lir take Anna, too, into the Otherworld? Mary knees trembled at the thought of the merciless depths of the Thames.

"Put the knife away Anna. Before someone gets hurt."

Not by a flicker of an eyelash did Anna give any sign of hearing Mary. A giggle came from Colin. "I bet someone said to my grandfather, 'Come down before someone gets hurt.' Well, guess what, you fucking morons, we're all hurt."

Colin was yelling now, "We're all dying. The world is dying. Too many immigrants. Too much pollution. Just ask my fucking mother."

"You're right, Colin." Simmy materialized from behind Mary and Caroline. Her handcuffs had been removed. Mr. Jeffreys puffed to a standstill beside Mary. He bent over backwards, in agony again. Simmy was oblivious to anything but Colin.

"Racism was never part of my father's Reborn Celts."

"It is now!" yelled Colin. He was getting more hysterical. "It's *my* Reborn Celts. *I'm* the true Morrigan. *I'm* the heir of Albert Edward."

"No." Simmy's voice shook. "My son, my darling boy. Come down now. We failed. The Reborn Celts are finished." She paused. "No one else has to die!" Simmy almost screamed. Mary shivered, remembering her voice from hours earlier around the fire.

Simmy held out her arms to the boy with the gold sun on his chest.

"The world is dying," she said, in a voice for him alone. "Not you, bursting with the springs of life. Come down, my love."

Mary felt lightheaded. Simmy's longing was real, and yet she sounded as if she was performing a part. She so wanted to be a mother. Unfortunately, behind the mother fighting for her son's life was the priestess of the forest and the cup. 'Bursting with the springs of life,' could mean the birth of the Eponia— in blood.

"Simmy, remember he's just a boy," called Mary, knowing a mother's pain never ends.

The woman kept her eyes on teetering Colin, but Mary knew she'd heard her.

Simmy's words were raw. "Don't be my father. He *left* us. He left *me*."

Colin shot a look of anguish at Simmy. She started to move towards him.

"No, no, don't! Let him come to you."

That was Caroline. Mary pulled her back from Anna, who was edging too close to Colin.

Colin disentangled his foot from the rails. Mary breathed again. He was going to come down. Younger now, even his unnatural blue eyes looked too young, as the boy and his mother exchanged a silent communication.

The end came fast. No one on the bridge saw the gulls flying in from the east. On the bridge, the tiny figure poised on the railing rose to embrace the sunrise that streaked across the river and set his robe ablaze. His face brimmed with red light. Without warning, he tore off the robe and jeans. Naked but for his shoes, Colin flung his arms wider than the sky.

"Mabon, son of light!" he screamed into the other world.

"Don't leave me Colin," Simmy cried.

He dived rather than jumped into the river. Mary lunged forward too late. Her nails brushed the scuffed leather of his muddy trainers. A second behind her was Mr. Jeffreys.

Another scream shattered the group on the bridge.

"Anna, nooooo!"

Anna followed Colin into the Thames. She was still holding her knife.

CHAPTER 45
RISING FROM THE RIVER

Waves wrapped around the bodies and sucked them down. A plume of blood broke the surface to a general gasp. Mary heard Caroline choking as the red swirled like a snake eating its tail. Colin, thought Mary, please, let it be Colin. Another thing to feel guilty about, as her grip tightened on Caroline.

"Anna. . .Anna," moaned Caroline. Mary had no words until there was a second eruption from below. It took forever; it was only a couple of minutes. Anna's head popped up from the depths. Colin's did not.

"Look, look, the police diver. He's got someone. Long black hair, it's Anna. Stop crying Caroline! He's got her!"

Mary stopped as a bleeding torso broke the surface. Yes, that was Colin. Two water demons in rubber suits handed Anna and Colin to waiting figures in the boat. Anna, not Colin, they later learned, responded to CPR. A miracle, said the River Police.

Almost no one survives that fall, they repeated. Briefed by Mr. Jeffreys and primed by the paramedics, the river Police had stationed their boat under Waterloo bridge. With professional speed they fished out the two unconscious bodies. Colin's ribs gushed blood from what appeared to be a savage swipe.

Much later, a diving team recovered what was deemed to be the weapon. A grotesquely twisted metal sheet was hauled onto the shingle near the Eponia outlet. Probably the remains of a garden shed, said the forensics team. After being knocked out by hitting the river at such speed, Colin had spun towards the gaping debris on the riverbed. The rusty iron pierced his heart.

The hospital staff found Anna's story impressive. She was a rare survivor from jumping off a bridge as high as Waterloo. After Mary and Caroline (with a few quiet words from Mr. Jeffreys) convinced the doctors that the psychotherapy offered to would-be suicides would be wasted on Anna, they were allowed to take her home.

First stop was the rented house in Oxford. Then, as soon as they had packed, and Mary was fit to drive, they travelled with Sarah to their shabby mock-Tudor home in Surrey. If DEA was to be disbanded on Mr. Jeffreys orders, their time was limited. Their home would be repossessed by the mortgage company. Mary could see some hard conversations ahead.

"The wife of Lir has gone to the Otherworld," was all Anna would say of her time in the river. Neither Mary nor Caroline asked her about the knife. The police did not mention finding it, and Mary did not inquire when Walbrook phoned. However, Anna did mention that she would be getting another.

"Don't bother, Anna!" muttered Mary from the sofa. She was still very tired, or she would have said a lot more.

"My knife is an offering to the river gods. Sacrifices have to be replaced."

"Of course, darling," said Caroline, her face full of shadows.

Mary remembered Barin's office, and all the Celtic objects recovered from lakes, rivers and, yes, wells. Surely the ritual did not demand the instant replacement of votive objects?

Anna stood at the window with the light behind her. Only she could be implacable while also wanting approval from Mary. With the stench of the river in her nostrils, Mary decided to let it go. She gave one of her tiny nods and Anna vanished. The three of them were on sick leave, with Sarah waiting to be invited back to Holywell. None of the four wanted to deal with the messy aftermath of the Reborn Celts.

The police informed Mary that Barin would be tried for the stealing of antiquities, abduction, and as an accomplice to murder. Too exhausting to contemplate, thought Mary. Then there was Simmy, recovering from a suicide attempt in a police cell. After several psych evals, the Crown Prosecution Service was considering the insanity plea offered by her defense team. Otherwise, it would be charges of aiding and abetting murder, in addition to kidnapping.

Other members of the Reborn Celts faced lesser charges particularly around Mary's abduction. Unfortunately, Mary failed to identify any of her captors apart from Simmy. At that point she was excused from the laborious process of building evidence that would convict Gav and Steve.

It was the fate of the Morrigan siblings that depended in part upon the testimony of the DEA, said Inspector Walbrook by phone. Mary knew that it would fall to her to find out whether Anna *could* give evidence in court without becoming the "wife of Lir" and whether Caroline, suffering from a down-swing after the stress, *should* testify.

CHAPTER 46
WHILE YOU WERE SLEEPING

Back in Surrey, and with court cases to come, Mary let the memories return. They crept back like domesticated animals who had fled to the woods during a storm. One of the most troubling derived from her second night in hospital after the drama on Waterloo Bridge. There she dreamed what was not a dream. For it was an exchange between the women at her bedside who thought she could not overhear.

"Sit back down, Anna. We're waiting for Mary and your blood tests will be back any minute. No, don't touch me, I don't want to do this now."

"You're angry?"

"Hurt. I know you don't understand. You hurt me, Anna. That kind of pain doesn't just go away."

"You go away. More than I."

Caroline gasped. "What? I never. . ."

"Often you go. Into the dark. I try, I walk with you all night long, but I cannot find you."

Those squeaks must be Caroline must be shifting on her chair. The next words were fraught.

"Depression is not the same. It's an illness. I can't do anything about it when it comes. This is about love."

Mary wanted to open her eyes more than anything in the world. Why were her lids weighted with iron bars? Caroline's depressed voice cracked. Mary had to stop her going into Anna's dark world. That place was forbidden.

"I know you don't know about love, that you grew up without love. Somehow you survived. I love you, but you left me for that man, Joe Griffith."

There was a pause and a shuffling. Mary's face and arms prickled. She could not move or speak. Someone coughed as if they were choking. It was Anna.

"The river," she rasped. "It is inside me, perhaps forever. No, don't get a nurse, Caroline. I am alright, I know it. Just listen."

Mary heard a shuddering breath. That must be Caroline.

"Remember when we were in Oxford with the wife of Lir? Caroline, when I saw that man attack you at the Boathouses, I ran to you. The wife of Lir ran. A knife in my stomach at the thought you might die. Is that not love?"

"I don't know."

Mary could hear the weariness in Caroline. "Do you really believe that depression is when I leave you?"

"And Mary. It pains her when you go."

"I can't help it. I'll 'go' again as you put it and I suppose you will too."

"You choose to return from the depression underworld. I chose to come back. That is love."

A sigh. "Oh Anna, I don't know if I am strong enough for this."

"Mary will make you strong. Her spirit rises."

At that, Mary opened her eyes.

CHAPTER 47
TWO VISITORS

A week later, Mary rested on the sofa, watching through French windows as Anna and Caroline planted apple trees. Entirely the wrong time of year, Mary pointed out. She knew however Caroline's depression took a beating if she could do anything to make things grow. Plus, it was good preparation for her recuperative visit to Holywell.

They were going the next day, all four of them. Sarah had been summoned back for her ongoing rehab, her blood magic forgiven, if not forgotten. Caroline would be taking a course on herbal anti-depressants known only to the witches. Anna was going to reassure Caroline (and for Janet to reassure Mary about Anna). That left only Mary. She had to decide what to do to save the DEA.

So, none of them were pleased when their last morning as a foursome was interrupted by two visitors, one then another. Mary sighed as she saw a whale of a limousine swamp their modest cul de sac. Their first visitor looked stunned by English suburbia.

"Mr. North. Please come in," said Mary.

He did not reply, merely strode past her. His lack of shaving was not a style statement, Mary judged. Gray stubble clashed with his grey silk suit and drew attention to bloodshot pale blue eyes. Even so, his hair remained coiffed. Sculpted ice, Mary thought. She could not warm to him.

"Miss Wandwalker, we need to talk."

She raised her eyebrows and indicated the best armchair. He stared at the room like a man used to grander domestic spaces. The sudden entrance of Caroline halted him. She had soil on her t-shirt, and grass stains on her hands. However, the dark crescents beneath her eyes were the most shocking. She chose the seat next to Mary.

Anna materialized in clean designer jeans and bright red lipstick. She scowled magnificently from the table as she snapped open the silver lid of her laptop. It was then Mary remembered that Mer-Corp was suing the DEA (or was it just herself?), for the alleged neglect of Rhiannon. She gulped, smelling again the rancid water of the Exmoor well.

"What can we do for you, Mr. North?" she said, sitting up very straight. "It goes without saying that we all grieve for your loss."

What that a snort from below? Mary hoped not. She had been free of that voice since Waterloo bridge.

Yes, I remember him, said Rhiannon, this time obviously from the deep. There was something inhuman in her words—from a daughter of her father.

Mr. North opened his mouth, then closed it again. He bent to fiddle with the brass lock of his leather briefcase; then changed his mind about opening it. At that moment he noticed Anna for the first time. That is, he really noticed her extraordinary beauty, and her dark hostile eyes. Frederic North flinched. Mary began to feel a flicker of sympathy. Rhiannon was back, and in her mood of malicious glee.

Mary's knuckles were white in her lap. Mr. North had set in motion the destruction of the DEA and the family it sustained. She should try to save them from the corporate power represented by this sad man. No wonder the room bristled with tension. And he still wasn't talking.

"Should we have a lawyer if you are here?"

It was unlike Caroline to ignore the anguish that seeped from North. Mary was proud of her.

"Keep fighting it, Caroline," Mary said in low tones. Don't drown, she meant. Don't let the depression pull you under.

Mr. North raised both hands, then returned them to his knees as Sarah, her dark skin glowing, entered with a tray of coffee and a questioning look. Mary nodded, and Sarah scuttled off to continue packing for Holywell. This is our home, thought Mary; mine, Caroline, and Anna's, even if we don't have it much longer.

"I've come for the torc," said Mr. North, at last. His hands curled into fists. He stared at each of the three women in turn.

"The torc," he repeated, his upper-class American drawl grating on Mary.

"Just like that?" said Anna. She was becoming ferocious. "You expect us to hand it over. It may have Mary's blood on it."

Mary was startled. She'd forgotten. Well, yes, untouched since that night, it could have traces of her blood. They'd wrapped it in a t-shirt Sarah had provided. She'd been wearing the top under her khakis, so it might still have her DNA as well. Mary realized that they should have handed it over to Mr. Jeffreys. Why hadn't he, or the police, demanded the torc?

Mr. North passed a damp hand over his forehead. "You don't understand, he said, sounding sad. Mr. Jeffreys approved it. And. . ." he motioned to Caroline, now hunched up at the other end of his sofa. "Mrs. Jones, you don't need to worry about lawyers. I won't be suing you."

"Her, or any of us?" said Mary. She ran her hand down her newly dry-cleaned skirt. There was something she wasn't seeing. Ah ha!

"You've done a deal," she said, coldly. "No lawsuit in return for the torc. I'm surprised at Mr. Jeffreys."

"No, no, it's not like that at all. I've cancelled the lawsuit and. . ." his voice dried. Mary handed him a coffee cup and silently indicated cream and sugar on the tray in front of him.

It's not like that at all, repeated mocked Rhiannon, although only Mary could hear her.

"You should listen with more subtlety, Miss Wandwalker," came a stronger masculine voice from the door. Mr. Jeffreys had let himself in. He knew it annoyed Mary, who had never given him a key. Mary stood up.

"We're not ready for visitors," she announced, not minding the rudeness to both men. "And we're not giving up the torc. After all the. . .the horror, the murders, it belongs. . ." she hesitated, taking in her companions. She was back in solstice night with the metal circling her neck. She knew it flickered in the firelight with the moon beyond.

"The torc must have reverence." That was Caroline, hugging her knees.

"It will," said Mr. Jeffreys bracingly. "It's going to the British Museum as part of a big donation by Mer-Corp. The torc will be studied by scientists, historians, anthropologists, metallurgists, you name it, from all over academia. Then it will be displayed for anyone to see, or worship if they please. The Great British Public will be able to imagine the warriors it adorned."

"Donated? Are you sure?" Mary sat back on the sofa and stuck an arm around Caroline who stopped rocking.

"There's no deal," said Mr. North, his voice cracking. His hand shook on the coffee cup. Everyone waited while he took a few sips. Mary remained suspicious. Anna narrowed her eyes.

"Let's give Mr. North a chance to explain himself," Mary said at last.

"No deal," he repeated. "A donation and a withdrawal of the lawsuit. It. . . it seems for the best."

"Of course, the British government is prepared to drop the matter of the original theft of the torc," said Mr. Jeffreys, smoothly.

"Not least because the original thief is dead?" Mary queried.

"Exactly," replied Mr. Jeffreys. "Well, in fact, Dr. Barin Morrigan handled the negotiations for Albert Edward," he continued, glancing at Frederic North, who was not paying attention. "He's desperate that his father's legacy be detached from the racist stain acquired by the Reborn Celts. We could still charge him for assisting his father over the torc, but that would be er. . ."

"Embarrassing," said Mary.

"Too complicated," retorted Mr. Jeffreys. He took a seat at the other end of the sofa and smiled at Caroline. Mary wanted Mr. Jeffreys to leave. She could tell by his demeanor that he had further business with the DEA. It was Frederic North who would have to go first.

"Um, thank you, Mr. North," she said. Why didn't he just go? "The. . .er museum will be grateful."

"Wife of Lir will speak to Rhiannon," Anna's voice rang out.

Shock rippled through the room. Mr. North fell back in the chair. Then he leaned forward, grasping the table in front of him.

"My daughter! You talk of *my* daughter." He choked. Mary went to the door and called to Sarah to fetch water.

"Anna," said Caroline in a small voice. "You shouldn't."

Anna ignored everyone, except Mr. North.

"Rhiannon says. . ."

Mary had to do something. "She's been talking to me, too."

Frederic North started to rise from his chair, then collapsed. Caroline was frozen. Anna did not look surprised.

"Indeed, Miss Wandwalker." Mr. Jeffreys was making fun of her. Never mind him.

"Is this your guilt speaking?" Frederic North rasped. Mary saw fear flicker in his eyes.

Sarah arrived with a glass of water. He waved her away. She made a face at Mary and vanished.

"Yes," Mary did not know what else to say. "I. . .I feel that I did not do my best for. . .for Miss North. My bad memories must have made up this person inside. . .I do apologize. . ."

NOOOOOO. Rhiannon shrieked. Don't say sorry to *him*. He'll sue you anyway. And I am real, real I say. More real than you.

Mary gasped and found herself holding her chest. Wishing she could sink into the carpet, she made herself meet Frederic North's outrage. "Your daughter says she's more real than me."

Fuck you, Mary Wandwalker, continued Rhiannon. You learn nothing. She disappeared. Mary saw Anna's ironic expression.

"Wife of Lir say you learn nothing."

"Thank you very much, Anna," snapped Mary. She noticed Mr. North's shoulder shaking. He held a rose handkerchief to conceal his eyes. Before Mary could do anything, Caroline had moved a chair next to him. She put an arm around his shoulders. He let out one large sob and leaned into her large chest.

"I'll wait outside," mouthed Mr. Jeffreys to Mary. She followed him to the door. "You could leave us in peace," she suggested.

"Business. You and I," he said, and went to the garden. Luckily it had an abandoned bird bath big enough to seat Jeffreys once he brushed out some leaves.

Back in the living room, Frederic North addressed Caroline with Anna a silent sentinel. Mary decided to leave them to it and fled into the kitchen for another pot of coffee.

When she returned, the atmosphere had thawed. Caroline could be heard assuring Frederic North that Mary and Anna meant no harm by talking to Rhiannon's ghost.

"We, erm, have unusual methods. Rhiannon herself appreciated them," she said, more confident than Mary of the murdered girl's support.

"I'll never understand her now."

His bleakness was better than rage, Mary supposed.

With Anna remote, it would be up to Mary to get their fragile visitor to leave.

"Mr. North, as Caroline says, I meant no disrespect. I've come to. . .to appreciate your daughter these last few weeks."

"She means she loves. . .erm loved, Rhiannon," said Caroline.

Mary cleared her throat. Anna intervened.

"You give hoard to native tribe," she said in the tones of the wife of Lir.

"I beg your pardon?"

"I'm saying. . ." She smiled. "You are making a considerable financial sacrifice to donate the Sacred Well Torc to the British Museum," said Anna. Her upper-class British accent was impeccable.

Mary's jaw dropped. "We are indeed most grateful," Mary got out.

Anna made a rude gesture to Mary.

A wintry Mr. North looked confused for a moment. He turned back to Caroline.

"I'll make the gift in the name of Rhiannon," he said in that clipped New England accent.

"She would have appreciated that." Caroline was calm, sure that the best would prevail. Mary admired how she could push her own pain aside for another person.

Donated? No way Jose, snorted Rhiannon from inside Mary. I'd have sold it by now and be on my way to the best parties in Italy. Those guys are *hot*.

I thought you planned to give it to Joe Griffith, thought Mary. Warrior king to your goddess and so on.

Yeah, well after the crazy guy cut my head off, my plans changed. *I* changed; in case you didn't notice. Why be a goddess when a girl can wallow in all that great food, art, and *romance*?

So now you're playing at being a real teenager. Mary was saddened. A dead one, too.

"Well, Miss Wandwalker? The torc? Can I take it?" That was Frederic North.

There was a flush on the cheekbones of his taut face.

"My. . .my associates and I will have to discuss your proposition," she said. He wasn't used to being stalled. Rhiannon wasn't impressed either.

Oh, go on! Give the Norths a break. Trust us for once.

Mary jumped up and went to the window, where she could think for a moment without being observed.

OK Rhiannon, she said to the dead girl. We'll hand over the torc on one condition. You go with him. Without waiting for a reply from the ghost she cleared her throat and turned back to face Frederic.

"Mr. North, I recommend that you take a trip to Italy. See the sights, try the er. . .amazing cuisine; experience the art, and the people. That's what Rhiannon would want for you. I'm certain of it."

For me, for me, came a spoiled teenager's cry inside her.

"You can take the torc to the British Museum on your way to the airport."

Frederic North showed surprise. He wasn't used to anyone, especially an older woman, telling him what to do.

Sarah came into the room holding the torc. She must have been listening at the door, Mary realized. The torc shone just as when he had given it to Rhiannon in what seemed like several lifetimes ago. When he handed it to her, she had become a princess, his princess. He took the torc from Sarah. Anna handed him a purple silk square and he wrapped it up, as if it were as delicate as an eggshell.

"Rhiannon wanted me to pay for a trip to Italy," he found himself saying. "Before she discovered the Reborn Celts, that is. Her school was doing something called a Grand Tour."

He looked straight at Mary. "Instead, I grounded her for some minor episode with pot. She spent that vacation exploring Europe on the internet and found the Reborn Celts website and its Summer School. She knew I'd acquired the torc because of our ancestry. I thought. . .I thought. . ." His voice dried up.

"You thought it might bring you closer," said Caroline.

It did, Mary thought to herself. Bring them closer. In terrible, unplanned ways.

"Go to Italy," she found herself repeating.

He stood up. With one hand curled around the torc, with the other he picked up his briefcase. The oligarch was ready to go and, if he was to be believed, to surrender the precious torc to claims he could not control.

"Italy, you said. For Rhiannon and me, it's too late."

"Not too late."

This time Rhiannon spoke through Mary. There was an inner sigh, a kind of release.

Mr. North looked thoughtful.

"I wonder if you can be right. I might just try a trip to Italy. Thank you, Miss Wandwalker, you and your team."

Sarah saw him out the door. Mary watched as he got into his great wheeled beast.

Yes, I'm going with him, said Rhiannon. Italy will be cooling off next month so perhaps we'll go to the mountains. Goodbye Mary Wandwalker.

The car door slammed shut and the beast began to move.

"Goodbye Rhiannon North," said Mary aloud. "Thank you for not being a goddess."

"What do you mean, Mary?" Caroline's mouth hung open.

"Oh, nothing, nothing. Something about Rhiannon. She's gone now. I might even miss her."

Caroline looked curious, then not, as Anna quickly kissed her cheek.

"You and I have to discuss the future of the DEA." Mr. Jeffreys was back. Anna was dragging Caroline up the stairs. If that was a hint, Mr. Jeffreys ignored it.

Tired of psychic drama, yet fearful for the DEA, Mary allowed him back into the house, then slammed the front door. It made a satisfying bang.

EPILOGUE:
THE WIFE OF LIR

The next morning Mary slept through the Big Ben chimes of her alarm. Caroline waited for as long as possible before waking her. They had to make an early start for Holywell if they were to arrive before lunch. Mary was keen to check out its old well.

"Just to put this case to bed," she said as she backed the car out of the driveway. She did not look at Sarah. That young woman self-consciously glanced at her hands. At last, the rough patches from the scrubbing bleach had faded.

"Janet's very proud of you," whispered Caroline into her ear. Sarah smiled gratefully.

"Janet so wants to see us," Caroline continued. "You know Mary, she and Jez Wiseman have been emailing."

"Um. . ." Relieved to avoid Surrey's gridlock, Mary steered the car towards channels flowing to the main highway. She too had heard from Dr. Wiseman, who was now back in California. With his Indigenous Studies degree on hold while Frederic North sorted out the priorities of Mer-Corp, Jez wrote of his decision regarding artificial legs.

"I'm getting them. Enough of being a hero who walks on dead legs. Off they come."

Mary thought long and hard about her reply. Instead of talking it over with Caroline and Anna, she watched them tend the garden, prepare meals, and rebuild their closeness. Their tense exchange in the hospital had served to irrigate their arid land, Mary discovered. Her observations of renewed affection fed into her correspondence with Wiseman.

325

"You talk of not being a hero. Yet there are all sorts of heroes, like those who can find forgiveness after betrayal," she'd written back, trying not to sound too pointed.

Caroline would have said that there were all sorts of gods. As well as forgiveness and compassion, there is divinity in regrowth and restoration. Such work invited the hearth goddess to re-make the home. Mary could not write that. Even though she could hear Caroline say it.

For was she not living amongst rebirth as a sacred process? During her convalescence, Caroline and Anna showed respect for Mary's wounds inside and out. Despite their curiosity about her imprisonment, they allowed her natural reserve to re-gather its silt. In her weakness, Mary found herself bathing in their wordless, loving attention.

What kind of bond the three of them had, Mary did not yet know. Yet they had survived the old serpent Thames. Water and blood: these divine liquids surrounded her in drinks and helpful bodies. After a while, Mary perceived that she was letting go of the anxiety about losing her family.

To Jez, Mary emailed that he might consider extending his relationships in the UK once his new legs were fitted. Holywell specializes in support through a time of transition, she wrote. Remember, Oxford's clinics are just minutes away. Joe Griffith never visited Holywell. If he had, he might have been able to let go the savage gods he found (or who had found him). By contrast, Holywell honored deities who could repair the nature of the earth. and human nature as part of it.

Mary stopped typing the email with a smile. Learning to live with new legs, instead of clutching at what was gone, Jez would discover that kind of heroism for himself.

Back on the road with Caroline, Anna, and Sarah, Mary turned the car off the motorway and towards the bumpy track that led to the Retreat Center. With the worst of the road works over, Mary was ready to continue the conversation.

"Yes, Dr. Wiseman could benefit from Holywell," she said. "I suggested he might visit."

"Janet. Witch. Teacher." That was Anna, stroking Caroline's hair.

Sarah intervened. "Yeah, that's right. Caroline suggested Janet might teach on Dr. Wiseman's next Veteran's field trip."

"Goodness," said Mary. "That didn't occur to me. How. . .how unusual. Are you feeling better, Caroline?"

The younger woman had refused breakfast, never a good sign.

"I'm OK." Caroline cleared her throat. "You know me." She was in the back with Anna and took her hand. "And Mary, um. . ."

"Yes?"

"Do we. . .should we be talking about Mr. Jeffreys' visit yesterday?"

Mary grinned with a touch of mischief. She'd been waiting for this.

"You mean because you and Anna were making so much noise upstairs. You were too enthusiastic to overhear us."

From the front seat, Sarah swiveled to catch Caroline's blushes, Anna's equanimity.

"Did he say anything about closing down the DEA?" Caroline was getting nervous, and so Mary, decreasing speed on the narrow lane, prepared to be reassuring.

"Not closing down. Just money stuff," she said. "And insurance. We are allowed to carry on, for now. There was more on clearing up the case. His people are dismantling online traces of the Reborn Celts. It won't eliminate all such craziness, and he knows it.

"White supremacists?" That was Sarah.

"Still out there, I'm afraid," confirmed Mary. "Many who attached themselves to the Reborn Celts melted away before Mr. Jeffreys' team could attach their tracing. . .er bots, I think he said. But they were able to identify and arrest the most violent."

Anna sniffed knowledgeably, so Mary continued. "Although his inquiries do back up what we thought. Racism was not in Albert Edward's original project. Seems to have been an infection from recent recruits."

"I guess the Reborn Celts won't save us from climate change." Anna's tone was sardonic.

"No," said Mary. Anna really should be more careful when it came to Caroline's frame of mind. Then again, Mary's daughter-in-law could surprise her.

"Holywell will carry on working on the climate emergency," Caroline said. "That's right, isn't it, Sarah? Moon magic, Woman magic, even some Celtic spells. No blood, though. Rather spells of water as the blood of life. To show that the earth is sacred."

"Yes, I'm going to help," said Sarah. "Janet says I've started my apprenticeship with you three. After my adventures with the DEA, I can go on to proper spell-making."

Mary muttered something as she put her foot on the brake so she could negotiate the twisty bits of the Holywell track.

"What was that, Mary Wandwalker? You don't think that witch consciousness will save the world?" Anna's mockery flooded the car.

Mary wished she could see the young woman's face rather than bits of it in the mirror as the car bumped along. In the distance she glimpsed a green hill where the motorway, big as the Thames itself, wound through the chalk downs. A green wave, she thought. The curves in the land are a green wave rooted in the rivers. Their springs rise in the holy wells of Oxford, London, and Holywell.

An image of Rhiannon's ecstatic eyes surfaced in Mary's mind. She blinked back the prickling in her own. I never cry, she repeated to herself. I don't need to answer Anna's provocation.

"Don't forget that the Otherworld is real," said Sarah from the front seat. She squeezed Mary's arm.

"I've been there," added Anna.

"No one knows what that energy can do if. . .*tapped,*" said Caroline.

Mary's smile was rueful. Perhaps she could let go of her disbelief? Not to believe as the other women did, but neither to dismiss it. After all, it was not just the Otherworld that was real between them. She remembered what she had meant to tell them today.

"Hey, I found something out," said Mary. "Wife of Lir." The words leapt in her throat. "She's actually the wife of *Lear*. Shakespeare, I just got it. After all this time. It's his *King Lear*. In the play, he has three daughters. . ."

"And no wife!" broke in Caroline. "Typical! The wife of Lear has no name. She isn't even present."

"She's there," said Anna.

"Anna? You've seen *King Lear*?" Mary didn't expect that. Even though she was always saying that nothing about Anna could astonish her.

"In the theatre, once in Berlin and several times on film. Wife of Lear is the terror in the old king's eyes. His craziness in the storm. And. . ." She stopped. Mary and Caroline drew breath, sensing something was coming. "And in Cordelia," added Anna. "Wife of Lir is there too. She's a queen."

With that, Anna curled up and prepared to sleep.

"Anna did say the wife of Lir had left her?" whispered Mary.

"Yes," said Caroline. "She said, 'for now.'"

CPSIA information can be obtained
at www.ICGtesting.com
Printed in the USA
LVHW100817060822
725337LV00022B/179